BOOKS AND PORTRAITS

BOOKS BY VIRGINIA WOOLF

BOOKS
AND PORTRAITS

Some further selections from the
literary and biographical writings of

VIRGINIA WOOLF

Edited and with a Preface by
Mary Lyon

Harcourt Brace Jovanovich
New York and London

Printed in the United States of America

Library of Congress Cataloging in Publication Data

Woolf, Virginia Stephen, 1882–1941.
   Books and portraits.

    I. Title.
PR6045.O72A6   1978   823′.9′12   77-85206
ISBN 0-15-113478-2

First American edition 1978

B C D E

CONTENTS

CONTENTS

PART II: MAINLY PORTRAITS

Preface

VIRGINIA WOOLF'S importance as a novelist has to a large extent eclipsed her significance as a literary critic and reviewer. In fact, it is quite likely that many admirers of her fictional and feminist work are scarcely aware of her significant role as a critic. Her first published works, however, were reviews or essays, and she continued to write criticism up until her death in 1941. Two volumes of her essays were published during her lifetime: *The Common Reader: First Series*, in 1925, and *The Common Reader: Second Series*, in 1932. Most of the essays appearing in these two collections derived from reviews which she had done for the *Times Literary Supplement* and other periodicals. No further volume of her essays appeared until after her death, although her husband, Leonard Woolf, in his Editorial Note to the posthumously published *The Death of the Moth* (1942) tells us that she was in the process of collecting a group of pieces for a new book at the time of her death. Presumably, many of these essays appeared in that posthumous volume. Five years later, a further collection of essays—*The Moment*—appeared, and in 1950 yet another—*The Captain's Death Bed*. At that time Leonard Woolf felt that he had published virtually all her critical work that would be of significance and interest to readers. However, further bibliographical research, undertaken by Miss B. J. Kirkpatrick, revealed a considerable number of hitherto unrepublished essays and reviews, many of which were written prior to Virginia Woolf's marriage. *Granite and Rainbow* (1958) contained a selection of some of the best of these pieces. In 1966-67 all the essays contained in these six volumes were republished in four volumes of *Collected Essays*. Meanwhile, Jean Guiguet had collected and edited a number of reviews which Virginia Woolf had done, principally of contemporary novelists; these were published as *Contemporary Writers* in 1965.

In 1967 B. J. Kirkpatrick published a revised *Bibliography* of Virginia Woolf's writings, and in doing so added a considerable number of entries to her previous list of published essays and reviews. A quick perusal of the 1967 *Bibliography* reveals that well over a hundred reviews and articles have still not been republished in volume form. These pieces I was invited to sort through, and asked to bring together those that seemed from both the reader's and the scholar's point of view most important to preserve. The task has proved a difficult one, largely because of the interest inherent in nearly every piece that Virginia Woolf wrote. Leonard Woolf mentions in his Editorial Note to *The Death of the Moth* the tremendous amount of effort and rewriting that went into each one of her essays. She was a perfectionist who always wrote with her whole mind and critical faculties deeply engaged. I have, however, eliminated some pieces that seemed to me too repetitive or close in content to other essays of hers that have been preserved. For instance, during the early part of the century she did reviews of several of Conrad's novels; I have not included these, because we have two very fine pieces on Conrad among the previously collected essays, which tend to recapitulate the principal points made in the earlier reviews. I have also tended not to include reviews of books by writers who may have been well known forty or fifty years ago, but have long since faded into obscurity, although it must be confessed that Virginia Woolf was often most engaging when demolishing the pretensions of a minor literary figure.

Of the essays I have preserved, many are very early. It would appear that when Virginia Woolf came to consider collecting her critical pieces in volume form, she did not look so far back as the first decade of the century; yet she had a firm, distinctive critical style right from the start, and some of these early reviews remain among her best. She was also at her best when reviewing her literary ancestors, not her contemporaries. She had the imaginative capacity to place herself in a previous literary period and savour the total atmosphere of that era. Her critical judgment was often less sure in dealing with writers of her own time, and it may well be that the spirit of competition entered into, and somewhat distorted, her otherwise sound judgment. Certainly she accorded a respect to Jane Austen, Charlotte Brontë and the like that she was unable to extend to any contemporary novelist writing in English, save perhaps Conrad.

Her critical sureness in dealing with the great figures of English literature derived in large part from her own family heritage. Nowhere is her literary debt to her father more apparent than in her critical writing. From her earliest childhood she had access not only to Sir Leslie Stephen's extensive library, but also to his taste and judgment. Had she not emerged predominantly as a novelist, she might well have occupied a position in twentieth-century criticism comparable to that which he occupied in the late Victorian era. Her earliest reviews seem most reflective of her father's influence, but this may well be true because periodicals sent her initially the sort of books that they felt Sir Leslie Stephen's daughter would be best equipped to criticise. When she emerged as a novelist and critic in her own right, they perhaps tended more frequently to assign to her works of contemporary fiction or books by women writers. But this is mere speculation. It is important to keep in mind, however, that nearly all her critical pieces originated as reviews, and that therefore the selection as a whole reflects not so much what she liked as what the periodicals for whom she reviewed expected her to like.

I have divided the essays into two major sections. The first, and larger, section deals with literary matters or with writers. The second section contains reviews of books in which one gets a vivid portrait of a man or woman, but not necessarily of a literary figure.

The first pieces in the book are largely informal essays or literary sketches, a few of which derive from reviews. The informal, or personal, essay was a genre which she admired greatly, largely because of the personality or "self" which it allowed the writer to expose, and these few pieces give some indication of the skill which she brought to the task. Essays on various men writers follow, and these, in turn, are succeeded by reviews of books about women writers and their works. The division may appear to be an arbitrary one, but I have made it because of her special awareness of what it meant to be a woman—and a woman writer. She tends to see women within their own tradition, rather than the more general one, and this is an important factor in her treatment of them.

The final section of Part I is devoted to reviews of collections of letters and to a few essays that reveal Virginia Woolf's appreciation of "literary geography"—her realization of the importance that a sense of place has in the work of many English writers. Any reader of her novels is aware of the significance that certain settings had for her personally: London, Cambridge, and Cornwall. Therefore, she was deeply aware of the influence of surroundings on other writers: the Yorkshire moors for the Brontës, the Lake District for

Wordsworth, the streets of London for Dickens; and indeed it is important to realize to what a degree her love of English literature is bound to her love of England itself, both its history and its geography.

The portraits in Part II have been separated by sex, just as the essays on writers were, and for similar reasons. Virginia Woolf rarely wrote about women without showing a consciousness of the limitations and restrictions imposed on her sex. In reviewing the lives of women she reveals with exceptional skill the roles society has expected them to play, varying from age to age, but always, in one sense or another, oppressive. One is undoubtedly more aware of the oppression in the case of nineteenth-century women than in the Elizabethan Age, and this in itself is a significant revelation which the arrangement of the essays chronologically by sex permits the reader to make.

Finally, it is important in reading Virginia Woolf's essays to keep her preëminent role as a writer of fiction in mind. The critic who writes only criticism approaches his subject from a somewhat different angle. If Virginia Woolf's criticism of prose is generally judged to be superior to her criticism of poetry, the fact that she was a practitioner has a good deal to do with that judgment. She saw the difficulties that confronted a novelist in conveying what she would probably call his vision of reality, and she also appreciated the successful accomplishment of that task, no matter how greatly his "reality" might differ from hers. Similarly, from a careful perusal of Virginia Woolf's essays, we derive a better sense of what her aims and objectives as a writer of fiction were; and we may turn from these essays back to her other books with a renewed sense of her achievement as a novelist.

MARY LYON

Acknowledgements

I am very much indebted to Ian Parsons for his editorial advice and wise guidance throughout my work on this book. I am also grateful to Miss B. J. Kirkpatrick both for her personal research on my behalf and for her excellent *Bibliography*, an invaluable book for all Virginia Woolf scholars.

PART ONE

OF WRITING AND WRITERS

In the Orchard[1]

MIRANDA slept in the orchard, lying in a long chair beneath the apple-tree. Her book had fallen into the grass, and her finger still seemed to point at the sentence "Ce pays est vraiment un des coins du monde où le rire des filles éclate le mieux . . ." as if she had fallen asleep just there. The opals on her finger flushed green, flushed rosy, and again flushed orange as the sun, oozing through the apple-trees, filled them. Then, when the breeze blew, her purple dress rippled like a flower attached to a stalk; the grasses nodded; and the white butterfly came blowing this way and that just above her face.

Four feet in the air over her head the apples hung. Suddenly there was a shrill clamour as if they were gongs of cracked brass beaten violently, irregularly, and brutally. It was only the school-children saying the multiplication table in unison, stopped by the teacher, scolded, and beginning to say the multiplication table over again. But this clamour passed four feet above Miranda's head, went through the apple boughs, and, striking against the cow-man's little boy who was picking blackberries in the hedge when he should have been at school, made him tear his thumb on the thorns.

Next there was a solitary cry—sad, human, brutal. Old Parsley was, indeed, blind drunk.

Then the very topmost leaves of the apple-tree, flat like little fish against the blue, thirty feet above the earth, chimed with a pensive and lugubrious note. It was the organ in the church playing one of Hymns Ancient and Modern. The sound floated out and was cut into atoms by a flock of fieldfares flying at an enormous speed—somewhere or other. Miranda lay asleep thirty feet beneath.

Then above the apple-tree and the pear-tree two hundred feet above Miranda lying asleep in the orchard bells thudded, intermittent, sullen, didactic, for six poor women of the parish were being churched and the Rector was returning thanks to heaven.

[1] *The Criterion*, April 1923.

And above that with a sharp squeak the golden feather of the church tower turned from south to east. The wind had changed. Above everything else it droned, above the woods, the meadows, the hills, miles above Miranda lying in the orchard asleep. It swept on, eyeless, brainless, meeting nothing that could stand against it, until, wheeling the other way, it turned south again. Miles below, in a space as big as the eye of a needle, Miranda stood upright and cried aloud: "Oh, I shall be late for tea!"

Miranda slept in the orchard—or perhaps she was not asleep, for her lips moved very slightly as if they were saying, "Ce pays est vraiment un des coins du monde . . . où le rire des filles . . . éclate . . . éclate . . . éclate . . . " and then she smiled and let her body sink all its weight on to the enormous earth which rises, she thought, to carry me on its back as if I were a leaf, or a queen (here the children said the multiplication table), or, Miranda went on, I might be lying on the top of a cliff with the gulls screaming above me. The higher they fly, she continued, as the teacher scolded the children and rapped Jimmy over the knuckles till they bled, the deeper they look into the sea—into the sea, she repeated, and her fingers relaxed and her lips closed gently as if she were floating on the sea, and then, when the shout of the drunken man sounded overhead, she drew breath with an extraordinary ecstasy, for she thought that she heard life itself crying out from a rough tongue in a scarlet mouth, from the wind, from the bells, from the curved green leaves of the cabbages.

Naturally she was being married when the organ played the tune from Hymns Ancient and Modern, and, when the bells rang after the six poor women had been churched, the sullen intermittent thud made her think that the very earth shook with the hoofs of the horse that was galloping towards her ("Ah, I have only to wait!" she sighed), and it seemed to her that everything had already begun moving, crying, riding, flying round her, across her, towards her in a pattern.

Mary is chopping the wood, she thought; Pearman is herding the cows; the carts are coming up from the meadows; the rider—and she traced out the lines that the men, the carts, the birds, and the rider made over the countryside until they all seemed driven out, round, and across by the beat of her own heart.

4

Miles up in the air the wind changed; the golden feather of the church tower squeaked; and Miranda jumped up and cried: "Oh, I shall be late for tea!"

Miranda slept in the orchard, or was she asleep or was she not asleep? Her purple dress stretched between the two apple-trees. There were twenty-four apple-trees in the orchard, some slanting slightly, others growing straight with a rush up the trunk which spread wide into branches and formed into round red or yellow drops. Each apple-tree had sufficient space. The sky exactly fitted the leaves. When the breeze blew, the line of the boughs against the wall slanted slightly and then returned. A wagtail flew diagonally from one corner to another. Cautiously hopping, a thrush advanced towards a fallen apple; from the other wall a sparrow fluttered just above the grass. The uprush of the trees was tied down by these movements; the whole was compacted by the orchard walls. For miles beneath the earth was clamped together; rippled on the surface with wavering air; and across the corner of the orchard the blue-green was slit by a purple streak. The wind changing, one bunch of apples was tossed so high that it blotted out two cows in the meadow ("Oh, I shall be late for tea!" cried Miranda), and the apples hung straight across the wall again.

A Woman's College from Outside[1]

THE feathery-white moon never let the sky grow dark; all night the chestnut blossoms were white in the green, and dim was the cow-parsley in the meadows. Neither to Tartary nor to Arabia went the wind of the Cambridge courts, but lapsed dreamily in the midst of grey-blue clouds over the roofs of Newnham. There, in the garden, if she needed space to wander, she might find it among the trees; and as none but women's faces could meet her face, she might unveil it, blank, featureless, and gaze into rooms where at that hour, blank, featureless, eyelids white over eyes, ringless hands extended upon sheets, slept innumerable women. But here and there a light still burned.

A double light one might figure in Angela's room, seeing how bright Angela herself was, and how bright came back the reflection of herself fron the square glass. The whole of her was perfectly delineated—perhaps the soul. For the glass held up an untrembling image—white and gold, red slippers, pale hair with blue stones in it, and never a ripple or shadow to break the smooth kiss of Angela and her reflection in the glass, as if she were glad to be Angela. Anyhow the moment was glad—the bright picture hung in the heart of night, the shrine hollowed in the nocturnal blackness. Strange indeed to have this visible proof of the rightness of things; this lily floating flawless upon Time's pool, fearless, as if this were sufficient—this reflection. Which meditation she betrayed by turning, and the mirror held nothing at all, or only the brass bedstead, and she, running here and there, patting, and darting, became like a woman in a house, and changed again, pursing her lips over a black book and marking with her finger what surely could not be a firm grasp of the science of economics. Only Angela Williams was at Newnham for the purpose of earning her living, and could not forget even in moments of impassioned adoration the cheques of her father at Swansea: her mother washing in the scullery: pink frocks out to dry on the line; tokens that even the lily no longer floats flawless upon the pool, but has a name on a card like another.

[1] *Atalanta's Garland*, Edinburgh University's Women's Union, 1926.

6

A. Williams—one may read it in the moonlight; and next to it some Mary or Eleanor, Mildred, Sarah, Phoebe upon square cards on their doors. All names, nothing but names. The cool white light withered them and starched them until it seemed as if the only purpose of all these names was to rise martially in order should there be a call on them to extinguish a fire, suppress an insurrection, or pass an examination. Such is the power of names written upon cards pinned upon doors. Such too the resemblance, what with tiles, corridors, and bedroom doors, to dairy or nunnery, a place of seclusion or discipline, where the bowl of milk stands cool and pure and there's a great washing of linen.

At that very moment soft laughter came from behind a door. A prim-voiced clock struck the hour—one, two. Now if the clock were issuing his commands, they were disregarded. Fire, insurrection, examination, were all snowed under by laughter, or softly uprooted, the sound seeming to bubble up from the depths and gently waft away the hour, rules, discipline. The bed was strewn with cards. Sally was on the floor. Helena in the chair. Good Bertha clasping her hands by the fire-place. A. Williams came in yawning.

"Because it's utterly and intolerably damnable," said Helena.

"Damnable," echoed Bertha. Then yawned.

"We're not eunuchs."

"I saw her slipping in by the back gate with that old hat on. They don't want us to know."

"They?" said Angela. "She."

Then the laughter.

The cards were spread, falling with their red and yellow faces on the table, and hands were dabbled in the cards. Good Bertha, leaning with her head against the chair, sighed profoundly. For she would willingly have slept, but since night is free pasturage, a limitless field, since night is unmoulded richness, one must tunnel into its darkness. One must hang it with jewels. Night was shared in secret, day browsed on by the whole flock. The blinds were up. A mist was on the garden. Sitting on the floor by the window (while the others played), body, mind, both together, seemed blown through the air, to trail across the bushes. Ah, but she desired to stretch out in bed and to sleep! She believed that no one felt her desire for sleep; she believed humbly—sleepily—with sudden nods and lurchings, that other people were wide awake. When they laughed all together a bird chirped in its sleep out in the garden, as if the laughter—

Yes, as if the laughter (for she dozed now) floated out much like mist and attached itself by soft elastic shreds to plants and bushes, so that the garden was vaporous and clouded. And then, swept by the wind, the bushes would bow themselves and the white vapours blow off across the world.

From all the rooms where women slept this vapour issued, attaching itself to shrubs, like mist, and then blew freely out into the open. Elderly women slept, who would on waking immediately clasp the ivory rod of office. Now smooth and colourless, reposing deeply, they lay surrounded, lay supported, by the bodies of youth recumbent or grouped at the window; pouring forth into the garden this bubbling laughter, this irresponsible laughter: this laughter of mind and body floating away rules, hours, discipline: immensely fertilising, yet formless, chaotic, trailing and straying and tufting the rose-bushes with shreds of vapour.

"Ah," breathed Angela, standing at the window in her nightgown. Pain was in her voice. She leant her head out. The mist was cleft as if her voice parted it. She had been talking, while the others played, to Alice Avery, about Bamborough Castle; the colour of the sands at evening; upon which Alice said she would write and settle the day, in August, and stooping, kissed her, at least touched her head with her hand, and Angela, positively unable to sit still, like one possessed of a wind-lashed sea in her heart, roamed up and down the room (the witness of such a scene) throwing her arms out to relieve this excitement, this astonishment at the incredible stooping of the miraculous tree with the golden fruit at its summit—hadn't it dropped into her arms? She held it glowing to her breast, a thing not to be touched, thought of, or spoken about, but left to glow there. And then, slowly putting there her stockings, there her slippers, folding her petticoat neatly on top, Angela, her other name being Williams, realised—how could she express it?—that after the dark churning of myriad ages here was light at the end of the tunnel; life; the world. Beneath her it lay—all good; all lovable. Such was her discovery.

Indeed, how could one then feel surprise if, lying in bed, she could not close her eyes?—something irresistibly unclosed them—if in the shallow darkness chair and chest of drawers looked stately, and the looking-glass precious with its ashen hint of day? Sucking her thumb like a child (her age nineteen last November), she lay in this good world, this new world, this world at the end of the tunnel, until a desire to see it or forestall it drove her, tossing her blankets, to guide herself to the window, and there, looking out upon the garden, where the mist lay, all the windows open, one fiery-bluish, something murmuring in the distance, the world of course, and the morning coming, "Oh," she cried, as if in pain.

On a Faithful Friend[1]

THERE is some impertinence as well as some foolhardiness in the way in which we buy animals for so much gold and silver and call them ours. One cannot help wondering what the silent critic on the hearthrug thinks of our strange conventions—the mystic Persian, whose ancestors were worshipped as gods whilst we, their masters and mistresses, grovelled in caves and painted our bodies blue. She has a vast heritage of experience, which seems to brood in her eyes, too solemn and too subtle for expression; she smiles, I often think, at our late-born civilisation, and remembers the rise and fall of dynasties. There is something, too, profane in the familiarity, half contemptuous, with which we treat our animals. We deliberately transplant a little bit of simple wild life, and make it grow up beside ours, which is neither simple nor wild. You may often see in a dog's eyes a sudden look of the primitive animal, as though he were once more a wild dog hunting in the solitary places of his youth. How have we the impertinence to make these wild creatures forego their nature for ours, which at best they can but imitate? It is one of the refined sins of civilization, for we know not what wild spirit we are taking from its purer atmosphere, or who it is—Pan, or Nymph, or Dryad—that we have trained to beg for a lump of sugar at tea.

I do not think that in domesticating our lost friend Shag we were guilty of any such crime; he was essentially a sociable dog, who had his near counterpart in the human world. I can see him smoking a cigar at the bow window of his club, his legs extended comfortably, whilst he discusses the latest news on the Stock Exchange with a companion. His best friend could not claim for him any romantic or mysterious animal nature, but that made him all the better company for mere human beings. He came to us, however, with a pedigree that had all the elements of romance in it; he, when, in horror at his price, his would-be purchaser pointed to his collie head and collie body, but terribly Skye-terrier legs—he, we were assured, was no less a dog than the original Skye—a chieftain of the same importance as the O'Brien or the O'Connor Don in human

[1] *Guardian*, January 18th, 1905.

aristocracy. The whole of the Skye-terrier tribe—who, that is, inherited the paternal characteristics—had somehow been swept from the earth; Shag, the sole scion of true Skye blood, remained in an obscure Norfolk village, the property of a low-born blacksmith, who, however, cherished the utmost loyalty for his person, and pressed the claims of his royal birth with such success that we had the honour of buying him for a very substantial sum. He was too great a gentleman to take part in the plebeian work of killing rats for which he was originally needed, but he certainly added, we felt, to the respectability of the family. He seldom went for a walk without punishing the impertinence of middle-class dogs who neglected the homage due to his rank, and we had to enclose the royal jaws in a muzzle long after that restriction was legally unnecessary. As he advanced in middle life he became certainly rather autocratic, not only with his own kind, but with us, his masters and mistresses; such a title though was absurd where Shag was concerned, so we called ourselves his uncles and aunts. The solitary occasion when he found it necessary to inflict marks of his displeasure on human flesh was once when a visitor rashly tried to treat him as an ordinary pet-dog and tempted him with sugar and called him "out of his name" by the contemptible lap-dog title of "Fido." Then Shag, with characteristic independence, refused the sugar and took a satisfactory mouthful of calf instead. But when he felt that he was treated with due respect he was the most faithful of friends. He was not demonstrative; but failing eyesight did not blind him to his master's face, and in his deafness he could still hear his master's voice.

The evil spirit of Shag's life was introduced into the family in the person of an attractive young sheep-dog puppy—who, though of authentic breed, was unhappily without a tail—a fact which Shag could not help remarking with satisfaction. We deluded ourselves into the thought that the young dog might take the place of the son of Shag's old age, and for a time they lived happily together. But Shag had ever been contemptuous of social graces, and had relied for his place in our hearts upon his sterling qualities of honesty and independence; the puppy, however, was a young gentleman of most engaging manners, and, though we tried to be fair, Shag could not help feeling that the young dog got most of our attention. I can see him now, as in a kind of blundering and shamefaced way he lifted one stiff old paw and gave it me to shake, which was one of the young dog's most successful tricks. It almost brought the tears to my eyes. I could not help thinking, though I smiled, of old King Lear. But Shag was too old to acquire new graces; no second place should be his, and he determined that the matter should be decided by force. So after some weeks of growing tension the battle was fought; they went for each other with white teeth gleaming—Shag was the aggressor—and rolled round and round on the grass, locked in each other's grip. When at last we got them apart, blood was running, hair was flying, and both dogs bore scars. Peace after that was impossible; they had but to see each other to growl and stiffen; the question was —Who was the conqueror? Who was to stay and who to go? The decision we came to was base, unjust, and yet, perhaps, excusable. The old dog has had his day, we said, he must give place to the new generation. So old Shag was deposed, and sent to a kind of dignified dower-house at Parson's-green, and the young dog reigned in his stead. Year after year passed, and we never saw the old friend who had known us in the days of our youth; but in the summer holidays he revisited the house in our absence with the caretaker. And so time went on till this last year, which, though we did not know it, was to be the last year of his life. Then, one winter's night, at a time of great sickness and anxiety, a dog was heard barking repeatedly, with the bark of a dog who waits to be let in, outside our kitchen-door. It was many years since that bark had been heard, and only one person in the kitchen was able to recognise it now. She opened the door, and in walked Shag, now almost quite blind and stone deaf, as he had walked in many times before, and, looking neither to right nor left, went to his old corner by the fireside, where he curled up and fell asleep without a sound. If the usurper saw him he slunk guiltily away, for Shag was past fighting for his rights any more. We shall never know—it is one of the many things that we can never know—what strange wave of memory or sympathetic instinct it was that drew Shag from the house where he had lodged for years to seek again the familiar doorstep of his master's home. And it befell that Shag was the last of the family to live in the old house, for it was in crossing the road which leads to the gardens where he was taken for his first walks as a puppy, and bit all the other dogs and frightened all the babies in their perambulators, that he met his death. The blind, deaf dog neither saw nor heard a hansom; and the wheel went over him and ended instantly a life which could not have been happily prolonged. It was better for him to die thus out among the wheels and the horses than to end in a lethal-chamber or be poisoned in a stable-yard.

So we say farewell to a dear and faithful friend, whose virtues we remember—and dogs have few faults.

English Prose[1]

I F it should be proposed to appoint Mr Pearsall Smith Anthologist Royal to the English-speaking races, I, for one, would
willingly contribute rather more than I can afford to his stipend.
For three hundred years and more a dead preacher called John
Donne has cumbered our shelves. The other day Mr Pearsall
Smith touched him with his wand, and behold!—the folios quake,
the pages shiver, out steps the passionate preacher; the fibres of our
secular hearts are bent and bowed beneath the unaccustomed
tempest. But no figure could be more misleading than this of the
wand and the wizard. Conceive, rather, a table piled with books;
folio pages turned and turned again; collations, annotations,
emendations, expurgations; voyages in omnibuses; hours of disillusionment—for who reads prose? life wasting under the rays of a
green lamp; the prize of months one solitary paragraph—truly if
Mr Pearsall Smith is a wizard he has learned his craft where none
but the bold and the faithful dare follow him. Therefore if I go on to
say that in one respect I am his superior, it will be understood that it
is not to his learning that I refer. I refer to his taste. In reading the
"Treasury of English Prose" I became aware that my taste is far
better than Mr Pearsall Smith's; it is in fact impeccable. But I need
scarcely hasten to add what everyone knows for himself; in matters
of taste each man, woman and child in the British Isles is impeccable; so are the quadrupeds. A dog who did not rate his own taste
better than his master's would be a dog not worth drowning.

This being said, let us waste no more time but proceed at once
to Stevenson. I had hoped, not very confidently, to look for
Stevenson in vain. I had hoped that the habit of cutting out passages
from Stevenson about being good and being brave and being happy
was now confined to schoolmasters and people at the head of public
institutions. I had hoped that private individuals were beginning
to say, "What is the point of Stevenson? Why did they call him a
master of prose? What did our fathers mean by comparing this
thin-blooded mummery with Scott or Defoe?"—but I had hoped in

[1] *A Treasury of English Prose*, edited by Logan Pearsall Smith. *The Athenæum*,
January 30, 1920.

vain. Here is Stevenson occupying one of two hundred and fifteen pages with reflections upon Happiness—reflections addressed in a private letter to a friend. It begins all right. Nobody can deny that it needs every sort of good quality to step along so briskly, with such apparent ease, such a nice imitation of talk running down the pen and flowing over the paper. Nor do I shiver when the pen steps more circumspectly. A writer's letters should be as literary as his printed works. But all my spines erect themselves, all my prejudices are confirmed when I come to this: "But I know pleasure still; pleasure with a thousand faces, and none perfect, a thousand tongues all broken, a thousand hands and all of them with scratching nails. High among these I place this delight of weeding out here alone by the garrulous water, under the silence of the high wood, broken by incongruous sounds of birds." Then I know why I cannot read the novels; then I know why I should never allow him within a mile of the anthologies.

Skipping (for no one reads an anthology through), we next alight upon Walter Pater—nervously, prepared for disappointment. Can he possibly be what he once seemed?—the writer who from words made blue and gold and green; marble, brick, the wax petals of flowers; warmth too and scent; all things that the hand delighted to touch and the nostrils to smell, while the mind traced subtle winding paths and surprised recondite secrets. This, and much more than this, comes back to me with renewed delight in Mr Pearsall Smith's quotations. The famous one still seems to me to deserve all its fame; the less famous, about a red hawthorn tree in full flower—"a plumage of tender crimson fire out of the heart of the dry wood"—revives the old joys and makes the nerve of the eye vibrate again; but if one cannot praise fitly it is better to be silent and only say that there can be no doubt—from the quotations at least—about Walter Pater.

About Emerson there is I think considerable doubt; or rather there is no doubt at all that he must be altogether different from what we supposed to deserve eleven full pages where there is no room for a single line of Dryden, Cowper, Peacock, Hardy, the Brontës, Jane Austen, Meredith (to take the obvious omissions); only two scraps of Sterne and a page and a bit of Conrad. Yet one sees what Mr Pearsall Smith means. Emerson wrote for anthologies. Passages seem to break off in one's hands like ripe fruit without damage to the tree. The first passage reads beautifully; the second almost as well. But then—what is it? something bald and bare and glittering—something light and brittle—something which suggests that if this precious fruit were dropped it would shiver into particles of silvery dust like one of those balls that were plucked from the boughs of ancient Christmas trees, and slipped and fell—is Emerson's fruit *that* kind of fruit? Of course the lustre is admirable—the dust, the dust of the stars.

But if Mr Pearsall Smith puts in and leaves out according to a rule of his own, that is an indispensable merit in an anthologist. He puts in, for example, Jeremy Taylor, and so reveals a great English writer who, to my shame, had been no more than an obscure clerical shade among the folios. For that I could forgive him—I was going to say the neglect of Mr Hardy; but Mr Pearsall Smith can hardly have neglected all, or almost all, the great English novelists. He has rejected them, and that is another matter, that leads one to consider what may be his reasons. I suppose there are at least twenty of them, and all so profound and lying at the roots of things that to lay bare a single one would need more columns than I have words. Lightly then will I run over a few suggestions and leave them to wither or perhaps fall on fertile soil. To begin with, every novelist would, I suppose, suspect a critic who complimented him on the beauty of his writing. "But that's not what I'm after," he would say, and add, a moment later, with the susceptibility of his kind, "You mean, I'm dull." And as a matter of fact the great novelists very seldom stop in the middle or in the beginning of their great scenes to write anything that one could cut out with a pair of scissors or loop round with a line of red ink. The greatest of novelists—Dostoevsky—always, so Russian scholars say, writes badly. Turgenev, the least great of the Russian trinity, always, they say, writes exquisitely. That Dostoevsky would have been a greater novelist had he written beautifully into the bargain no one will deny. But the novelist's task lays such a load upon every nerve, muscle, and fibre that to demand beautiful prose in addition is, in view of human limitations, to demand what can only be given at the cost of a sacrifice. Let us choose two instances from among the writers of our own tongue. There is no novel by Mr Conrad which has not passages of such beauty that one hangs over them like a humming-bird moth at the mouth of a flower. Yet I believe that one pays for such beauty in a novel. To achieve it the writer has had to shut off his energy in other directions. Hence, I think, so many pages of Mr Conrad's novels are slack and slumberous, monotonous like the summer sea. Mr Hardy, on the other hand, has not in the course of some twenty volumes written a single passage fit to be included in a treasury of English prose. Impossible! Yet I could not, at a moment's notice, lay my hand on one. The greater number of our novelists are in the same boat with him. But what, then, can we be talking about? What is this "beautiful English prose"?

Surely the most beautiful of all things! the reader of Mr Pearsall Smith's selection will exclaim—the most subtle, the most profound, the most moving and imaginative. And who are the people who keep it alive, extend its powers, and increase its triumphs? The novelists. Only we must not go to them for perfect passages, descriptions, perorations, reflections so highly wrought that they can stand alone without their context. We must go to them for chapters, not for sentences; for beauty, not tranquil and contained, but wild and fleeting like the light on rough waters. We must seek it particularly where the narrative breaks and gives way to dialogue. But it must be conceded that the novelists put their English to the most menial tasks. She has to do all the work of the house; to make the beds, dust the china, boil the kettle, sweep the floors. In return she has the priceless privilege of living with human beings. When she has warmed to her task, when the fire is burning, the cat here, the dog there, the smoke rising from the chimney, the men and women feasting or love-making, dreaming or speculating, the trees blowing, the moon rising, the autumn sun gold upon the corn—then read Mr Hardy and see whether the common prose of English fiction does not carry herself like the Queen she is—the old Queen, wise in the secrets of our hearts; the young Queen with all her life before her. For though English poetry was a fine old potentate—but no, I dare not breathe a word against English poetry. All I will venture is a sigh of wonder and amazement that when there is prose before us with its capacities and possibilities, its power to say new things, make new shapes, express new passions, young people should still be dancing to a barrel organ and choosing words because they rhyme.

Impressions at Bayreuth[1]

THE commonplace remark that music is in its infancy is best borne out by the ambiguous state of musical criticism. It has few traditions behind it, and the art itself is so much alive that it fairly suffocates those who try to deal with it. A critic of writing is hardly to be taken by surprise, for he can compare almost every literary form with some earlier form and can measure the achievement by some familiar standard. But who in music has tried to do what Strauss is doing, or Debussy? Before we have made up our minds as to the nature of the operatic form we have to value very different and very emphatic examples of it. This lack of tradition and of current standards is of course the freest and happiest state that a critic can wish for; it offers some one the chance of doing now for music what Aristotle did 2,000 years ago for poetry. The fact however that so little has yet been done to lay bare the principles of the art accounts for the indecision which marks our attempts to judge new music. As for the old, we take it for granted, or concentrate our minds upon the *prima donna*'s cold. It is criticism of a single hour, in a particular day, and tomorrow the mark has faded.

There is only one way open thus for a writer who is not disposed to go to the root of the matter and is yet dissatisfied with the old evasions—he may try to give his impressions as an amateur. The seats in the great bare house in Bayreuth are packed with them; they have a secret belief that they understand as well as other people, although they seldom venture an opinion; and, at any rate, there is no doubt that they love music. If they hesitate to criticize, it is perhaps that they have not sufficient technical knowledge to fasten upon details; a criticism of the whole resolves itself into vague formulas, comparisons, and adjectives. Nevertheless, no one can doubt that the audience at Bayreuth, pilgrims many of them from distant lands, attend with all their power. As the lights sink, they rustle into their seats, and scarcely stir till the last wave of sound has ceased; when a stick falls, there is a nervous shudder, like a ripple in water, through the entire house. During the intervals between the acts, when they come out into the sun, they seem

[1] *The Times*, August 21, 1909.

oppressed with a desire to disburden themselves somehow of the impression which they have received. *Parsifal*, in particular, lays such a weight upon the mind that it is not until one has heard it many times over that one can begin, as it were, to move it to and fro. The unfamiliarity of the ideas hinders one at the outset from bringing the different parts together. One feels vaguely for a crisis that never comes, for, accustomed as one is to find the explanation of a drama in the love of man and woman, or in battle, one is bewildered by a music that continues with the utmost calm and intensity independently of them. Further, the change from the Temple of the Grail to the magic garden, with its swarms of flower-maidens and its hot red blossoms, is too violent a break to be bridged conveniently.

Nevertheless, although they are great, these difficulties scarcely do more than disturb the surface of a very deep and perhaps indescribable impression. Puzzled we may be, but it is primarily because the music has reached a place not yet visited by sound. An anthem sung with perfect skill in some great church will suggest a part of the scene in the vast hall, with its green distances, and yet a part only. Ecclesiastical music is too rigidly serene and too final in its spirit to penetrate as the music of *Parsifal* penetrates. Somehow Wagner has conveyed the desire of the Knights for the Grail in such a way that the intense emotion of human beings is combined with the unearthly nature of the thing they seek. It tears us, as we hear it, as though its wings were sharply edged. Again, feelings of this kind that are equally diffused and felt for one object in common create an impression of largeness and, when the music is played as it was played on the night of the 11th, of an overwhelming unity. The Grail seems to burn through all superincumbences; the music is intimate in a sense that none other is; one is fired with emotion and yet possessed with tranquillity at the same time, for the words are continued by the music so that we hardly notice the transition.

It may be that these exalted emotions, which belong to the essence of our being, and are rarely expressed, are those that are best translated by music; so that a satisfaction, or whatever one may call that sense of answer which the finest art supplies to its own question, is constantly conveyed here. Like Shakespeare, Wagner seems to have attained in the end to such a mastery of technique that he could float and soar in regions where in the beginning he could scarcely breathe; the stubborn matter of his art dissolves in his fingers, and he shapes it as he chooses. When the opera is over, it is surely the completeness of the work that remains with us. The earlier operas have always their awkward moments, when the illusion breaks; but *Parsifal* seems poured out in a smooth stream at white heat; its shape is solid and entire. How much of the singular atmosphere which surrounds the opera in one's mind springs from other sources than the music itself it would be hard to say. It is the only work which has no incongruous associations.

It has been possible, during these last performances, to step out of the opera-house and find oneself in the midst of a warm summer evening. From the hill above the theatre you look over a wide land, smooth and without hedges; it is not beautiful, but it is very large and tranquil. One may sit among rows of turnips and watch a gigantic old woman, with a blue cotton bonnet on her head and a figure like one of Dürer's, swinging her hoe. The sun draws out strong scents from the hay and the pine trees, and if one thinks at all, it is to combine the simple landscape with the landscape of the stage. When the music is silent the mind insensibly slackens and expands, among happy surroundings: heat and the yellow light, and the intermittent but not unmusical noises of insects and leaves smooth out the folds. In the next interval, between seven and eight, there is another act out here also; it is now dusky and perceptibly fresher; the light is thinner, and the roads are no longer crossed by regular bars of shade. The figures in light dresses moving between the trees of the avenue, with depths of blue air behind them, have a curiously decorative effect. Finally, when the opera is over, it is quite late; and half way down the hill one looks back upon a dark torrent of carriages descending, their lamps wavering one above another, like irregular torches.

These strange intervals in the open air, as though a curtain were regularly drawn and shut again, have no disturbing effect, upon *Parsifal* at least. A bat from the woods circled Kundry's head in the meadow, and little white moths dance incessantly over the footlights. It was curious, although scarcely fair, to test *Lohengrin* two days after one had heard *Parsifal*. The difference which a chorus, alive in all its parts so that eyes and arms are moving when the voice is silent, can make to a work in which the chorus means so much is surprising certainly; and yet, recognizing the admirable performance, other reflections were suggested by it. The same surroundings that were so congenial to *Parsifal* turn much of *Lohengrin* to tinsel and sham armour; one thinks of gorgeous skirts and the mantles of knights trailed along the dusty paths and pricked by the stubble. An opera house which shelters such a troop should be hemmed in by streets with great shop windows; their splendour somehow dwindles away and falls flat in the empty country.

But although this was one of the impressions that *Lohengrin* gave rise to, can it be held to be any reflection upon the music? No one, perhaps, save a writer properly versed in the science, can decide which impressions are relevant and which impertinent, and it is here that the amateur is apt to incur the contempt of the professional. We know the critic who, in painting, prefers the art of Fra Angelico because that painter worked upon his knees; others choose books because they teach one to rise early; and one has only to read the descriptive notes in a concert programme to be led hopelessly astray. Apart from the difficulty of changing a musical impression into a literary one, and the tendency to appeal to the literary sense because of the associations of words, there is the further difficulty in the case of music that its scope is much less clearly defined than the scope of the other arts. The more beautiful a phrase of music is the richer its burden of suggestion, and if we understand the form but slightly, we are little restrained in our interpretation. We are led on to connect the beautiful sound with some experience of our own, or to make it symbolize some conception of a general nature. Perhaps music owes something of its astonishing power over us to this lack of definite articulation; its statements have all the majesty of a generalization, and yet contain our private emotions. Something of the same effect is given by Shakespeare, when he makes an old nurse the type of all the old nurses in the world, while she keeps her identity as a particular old woman. The comparative weakness of *Lohengrin* urges one to such speculations, for there are many passages which fit loosely to the singer's mood, and yet carry one's mind out with a beauty of their own.

In the meantime, we are miserably aware how little words can do to render music. When the moment of suspense is over, and the bows actually move across the strings, our definitions are relinquished, and words disappear in our minds. Enormous is the relief, and yet, when the spell is over, how great is the joy with which we turn to our old tools again! These definitions indeed, which would limit the bounds of an art and regulate our emotions, are arbitrary enough; and here at Bayreuth, where the music fades into the open air, and we wander with *Parsifal* in our heads through empty streets at night, where the gardens of the Hermitage glow with flowers like those other magic blossoms, and sound melts into colour, and colour calls out for words, where, in short, we are lifted out of the ordinary world and allowed merely to breathe and see—it is here that we realize how thin are the walls between one emotion and another; and how fused our impressions are with elements which we may not attempt to separate.

Modes and Manners of the Nineteenth Century[1]

WHEN one has read no history for a time the sad-coloured volumes are really surprising. That so much energy should have been wasted in the effort to believe in something spectral fills one with pity. Wars and Ministries and legislation—unexampled prosperity and unbridled corruption tumbling the nation headlong to decay—what a strange delusion it all is!—invented presumably by gentlemen in tall hats in the forties who wished to dignify mankind. Our point of view they ignore entirely: we have never felt the pressure of a single law; our passions and despairs have nothing to do with trade; our virtues and vices flourish under all Governments impartially. The machine they describe; they succeed to some extent in making us believe in it; but the heart of it they leave untouched—is it because they cannot understand it? At any rate, we are left out, and history, in our opinion, lacks an eye. It is with unusual hope that we open the three volumes in which a nameless author has dealt with the Modes and Manners of the Nineteenth Century. Thin and green, with innumerable coloured pictures and a fair type, they are less like a mausoleum than usual; and modes and manners—how we feel and dress—are precisely what the other historian ignores.

The connexion between dress and character has been pointed out often enough. Because dress represents some part of a man picturesquely it lends itself happily to the satirist. He can exaggerate it without losing touch with the object of his satire. Like a shadow, it walks beside the truth and apes it. The device of making the smaller ridicule the greater by representing it recommended itself to Swift and Carlyle. But to discover soberly how far thought has expressed itself in clothes, and manners as we call them, is far more difficult. There is the temptation to hook the two together by the most airy conjectures. A gentleman had the habit, for example, of walking in the streets of Berlin with tame deer; that was character-

[1] Translated by M. Edwards. 3 vols. *The Times Literary Supplement*, February 24, 1910.

istic, we are told, of a certain middle-class section of German society, in the twenties, thirties, and forties, which was learned, pedantic, Philistine, and vulgar; for to make oneself conspicuous is a mark of the vulgarian, and to walk with tame deer is to make oneself conspicuous. But there are more solid links. The French Revolution, of course, sundered the traditions of ages. It decreed that man in future must be mainly black, and should wear trousers instead of breeches. The waistcoat alone remained aristocratic, and drew to itself all the reds and oranges of the other garments, and, as they became cotton, turned to plush and brocade. At length this rich territory was conquered, and sparks of colour only burnt in the cravat and on the fob. The different garments moved up and down, swelled and shrank at intervals, but after 1815 a man's clothes were "essentially the same as they are now." Men wished to obliterate classes, and a dress that could be worn at work became necessary. Women, on the other hand, were exposed to fewer influences, so that it may be easier to trace one idea in their clothes. The effect of the Revolution seems to be definite enough. Rousseau had bidden them return to nature; the Revolution had left them poor; the Greeks were ancient, and therefore natural; and their dress was cheap enough for a democracy. Accordingly, they dressed in pure white cottons and calicoes, without a frill or an exuberance; nature alone was to shape the lines; nature was to suffer not more than eight ounces of artificial concealment. The effect of these tapering nymphs, dancing on a hilltop among slim trees, is exquisite but chill. Because Greek temples were white, they white-washed their walls; the bed room was the Temple of Sleep; the tables were altars; the chair legs were grooved into columns; reticules were shaped like funeral urns, and classical cameos were worn at the neck. The absolute consistency of their attitude may be ridiculous, but it is also remarkable. In fact, the society of the Empire is the last to "boast a style of its own, owing to the perfect correspondence between its aims, ideas, and character, and their outward manifestations." Any unanimity is overwhelming; it is one of the great gifts we bestow upon the Greeks; and, although there were many beautiful episodes in the nineteenth century, no single style was again strong enough to make everything consistent. Before the Revolution some sort of order was stamped upon fashion by the will of the Queen, who could afford to make beauty the prime virtue; but in 1792 Mlle Bertin, Marie Antoinette's modiste, fled from Paris, and although she touched at other Courts, eventually settling in England, her rule was over; shops for ready-made clothing opened as she left. For ten years, 1794-1804, the didactic classic spirit served instead of the Royal will; and then a confusion set in which threatens never to grow calm. Still the author does his best to make one change account for another, at the risk of wide generalizations. "Feeling and sensibility took the place in this generation [the generation of the Napoleonic wars] of religion. . . . During the First Empire love and passion had been but the passing gratification of the moment, but now love was to be the one lasting object of life and being"—therefore puffs and ruffs were worn; the furniture became rococo, and Gothic cathedrals influenced the chairs and the clocks.

A woman's clothes are so sensitive that, far from seeking one influence to account for their changes, we must seek a thousand. The opening of a railway line, the marriage of a princess, the trapping of a skunk—such external events tell upon them; then there is the "relationship between the sexes"; in 1867 the Empress Eugénie, wearing a short skirt for the first time, went for a drive with the Emperor and Empress of Austria. As the ladies stepped into the carriage, the Emperor turned to his wife and said, "Take care, or some one may catch sight of your feet." The influences of beauty and of reason are always fighting in a woman's clothes; reason has won some remarkable triumphs, in Germany for the most part, but generally submits to a weak compromise. When we talk of fashion, however, we mean something definite though hard to define. It comes from without; we wake in the morning and find the shops alive with it; soon it is abroad in the streets. As we turn over the pictures in these volumes we see the spirit at work. It travels all over the body ceaselessly. Now the skirt begins to grow, until it trails for six feet upon the ground; suddenly the spirit leaps to the throat, and creates a gigantic ruff there, while the skirt shrinks to the knees; then it enters the hair, which immediately rises in the pinnacles of Salisbury Cathedral; a slight swelling appears beneath the skirt; it grows, alarmingly; at last a frame has to support the flounces; next the arms are attacked; they imitate Chinese pagodas; steel hoops do what they can to relieve them. The hair, meanwhile, has subsided. The lady has outgrown all cloaks, and only a vast shawl can encompass her. Suddenly, without warning, the entire fabric is pricked; the spirit moves the Empress Eugénie one night (January 1859) to reject her crinoline. In an instant the skirts of Europe melt away, and with pursed lips and acrimonious manners the ladies mince about the streets clasped tightly round the knees, instead of swimming. It is from the crinoline, no doubt, that Meredith got his favourite "she swam."

Fashion dealt more discreetly with men, and chiefly haunted their legs. Nevertheless, there was a great sympathy between the sexes. When her skirts ballooned, his trousers swelled; when she dwindled away, he wore stays; when her hair was Gothic, his was romantic; when she dragged a train, his cloak swept the ground. About 1820 his waistcoat was more uncontrollable than any garment of hers; five times within eight months it changed its shape; for a long time the cravat preserved a space for jewelry where the necklaces were rivalled. The only parts of men that survived the stark years of the thirties and forties were the hat and the beard; they still felt the sway of political changes. The democratic spirit required felt hats that drooped; in 1848 they dissolved about the ears; stiffening again as reaction set in. The same principle ruled the beard; to be clean shaven was a sign of unflinching respectability; a ragged beard, or even a beard alone, showed that one's opinions were out of control. At the present time "Only at home does the gentleman indulge in coloured gold-laced velvet, silk, or cashmere; when he appears in public he may only venture by the superior cut of his garments to aim at any distinction; if the male attire thereby loses in effect, it gains in tone."

With furniture we find the same thing. Quite slowly every chair and table round us changes its form; if one had fallen asleep in an early Victorian drawing-room, among the patterns and plush, one would wake up this year with a horrid start. The room would seem little better than an attic. Yet, if one had sat there open-eyed, one would scarcely have seen the things change. Dress and furniture are always moving, but, having done his utmost to make them depend upon "the spirit of the time," the author declares himself baffled. "The longer we study the question, the more certain do we become that though we know the how, we shall never know the wherefore." Are we truly in the grip of a spirit that makes us dance to its measure, or can it be laid without recourse to magic? When one compromises one delivers no clear message. Throughout the nineteenth century both dress and furniture were at the mercy of a dozen different aims, and the original meaning was further blunted by the intervention of machines. Only great artists, giving their minds to nothing else, represent their age; dressmakers and cabinet-makers generally caricature it or say nothing about it. As for manners, the term is so vague that it is difficult to test it; but it is probable that they too only approximate, and that people's behaviour is the roughest guide to what they mean. If manners are not rubbed smooth by a machine, the comfort of society depends upon using a common language, and only saying what can be misunderstood without disaster. For this reason a history of modes and manners must use phrases which are as empty as any in the language, and the history is not a history of ourselves, but of our disguises. The poets and the novelists are the only people from whom we cannot hide.

Men and Women[1]

IF you look at a large subject through the medium of a little book you see for the most part something of such vague and wavering outline that, though it may be a Greek gem, it may almost equally be a mountain or a bathing machine. But though Mlle Villard's book is small and her subject vast, her focus is so exact and her glass so clear that the outline remains sharp and the detail distinct. Thus we can read every word with interest because it is possible at a thousand points to check her statements; she is on every page dealing with the definite and the concrete. But how, in treating of a whole century, a whole country, and a whole sex, is it possible to be either definite or concrete? Mlle Villard has solved the problem by using fiction as her material; for, though she has read Blue-books and biographies, her freshness and truth must be ascribed largely to the fact that she has preferred to read novels. In novels, she says, the thoughts, hopes and lives of women during the century and in the country of her most remarkable development are displayed more intimately and fully than elsewhere. One might indeed say that were it not for the novels of the nineteenth century we should remain as ignorant as our ancestors of this section of the human race. It has been common knowledge for ages that women exist, bear children, have no beards, and seldom go bald; but save in these respects, and in others where they are said to be identical with men, we know little of them and have little sound evidence upon which to base our conclusions. Moreover, we are seldom dispassionate.

Before the nineteenth century literature took almost solely the form of soliloquy, not of dialogue. The garrulous sex, against common repute, is not the female but the male; in all the libraries of the world the man is to be heard talking to himself and for the most part about himself. It is true that women afford ground for much speculation and are frequently represented; but it is becoming daily more evident that Lady Macbeth, Cordelia, Ophelia,

[1] *La Femme Anglaise au XIXème Siècle et son Evolution d'après le Roman Anglais contemporain.* By Léonie Villard, *The Times Literary Supplement*, March 18, 1920.

Clarissa, Dora, Diana, Helen and the rest are by no means what they pretend to be. Some are plainly men in disguise; others represent what men would like to be, or are conscious of not being; or again they embody that dissatisfaction and despair which afflict most people when they reflect upon the sorry condition of the human race. To cast out and incorporate in a person of the opposite sex all that we miss in ourselves and desire in the universe and detest in humanity is a deep and universal instinct on the part both of men and of women. But though it affords relief, it does not lead to understanding. Rochester is as great a travesty of the truth about men as Cordelia is of the truth about women. Thus Mlle Villard soon finds herself confronted by the fact that some of the most famous heroines even of nineteenth-century fiction represent what men desire in women, but not necessarily what women are in themselves. Helen Pendennis, for example, tells us a great deal more about Thackeray than about herself. She tells us, indeed, that she has never had a penny that she could call her own, and no more education than serves to read the Prayer-book and the cookery-book. From her we learn also that when one sex is dependent upon the other it will endeavour for safety's sake to simulate what the dominant sex finds desirable. The women of Thackeray and the women of Dickens succeed to some extent in throwing dust in their masters' eyes, though the peculiar repulsiveness of these ladies arises from the fact that the deception is not wholly successful. The atmosphere is one of profound distrust. It is possible that Helen herself flung off her widow's weeds, took a deep draught of beer, produced a short clay pipe, and stuck her legs on the mantelpiece directly her master was round the corner. At any rate, Thackeray cannot forbear one glance of suspicion as he turns his back. But midway through the nineteenth century the servile woman was stared out of countenance by two very uncompromising characters—Jane Eyre and Isopel Berners. One insisted that she was poor and plain, and the other that she much preferred wandering on a heath to settling down and marrying anybody. Mlle Villard attributes the remarkable contrast between the servile and the defiant, the sheltered and the adventurous, to the introduction of machinery. Rather more than a century ago, after whirling for many thousands of years, the spinning-wheel became obsolete.

29

En fait, le désir de la femme de s'extérioriser, de dépasser les limites jusque-là assignées à son activité, prend naissance au moment même où sa vie est moins étroitement liée à toutes les heures aux tâches du foyer, aux travaux qui, une ou deux générations auparavant, absorbaient son attention et employaient ses forces. Le rouet, l'aiguille, la quenouille, la préparation des confitures et des conserves, voire des chandelles et du savon . . . n'occupent plus les femmes et, tandis que l'antique ménagère disparaît, celle qui sera demain la femme nouvelle sent grandir en elle, avec le loisir de voir, de penser, de juger, la conscience d'elle-même et du monde où elle vit.

For the first time for many ages the bent figure with the knobbed hands and the bleared eyes, who, in spite of the poets, is the true figure of womanhood, rose from her wash-tub, took a stroll out of doors, and went into the factory. That was the first painful step on the road to freedom.

Any summary of the extremely intelligent pages in which Mlle Villard has told the story of the Englishwoman's progress from 1860 to 1914 is impossible. Moreover, Mlle Villard would be the first to agree that not even a woman, and a Frenchwoman at that, looking with the clear-sighted eyes of her race across the Channel, can say for certain what the words "emancipation" and "evolution" amount to. Granted that the woman of the middle class has now some leisure, some education, and some liberty to investigate the world in which she lives, it will not be in this generation or in the next that she will have adjusted her position or given a clear account of her powers. "I have the feelings of a woman," says Bathsheba in "Far from the Madding Crowd," "but I have only the language of men." From that dilemma arise infinite confusions and complications. Energy has been liberated, but into what forms is it to flow? To try the accepted forms, to discard the unfit, to create others which are more fitting, is a task that must be accomplished before there is freedom or achievement. Further, it is well to remember that woman was not created for the first time in the year 1860. A large part of her energy is already fully employed and highly developed. To pour such surplus energy as there may be into new forms without wasting a drop is the difficult problem which can only be solved by the simultaneous evolution and emancipation of man.

Coleridge as Critic[1]

IN his preface to the "Anima Poetae" Mr E. H. Coleridge remarks that the "Table Talk", unlike other of Coleridge's prose
writings, still remains well known and widely read. We do not
know that the brief article by Coventry Patmore prefixed to this
new edition tells us much more than that Mr Patmore was himself a
Conservative, but if the preface had any share in the re-publication
of the "Table Talk", we owe it our thanks. It is always well to
re-read the classics. It is always wholesome to make sure that they
still earn their pedestals and do not merely cast their shadows over
heads bent superstitiously from custom. In particular it is worth
while to re-read Coleridge because, owing to his peculiarities of
character and to the effect which they had upon such portrait
painters as Hazlitt, De Quincey, and above all, Carlyle, we possess
a very visible ghost—Coleridge, a wonderful, ridiculous, impossibly loquacious old gentleman who lived at Highgate and could
never determine which side of the path to walk on. The loquacity
can hardly have been exaggerated, but read the "Table Talk" and
you will get what no portrait painter can possibly catch—the
divine quality of the old gentleman's mind, the very flash of his
miraculous eye. Whether or no it is a test of true greatness, his own
words give us at once not indeed a sense of perceiving the distinction
between the reason and the understanding, but of knowing him as
no second person can reveal him; there is a being in the book who
still speaks directly to the individual mind.

The comparison between Coleridge and Johnson is obvious in so
far as each held sway chiefly by the power of his tongue. The
difference between their methods is so marked that it is tempting,
but also unnecessary, to judge one to be inferior to the other.
Johnson was robust, combative, and concrete; Coleridge was the
opposite. The contrast was perhaps in his mind when he said of
Johnson:

> . . . his *bow-wow* manner must have had a good deal to do with
> the effect produced. . . . Burke, like all men of genius who love to

[1] *The Table Talk and Omniana of Samuel Taylor Coleridge.* With a Note on
Coleridge by Coventry Patmore. *The Times Literary Supplement*, February 7, 1918.

talk at all, was very discursive and continuous; hence he is not reported; he seldom said the sharp, short things that Johnson almost always did, which produce a more decided effect at the moment, and which are so much more easy to carry off.

Modesty may have required him to say Burke instead of Coleridge, but either name will do. The same desire to justify and protect one's type led him no doubt to perceive the truth that "a great mind must be androgynous. . . . I have known strong minds with imposing, undoubting, Cobbett-like manners, but I have never met a great mind of this sort."

But the chief distinction between the talk of Coleridge and that of Johnson, or indeed, between the talk of Coleridge and that of most of the famous talkers, lay in his indifference to, in his hatred of, "mere personality." That omission rules out more than gossip; it rules out the kind of portrait painting in which Carlyle excelled, or the profound human insight so often expressed by Johnson. One cannot suppose that Coleridge would ever have lifted a poor woman to his shoulders, but he could be "pained by observing in others, and was fully conscious in himself of a sympathy" with the upper classes which he had not for the lower, until, hearing a thatcher's wife cry her heart out for the death of her child, "it was given him all at once to feel" that, while sympathizing equally with poor and rich in the matter of the affections—"the best part of humanity"—still with regard to *mental* misery, struggles and conflicts, his sympathies were with those who could best appreciate their force and value. From this it is plain that if we seek Coleridge's company we must leave certain human desires outside, or rather we must be ready to mount, if we can, into an atmosphere where the substance of these desires has been shredded by infinite refinements and discriminations of all its grossness.

The incompatibility which certainly existed between Coleridge and the rest of the world arose, so the Table Talk persuades us, from the fact that even more than Shelley he was "a beautiful and ineffectual angel"—a spirit imprisoned behind bars invisible and intangible to the tame hordes of humanity, a spirit always beckoned by something from without. Very naturally, to his fellow prisoners behind the bars his interpretation was confused, and from a philosophic point of view inconclusive. But there has been no finer messenger between gods and men, nor one whose being kept from youth to age so high a measure of transparency. His criticism is the most spiritual in the language. His notes upon Shakespeare are, to our thinking, the only criticisms which bear reading with the sound of the play still in one's ears. They possess one of the marks which we are apt to discover in the finest art, the power of seeming to bring to light what was already there beforehand, instead of imposing anything from the outside. The shock, the surprise, the paradox, which so often prevail and momentarily illumine, are entirely absent from the art of Coleridge; and the purity of his criticism is further increased by his neglect here also of "mere personality." The possibility that one may throw light upon a book by considering the circumstances in which it was written did not commend itself to Coleridge; to him the light was concentrated and confined in one ray—in the art itself. We have, of course, to take into account the fact that he never produced any complete work of criticism. We have only imperfect reports of lectures, memories of talk, notes scribbled in the margins of pages. His views are therefore scattered and fragmentary, and it is usual to lament the ruin wrought by opium upon the vast and enduring fabric which should have been built from these broken stones. But this mania for size savours rather of megalomania. There is a great deal to be said for small books. It is arguable that the desire to be exhaustive, comprehensive, and monumental has destroyed more virtue than it has brought to birth. In literary criticism at least the wish to attain completeness is more often than not a will o' the wisp which lures one past the occasional ideas which may perhaps have truth in them towards an unreal symmetry which has none.

Coleridge's mind was so fertile in such ideas that it is difficult to conceive that, given the health of a coal-heaver and the industry of a bank clerk, he could ever have succeeded in tracking each to its end, or in embracing the whole of them with their innumerable progeny in one vast synthesis. A great number spring directly from literature, but almost any topic had power at once to form an idea capable of splitting into an indefinite number of fresh ideas. Here are some chosen for their brevity. "You abuse snuff! Perhaps it is the final cause of the human nose!" "Poetry is certainly something more than good sense, but it must be good sense at all events." "There is no subjectivity whatever in the Homeric poetry." "Swift was *anima Rabelaisii habitans in sicco*—the soul of Rabelais dwelling in a dry place." "How inimitably graceful children are before they learn to dance!" "There is in every human countenance either a history or a prophecy." "You see many scenes which are simply Shakespeare's, disporting himself in joyous triumph and vigorous fun after a great achievement of his highest genius." A respectable library could be, and no doubt has been, made out of these ideas; and Coleridge, not content with carrying the stuff of many libraries in his head, had what in England is more remarkable, the germs of an equal susceptibility to painting and to music. The gifts should go together; all three are perhaps needed to complete each one. But if such gifts complete a Milton or a Keats they may undo a Coleridge. The reader of the "Table Talk" will sometime reflect that although, compared with Coleridge, he must consider himself deaf and blind as well as dumb, these limitations, in the present state of the world, have protected him and most of his work has been done within their shelter. For how can a man with Coleridge's gifts produce anything? His demands are so much greater than can be satisfied by the spiritual resources of his age. He is perpetually checked and driven back; life is too short; ideas are too many; opposition is too great. If Coleridge heard music he wanted hours and hours of Mozart and Purcell; if he liked a picture he fell into a trance in front of it; if he saw a sunset he almost lost consciousness in the rapture of gazing at it. Our society makes no provision for these apparitions. The only course for such a one to pursue is that which Coleridge finally adopted—to sink into the house of some hospitable Gillman and there for the rest of his life to sit and talk. In better words, "My dear fellow! never be ashamed of scheming!—you can't think of living less than 4,000 years, and that would nearly suffice for your present schemes. To be sure, if they go on in the same ratio to the performance, then a small difficulty arises; but never mind! look at the bright side always and die in a dream!"

Patmore's Criticism[1]

BOOKS of collected essays are always the hardest to read, because, collected though they may be, it is often only the binding that joins them together. And when the author was a man whose main work in life was to write poetry, it is more than likely that his essays will be mere interjections and exclamations uttered spasmodically in the intervals of his proper pursuits. The list of contents makes us suspect the sort of thing we are to find. One day Coventry Patmore will write upon Mr Gladstone; another upon December in Garden and Field; again upon Coleridge; next upon dreams; and finally it will strike him to set down his views upon Liverpool Cathedral and Japanese houses. But our foreboding that we shall be jerked from topic to topic and set down in the end with a litter of broken pieces is in this case quite unfounded. For one thing, these thirty-seven papers were written within the compass of eleven years. Next, as Mr Page points out, Coventry Patmore's criticism was based upon considered principles. "The book is a book of doctrine, and is 'original' only in that it goes back to origins; the doctrines are those of Aristotle, of Goethe, of Coleridge, indeed, as one can imagine Patmore saying, 'of all sensible men.' The style only that holds them together is his own."

The style which holds so many separate parts so firmly is undoubtedly a good one. One would perhaps feel some discomfort, some unfitness in finding a column of such solid construction among the blurred print of an evening newspaper. Clearly one must look not among ephemeral scribblers but among established worthies if one is to find a writer against whom to test the merits and defects of Patmore's style. It is much in the eighteenth-century manner—concise, plain, with little imagery, extravagance, adventure, or inequality. Placed directly after one of Johnson's Lives of the Poets one of Patmore's essays can be read, so far as the diction goes, without any of that gradual loosening of the attention which attacks us as prose weakens under the adulteration of unnecessary words, slack cadences, and worn-out metaphors. But thus read we shall

[1] *Courage in Politics and Other Essays* by Coventry Patmore. *The Times Literary Supplement*, May 26, 1921.

somehow gather the impression that while Johnson is constantly outrageous and Patmore almost invariably civilized, Johnson's papers are the small visible fragment of a monster, Mr Patmore's essays have about them no such suggestion of unexpressed magnitude. A few pages seem to hold quite comfortably all that he has to say. He is small and wiry, rather than large and loose.

But the chief distinction of Mr Patmore's criticism is that to which Mr Page draws attention. He had a great dislike for the impressionist criticism which is "little more than an attempt to describe the feelings produced in the writers by the works they profess to judge" and tried consistently to base his own judgments upon doctrines set beyond the reach of accident and temperament. His pages provide many examples of the successful practice of this form of criticism, and some also of the defects which, though not inherent in the method, seem most apt to attack those who pursue it.

In the essay upon out-of-door poetry, for instance, instead of dallying with roses and cabbages and all the other topics which so pleasantly suggest themselves, he makes straight for the aesthetic problem. The quality which distinguishes good descriptive poetry from bad descriptive poetry is, he says, that the poet in the first case has seen things "in their living relationships." "The heather is not much, and the rock is not much; but the heather and the rock, discerned in their living expressional relationship by the poetic eye, are very much indeed—a beauty which is living with the life of man, and therefore inexhaustible . . . but true poets and artists know that this power of visual synthesis can only be exercised, in the present state of our faculties, in a very limited way; hence there is generally, in the landscapes and descriptions of real genius, a great simplicity in and apparent jealousy of their subjects, strikingly in contrast with the works of those who fancy that they are describing when they are only cataloguing." This is fruitful criticism because it helps us to define our own vaguer conceptions. Much of Wordsworth (here Mr Patmore would not agree) is oppressive because the poet has not seen nature with intensity either in relation to his poem, to himself, or to other human beings; but has accepted her as something in herself so desirable that description can be used in flat stretches without concentration. Tennyson is of course the master of those Victorian poets who carried descriptive writing to such a pitch that if their words had been visible the blackbirds would certainly have descended upon their garden plots to feed upon the apples and the plums. Yet we do not feel that this is poetry so much as something fabricated by an ingenious craftsman for our delight. Of the moderns, Mr Hardy is without rival in his power to make nature do his will, so that she neither satiates nor serves as a curious toy, but appears at the right moment to heighten, charm, or terrify, because the necessary fusion has already taken place. The first step towards this absorption is to see things with your own eyes, in which faculty Patmore held the English poets to be easily supreme.

Then, from poetry we turn to the little essay which is, of course, quite insufficient to deal with Sir Thomas Browne; but here again Patmore speaks to the point, drawing attention not to his own qualities, but to those which are in the work itself. "The prose of the pre-revolutionary period was a fine art. In proportion to the greatness of its writers, it was a continually varying flow of music, which aimed at convincing the feelings as the words themselves the understanding. The best post-revolutionary prose appeals to the understanding alone." The prose of the Religio Medici (oddly enough Patmore values neither Urn Burial nor Christian Morals) is certainly fine art. Yet in reading it again one is struck as much by the easy colloquial phrases as by the famous passages. There is an intensity of the modern sort as well as the poetic sonority of the ancient. The art of the deliberate passages is evident; but in addition to that Sir Thomas has something impulsive, something we may call, in default of a better word, amateurish about him as if he wrote for his own pleasure with language not yet solidified, while the best modern prose writers seem to remember, unwillingly no doubt, that prose writing is a profession.

Whether or not we agree with what Patmore says on these points, it is good criticism because it makes us turn to think about the book under consideration. But the criticism which is based upon the "doctrines of Aristotle, of Goethe, and of Coleridge," especially when practised in the columns of a newspaper, is apt to have the opposite effect. It is apt to be sweeping and sterile. The laws of art can be stated in a little essay only in so compressed a form that unless we are prepared to think them out for ourselves, and apply them to the poem or novel in question, they remain barren, and we accept them without thinking. "There is no true poem or novel without a moral; least of all such as, being all beauty (that is to say, all order), are all moral." A statement of that kind applied with little elaboration to the "Vicar of Wakefield" does not illumine the book, but, especially when coupled with an uncalled for fling at Blake, "who seems to have been little better than an idiot," withdraws attention from the "Vicar of Wakefield" and concentrates it upon Coventry Patmore. For it is evident that though the manner remains oracular this is the voice of a private person—of a person, moreover, who has written poetry himself, has been attacked by the critics, and has evolved a highly individual philosophy, into which Goldsmith and Coventry Patmore fit precisely as they are, but Blake, Shelley, and Miss Austen can only be made to fit by taking a knife to their edges. Blake was little better than an idiot; "Pride and Prejudice" was inferior to "Barchester Towers"; Shelley was an immoral writer; and by the side of Thomas Hardy, not indeed his equal but worthy of comparison and of the highest eulogy, appears the author of the "Mischief of Monica," a lady, it is now perhaps necessary to say, called Mrs Walford. For these freaks and oddities it is, of course, unnecessary to make Aristotle responsible. The Angel in the House is the undoubted parent. In an impressionist critic of the school which Patmore condemned you will meet precisely the same freaks of prejudice and partisanship, but with the difference that as no attempt is made to relate them to doctrines and principles they pass for what they are, and, the door being left wide open, interesting ideas may take the opportunity to enter in. But Patmore was content to state his principle and shut the door.

But if Patmore was an imperfect critic the very imperfections which make it sometimes useless to argue further about literature prove that he was a man of great courage and conviction, much out of harmony with his age, intolerant of the railway, a little strident we may think in his conservatism, and over-punctilious in his manners, but never restrained by sloth or cowardice from coming out into the open and testifying to his faith like a bright little bantam (if we may use the figure without disrespect) who objects to express trains, and says so twice a day, flying to the top of the farm-yard wall and flapping his wings.

Papers on Pepys[1]

THE number of those who read themselves asleep at night with Pepys and awake at day with Pepys must be great. By the nature of things, however, the number of those who read neither by night nor by day is infinitely greater; and it is, we believe, by those who have never read him that Pepys is, as Mr Wheatley complains, treated with contempt. The Pepys Club "may be considered", Mr Wheatley writes, "as a kind of missionary society to educate the public to understand that they are wrong in treating Pepys with affection, tempered with lack of respect." The papers published in the present volume would not have suggested to us so solemn a comparison. A missionary society, however, which dines well, sings beautifully old English songs, and delivers brief and entertaining papers upon such subjects as Pepys's portraits, Pepys's stone, Pepys's Ballads, Pepys's health, Pepys's musical instruments, although it differs, we imagine, in method from some sister institutions, is well calculated to convert the heathen. Lack of respect for Pepys, however, seems to us a heresy which is beyond argument, and deserving of punishment rather than of the persuasive voices of members of the Pepys Club singing "Beauty retire."

For one of the most obvious sources of our delight in the Diary arises from the fact that Pepys, besides being himself, was a great Civil Servant. We are glad to remember that it has been stated on authority, however well we guessed it for ourselves, that Pepys was "without exception the greatest and most useful Minister that ever filled the same situation in England, the acts and registers of the Admiralty proving this beyond contradiction." He was the founder of the modern Navy, and the fame of Mr Pepys as an administrator has had an independent existence of its own within the walls of the Admiralty from his day to ours. Indeed, it is possible to believe that we owe the Diary largely to his eminence as an official. The reticence, the pomposity, the observance of appearances which their duties require, or at least exact, of great public servants must make it more congenial to them than to others to unbend and

[1] *Occasional Papers of the Pepys Club.* edited by H. B. Wheatley. Vol I, 1903-14. *The Times Literary Supplement,* 4 April, 1918.

unbosom themselves in private. We can only regret that the higher
education of women now enables the wives of public men to receive
confidences which should have been committed to cipher. Happily
for us, Mrs Pepys was a very imperfect confidante. There were
other matters besides those naturally unfit for a wife's ear that
Pepys brought home from the office and liked to deliver himself
upon in private. And thus it comes about that the Diary runs
naturally from affairs of State and the characters of Ministers to
affairs of the heart and the characters of servant girls; it includes the
buying of clothes, the losing of tempers, and all the infinite curiosities, amusements, and pettinesses of average human life. It is a
portrait where not only the main figure, but the surroundings,
ornaments, and accessories are painted in. Had Mrs Pepys been as
learned, discreet, and open-minded as the most advanced of her sex
are now reputed to be, her husband would still have had enough
over to fill the pages of his Diary. Insatiable curiosity, and unflagging
vitality were the essence of a gift to which, when the possessor is able
to impart it, we can give no lesser name than genius.

It is worth reminding ourselves that because we are without his
genius it does not follow that we are without his faults. The chief
delight of his pages for most of us may lie not in the respectable
direction of historical investigation, but in those very weaknesses
and idiosyncrasies which in our own case we would die rather than
reveal; but our quick understanding betrays the fact that we are
fellow-sinners, though unconfessed. The state of mind that makes
possible such admission of the undignified failings even in cipher
may not be heroic, but it shows a lively, candid, unhypocritical
nature which, if we remember that Pepys was an extremely able
man, a very successful man and honourable beyond the standard of
his age, fills out a figure which is perhaps a good deal higher in the
scale of humanity than our own.

But those select few who survive the "vast and devouring space"
of the centuries are judged not by their superiority to individuals in
the flesh, but by their rank in the society of their peers, those solitary
survivors of innumerable and nameless multitudes. Compared
with most of these figures, Pepys is small enough. He is never
passionate, exalted, poetic, or profound. His faults are not great
ones, nor is his repentance sublime. Considering that he used cipher,
and on occasion double cipher, to screen him in the confessional, he

did not lay bare very deep or very intricate regions of the soul. He has little consciousness of dream or mystery, of conflict or perplexity. Yet it is impossible to write Pepys off as a man of the dumb and unanalytic past, or of the past which is ornate and fabulous; if ever we feel ourselves in the presence of a man so modern that we should not be surprised to meet him in the street and should know him and speak to him at once, it is when we read this Diary, written more than two hundred and fifty years ago.

This is due in part to the unstudied ease of the language, which may be slipshod but never fails to be graphic, which catches unfailingly the butterflies and gnats and falling petals of the moment, which can deal with a day's outing or a merrymaking or a brother's funeral so that we late comers are still in time to make one of the party. But Pepys is modern in a deeper sense than this. He is modern in his consciousness of the past, in his love of pretty, civilized things, in his cultivation, in his quick and varied sensibility. He was a collector and a connoisseur; he delighted not only in books, but in old ballads and in good furniture. He was a man who had come upon the scene not so early but that there was already a fine display of curious and diverting objects accumulated by an older generation. Standing midway in our history, he looks consciously and intelligently both backwards and forwards. If we turn our eyes behind us we see him gazing in our direction, asking with eager curiosity of our progress in science, of our ships and sailors. Indeed, the very fact that he kept a diary seems to make him one of ourselves.

Yet in reckoning, however imperfectly, the sources of our pleasure we must not forget that his age is among them. Sprightly, inquisitive, full of stir and life as he is, nevertheless Mr Pepys is now two hundred and eighty-five years of age. He can remember London when it was very much smaller than it is now, with gardens and orchards, wild duck and deer. Men "justled for the wall and did kill one another." Gentlemen were murdered riding out to their country houses at Kentish-town. Mr Pepys and Lady Paulina were much afraid of being set upon when they drove back at night, though Mr Pepys concealed his fears. They very seldom took baths, but, on the other hand, they dressed in velvet and brocade. They acquired a great deal of silver plate too, especially if they were in the public service, and a present of gloves for your wife might well

be stuffed with guineas. Ladies put on their vizards at the play—
and with reason if their cheeks were capable of blushing. Sir Charles
Sedley was so witty once with his companion that you could not
catch a word upon the stage. As for Lady Castlemaine, we should
never persuade Mr Pepys that the sun of beauty did not set once and
for all with her decline. It is an atmosphere at once homely and
splendid, coarse and beautiful, of a world far away and yet very
modern that is preserved in his pages.

The Pepys Club, which draws its life from so fertile a source, may
well flourish and multiply its members. The portraits reproduced
here, in particular a page of Mr Pepys's "individual features," are
of themselves sufficient to make this volume of memorable interest.
And yet there is one contribution which we would rather have left
unread. It consists only of a little Latin, a few signs, two or three
letters of the alphabet, such as any oculist in Harley-street will
write you out upon half a sheet of note-paper for a couple of guineas.
But to Samuel Pepys it would have meant a pair of spectacles, and
what that pair of spectacles upon that pair of eyes might have seen
and recorded it is tantalizing to consider. Instead of giving up his
Diary upon May 31, 1669, he might with this prescription have
continued it for another thirty years. It is some relief to be told that
the prescription is beyond the skill of contemporary oculists; but
this is dashed by Mr Power's statement that had Pepys chanced to
sit upon the "tube spectacall" of paper which his oculist provided
so that he must read through a slit,

> he would then have found his eye strain removed; his acute mind
> would have set itself to determine the cause; he would have
> pasted slips of black paper on each side of his glasses, and the
> Diary might have been continued to the end of his life; whilst the
> paper he would certainly have read upon the subject before the
> Royal Society would have added still greater lustre to his name,
> and might have revolutionized the laws of dioptrics.

But our regret is not purely selfish. How reluctant Pepys was to
close his Diary the melancholy last paragraph bears witness. He
had written until the act of writing "undid" his eyes, for the things
he wished to write were not always fit to be written in long-hand,
and to cease to write "was almost as much as to see myself go into
my grave." And yet this was a writing which no one, during his life
at any rate, was to be allowed to read. Not only from the last

sentence, but from every sentence, it is easy to see what lure it was that drew him to his Diary. It was not a confessional, still less a mere record of things useful to remember, but the storehouse of his most private self, the echo of life's sweetest sounds, without which life itself would become thinner and more prosaic. When he went upstairs to his chamber it was to perform no mechanical exercise, but to hold intercourse with the secret companion who lives in everybody, whose presence is so real, whose comment is so valuable, whose faults and trespasses and vanities are so lovable that to lose him is "almost to go into my grave." For this other Pepys, this spirit of the man whom men respected, he wrote his Diary, and it is for this reason that for centuries to come men will delight in reading it.

Sheridan[1]

AT first sight there may seem some incongruity between one's idea of Sheridan and the size of Mr Sichel's volumes. Nine people out of ten, if asked to give you their impression of Sheridan, would tell you that he wrote three standard plays, was famous for his debts, his wit, and his speech at the trial of Warren Hastings; they would add that he had played a distinguished but not a commanding part as a statesman, and flitted through the society of the Georgian era, a brilliant but slightly intoxicated insect, with gorgeous wings but an erratic flight. The important aspect of two stout volumes, numbering some 1,100 pages between them, seems strangely at variance with such a figure. How completely Mr Sichel corrects the popular view we shall attempt to show; but let us insist at once that the heaviness of the volumes is true in a literal sense only, and that, after reading from cover to cover, the importance of his subject seems to demand an even fuller treatment than it was possible to bestow. We should like more about the Linleys, more of Sheridan's own letters, and more of Mrs Tickell and her sister.

If only to enlighten the reader as to the extreme interest and complexity of his task, and to point out its true nature, it is best to read the "Overture" first, in which Mr Sichel seeks to "psychologize a temperament and a time." At first (let us own) the clash of contrasts, urged with unusual sharpness and precision, blinds our eyes to the form which they would reveal; simplicity and extravagance, generosity and meanness, rash confidence and moderation, passion and coldness—how are we to compose them all into one human shape? But later, when we begin to understand, it appears that the clue to Sheridan's baffling career must be sought among these contradictory fragments. For, looked at from the outside, the inconsistencies of his life fill us with a sense of dissatisfaction. Before he was thirty he had written three plays that are classics in our literature; then, once in Parliament, he turned to reform and finance and gave up writing altogether; "the Muses of Love and Satire beckoned to him from Parnassus, and to the last he persisted

[1] *The Life of Richard Brinsley Sheridan* by Walter Sichel. *The Times Literary Supplement*, December 2, 1909.

in declaring that they, and not politics, were his true vocation"; yet "his heart stayed in the Assembly of the nation, and to the last, like Congreve, he slighted his theatrical triumphs"; his married life, which began with two duels on his wife's behalf, and ended in an agony of grief as she lay dying in his arms, would present a perfect example of devotion were it not that he had been unfaithful while she lived, and married again, a girl of twenty, three years after her death; finally, his political career is as incomprehensible as the rest, for, with gifts as orator and statesman that made him famous over Europe, he never held high office; with a character of singular independence he acted "equivocally," and with a record of devotion to his Prince he lost his favour completely, and died, without a seat, dishonoured and in debt. Nothing tends to make us lose interest in a character so much as the suspicion that there is something monstrous about it, and the achievement of Mr Sichel's biography is that it restores Sheridan to human size and brings him to life again.

The first gift that makes itself felt is the gift that is always present and at work, but is yet the hardest to recapture—the gift of charm. "There has been nothing like it since the days of Orpheus," wrote Byron; it made the boys at Harrow love him; Sumner, the headmaster, overlooked his mischief because of it; it drew the bailiffs in later days to stand behind his chair; as for his sister, she confessed that she "admired—I almost adored him." In early days his face expressed only the finer part of him; "its half heaviness was lit up by the comedy of his smile, the audacity of his air," and the brilliance of those eyes that were to outshine the rest of him, and to "look up at the coffin lid as brightly as ever" when the mouth and chin had grown coarse as a Satyr's. There are only two letters from Sheridan at Harrow; and they are both about dress. In one he complains that his clothes are so shabby that he "is almost ashamed to wear them on Sunday"; in the other he is anxious to have the proper mourning sent him on his mother's death. Most schoolboys are conventional, but in addition to conforming to its laws, Sheridan liked the world to know that he grieved. A year or two later, when we come to Miss Linley and the famous elopement and the duels, the romance of Sheridan's nature blossoms out, with curious qualifications. He discovered that the beautiful Miss Linley, who sang like an angel, was tormented by a man called Mathews, who was married; she had flirted with him as a child and he now pressed her dishonour-ably. Sheridan became her knight; he snatched her away to France without her parents' knowledge, and placed her in a convent. It is probable that they went through "some form of marriage" near Calais. Mathews, meanwhile, proclaimed his rival a liar and a scoundrel in the *Bath Chronicle*, and Sheridan vowed that he "would never sleep in England till he had thanked him as he deserved." He left Miss Linley in her father's hands, fought with Mathews twice, and obliged him to fly the country. It is a tale no doubt that might be matched by others of that age, but in the romantic arrangement of the plot, in the delicate respect with which he treated his charge, and in the extravagance of the vow which constrained him to spend the night out of bed at Canterbury and to reach his rival starved for want of sleep, there are signs of something out of the ordinary. Nor was his behaviour ordinary in the months of separation that follow-ed. In his letters and his lyrics he luxuriated—for the passion that finds words has pleasure about it—in the shades of his emotion.

But love also started his brain into activity. Not only did he work at mathematics, make an abstract of the history of England, and comment upon Blackstone, but he thought about the principles upon which the world is run. It seemed to him that "all the nobler feelings of man," which he began to perceive in himself, were blunted by civilization, and sighed for the early days when the ties of friendship and of love "could with some safety be formed at the first instigation of our hearts." Now and perhaps throughout his life he believed that one's emotions are supreme, and that one should rate the obstacles that thwart them as tokens of bondage. He was fond of dreaming about the enchanted world of the Arcadia and of the Faëry Queen, liking rather to dwell upon "the characters of life as I would wish that they *were* than as they *are*," and persuading himself that his wish was really a desire to pierce beneath the corruptions of society to the true face of man beneath. Perhaps he felt that a world so simplified would be easier to live in than ours—but can one believe in it? He wished to replace all Fielding and Smollett with knights and ladies, but he did not believe in them either. The true romantic makes his past out of an intense joy in the present; it is the best of what he sees, caught up and set beyond the reach of change; Sheridan's vague rapture with the glamour of life was only sufficient to make him discontented, sentimental, and chivalrous. The strange admixture is shown in his behaviour when he was asked to allow his wife—for they had married with the consent of her father, but to the rage of his—to sing publicly for money. He refused to agree, although they were very poor and large sums were offered. It was said that the sight of George III ogling her decided him, and Johnson declared, "He resolved wisely and nobly, to be sure." But later, when he was struggling for a position in London drawing rooms he allowed her to advertise concerts "to the Nobility and Gentry" at which she was to sing without taking money. He gained a reputation for chivalry, for it implied that he cared for his wife's honour more than for gold, and spurned a friendship that was bought; but then he valued the favour of the great very highly, and if it is true that he never cared for money, he seldom paid his debts.

Sheridan would do anything to make the world think well of him; he would wear intense mourning; he would keep a fine establishment; he would faint if people wished it; he could anticipate the popular desires, and exaggerate them brilliantly. The actor's blood in him, which rises on applause like a ship on the waves, was responsible for the touch of melodrama; but the finer perceptions of artists were his too, and these, trained to discover emotions beneath small talk and domesticity, threw him off his balance in the uproar of the world. There is certainly a strange discrepancy between Sheridan in private and Sheridan in public—between his written words and his spoken. The three famous plays were written before he took to public life, and represent more of him than tradition or the imperfect reports of his speeches can now preserve. They show what Sheridan thought when there was no public to send the blood to his head. The way in which he takes the word "honour" in *The Rivals* and makes it the jewel of a frightened country bumpkin and the sport of his shrewd serving-man assures us that he fought his own duels with a full sense of their absurdity. "Odds blades! David," cries Acres, "no gentleman will ever risk the loss of his honour!" "I say, then," answers David, "it would be but civil in *honour* never to risk the loss of a *gentleman*. Look'ee, master, this *honour* seems to me to be a marvellous false friend: ay truly, a very courtier-like servant," and so on, until honour and the valiant man of honour are laughed out of court together.

Then again we have some reason to believe that Sheridan was an unthinking sentimentalist, and so slipshod in his morality that he acted upon no reasoned view, but used the current conventions. If that were so, he would have been the last to see the humour of Charles Surface in *The School for Scandal*. The good qualities of this character are lovable only because we know them to be slightly ridiculous; we are meant to think it a weak but endearing trait in him that he refuses to sell his uncle's picture. "No, hang it; I'll not part with poor Noll; the old fellow has been very good to me, and, egad, I'll keep his picture while I've a room to put it in." And Sheridan satirizes his own system of generosity by adding to Charles's offer of a hundred pounds to poor Stanley, "If you don't make haste, we shall have some one call that has a better right to the money." These are details, but they keep us in mind of the acutely sensible side of Sheridan's temperament. He laughs at the vapours of his age—at old women sending out for novels from the library, at bombastic Irishmen, picking quarrels for the glory of it, at romantic young ladies sighing for the joys of "sentimental elopements— ladder of ropes!—conscious moon—four horses—Scotch parson ... paragraphs in the newspapers." The pity is that his Irish gift of hyperbole made it so easy for him to heap one absurdity on another, to accumulate superlatives and smother everything in laughter. Mrs Malaprop would be more to the point if she could stay her tongue from deranging epitaphs; and the play scene in *The Critic* suffers from the same voluble buffoonery—but that it has such a rapture of fun in it that we can never cease to laugh.

> *The wind whistles—the moon rises—see,*
> *They have kill'd my squirrel in his cage!*
> *Is this a grasshopper?—Ha! no; it is my*
> *Whiskerandos—you shall not keep him—*
> *I know you have him in your pocket—*
> *An oyster may be cross'd in love!—Who says*
> *A whale's a bird?—"*

His humour makes one remember that he liked practical jokes. It is absolutely free from coarseness. The most profound humour is not fit reading for a girls' school, because innocence is supposed to ignore half the facts of life, and however we may define humour, it is the most honest of the gifts.

Among other reasons for the morality of the stage in Sheridan's day may be found the reason that it lacked vigour of every kind. Sheridan, the first of the playwrights, was prevented, partly by the fact that his audience would not like it, and partly by an innate prudery of his own—a touch of that sentimentality which led him to prefer unreal characters to real ones—from giving a candid account of his life. He took some thought of appearances, even in the study. His own view of the stage may be gathered in the first act of *The Critic*. Having regard to the limitations of an audience which could not brook Vanbrugh and Congreve, one should not "dramatize the penal laws" or make the stage the school of morality, but find the proper sphere for the comic muse in "the follies and foibles of society." That was Sheridan's natural province, in spite of a fitful longing, to write a romantic Italian tragedy. If we grant that he had not the power which moves us so keenly in Congreve of showing how witty people love, and lacked the coarse vigour which still keeps *The Rehearsal* alive, we are conscious that he has another power of his own; Sir Henry Irving found it in his "play of human nature"; Mr Sichel speaks of his sympathy —"a sympathy that Congreve lacked." It is that surely that gives his comedy its peculiar glow. It does not spring from insight, or from any unusual profundity. It lies rather in his power to get on with ordinary people— to come into a room full of men and women who know him for the cleverest man of his time, and to set them at once at their ease. Other dramatists would treat such a character as Charles Surface with condescension, for a blockhead, or with uneasy respect, because of his courage and muscle; but Sheridan liked him heartily; he was his "ideal of a good fellow." This humanity—it was part of his charm as a man—still warms his writing; and it has another quality which also appeals to us. He reminds us sometimes of our modern dramatists in his power to see accepted conventions in a fresh light. He tests the current view of honour; he derides the education that was given to women; he was for reforming the conventions of the stage. His interest in ideas was only a faint forecast of our own obsession; and he was too true an artist to make any character the slave of a theory. A great fastidiousness was one of the many gifts that were half-failings, and the more he wrote the less possible it became to make the drama an instrument of reform. *The School for Scandal* was polished and polished again; "after nineteen years he had been unable to satisfy himself" with his style. The excessive care was fatal; it helped to dry up his vein before he had fully explored it, and his last comedy *Affectation* has dwindled to a few careful sentences, very neatly written in a small copy-book.

An acute sense of comedy does not seem compatible with a reformer's zeal; and, when the success of his plays and the charm of his wife brought him into touch with the rulers of the country, the chance of acting among them proved irresistible. His success with the great ladies who came to his wife's drawing room showed him what kind of power might be his—he might lead human beings. From the first, too, he had had the political instinct—a sense of distress among the people and a desire to make their lives better by improving the laws of the land. "Government for the people, through the people, and by the people" was the creed with which he started his career under the guidance of Fox. A boyish essay shows how natural it was to him to think of man as a free being oppressed by the laws. ". . . all laws at present are Tyranny. . . . All Liberty consists in the Probability of not being oppressed. What assurance have we that we shall not be taxed at eight shillings in the pound? No more than the colonies have." One of the first causes that attracted him was the cause of the American colonies, and he urged passionately their right to independence. He resolved to "sacrifice every other object" to politics, and to "force myself into business, punctuality, and information."

But it is not necessary to trace Sheridan's Parliamentary career. Mr Sichel proves, if one can separate them, that it was more important than his career as a man of letters, and for this reason his second volume is even more interesting than his first. What is interesting, of course, is the spectacle of a man who tries to give some shape to his beliefs, and has great opportunities. He had to do what he could with questions like that of the American colonists, of the Irish Union, of Indian government, of the French Revolution, which sprang up one after the other. They have come to be facts now, lying sunk beneath a heap of results; but they were then in the making, composed of the united wills of individuals and shaped by the wills of individuals. This is one source of interest; but it happens very often that we lose sight of the aim in amazement at the spectacle. When Sheridan entered Parliament, Burke and Pitt and Fox, to take the leaders only, gave every question an extraordinary depth and complexity. It seems that we are not tracing ideas, but

watching a gigantic drama, like those old Homeric combats where
the motive may be the sack of Troy, but in which the episodes
represent every phase of human life. Sometimes the vast range of
the fight narrows itself to the will of one man; the central figure is
undraped; and we have to contemplate the absurd or touching
spectacle of a gentleman afflicted with the gout—"a poor, bare,
forked animal," touched in his mind, too, who for the moment
represents humanity. There are strange anecdotes in the Duchess of
Devonshire's diary. The King began to go mad, and said "the
Prince of Wales is dead, so women may be honest." He made Sir
George Baker go down on his knees to look at the stars; he ordered
a "tye wig, and danc'd with Dr Reynolds"; the courtiers had
to pretend that he could play chess when he could only play
draughts, and that they had all been a little mad and wore strait
waistcoats themselves. Such contrasts abound, but if we know
enough there appears to be some order in the tumult; it is shaped
something after a human form. We need only observe out of what
elements the conduct of a public man is made.

Sheridan, in spite of his vanity and irresponsibility, had an
unwavering sense of something more stable than any private
advantage. He could look beyond his own life, and judge clearly of
things to come. Again and again we find him on the side of reform,
courageous and "unpurchaseable," a statesman whose views grew
wider as he aged. And yet, how strangely little traits of character,
small vices unchecked since boyhood, assert themselves and corrupt
his actions! The speech upon the Begums of Oude, which made
great men tremble and women cry with ecstasy, lacks something
essential, for all its thunder of eloquence. Years afterwards he met
Warren Hastings, shook his hand, and begged him to believe that
"political necessity" had inspired some of his rage. When Hastings
"with great gravity" asked him to make that sentence public, he
could only "mutter," and get out of it as best he might. It is the
same with his friendship for the Regent; he could not care for
anything for its own sake. The man was a Prince, girt about with
romance, and hung with stars and ribbons; Mrs Fitzherbert was a
woman, beautiful and in distress; his sympathies were volatile, and
he moved in a world of gems and decorations, which might be had
for the asking. Yet gold was too gross to tempt him; he craved for
love, confidence, and demonstrative affection in the face of the

world. What he asked he could not get, or perhaps he asked it of the wrong people. From the first an uneasy note sounds beneath the rest. The beautiful Mrs Sheridan implored him, when they began to rise, to let his friends know of their poverty. He had not the courage to do it, and she was led on to bet and to flirt. "Oh, my own," she wrote him, "'ee can't think how they beat me every night." He condoned her frailties with the tact of a perfect gentleman. But once in the race there was no standing still. The Duchess of Devonshire, Lady Bessborough, Lady Elizabeth Foster—all the great ladies and the brilliant young men were there to egg him on. At their pressure such a fountain of wit and satire and imagery sprang from his lips as no one else could rival. His face might grow fiery and his nose purple, but his voice kept its melody to the end. Yet, in spite of all this, he was never at his ease, and always conscious of a certain misfit. When he stood on the Down where, twenty years before, he had fought and lain wounded, he considered his situation:—

> What an interval has passed since, and scarcely one promise that I then made to my own soul have I attempted to fulfil. . . . The irregularity of all my life and pursuits, the restless, contriving temper with which I have persevered in wrong pursuits and passions makes [some words erased, of which "errors" is legible] reflexion worse to me than even to those who have acted worse.

He thought he could foresee the "too probable conclusion," but even his imagination, though made intense by sorrow, could hardly have foreseen the end. Perhaps it was the humour of it that he could not have foreseen. He became "Old Sherry" to the younger generation, and was to be met "half seas over", a disreputable figure, but still talking divinely, a battered Orpheus, but still a very polite gentleman, a little bewildered by the course of events, and somewhat disappointed by his lot. He fell into sponging houses, escaped ingeniously from the "two strange men" who had followed him all his life, and begged as eloquently as ever, with a touch of Irish brogue in his voice. "They are going to put the carpets out of window, and break into Mrs Sheridan's room, and take me" he wrote, but was sanguine on the morrow. Then he lay dying, and the prescriptions were unopened in the bare parlour, and "there were strange people in the hall." But so long as life promised adventures

Sheridan had a part to act, and could welcome a future. It is not in any event that his tragedy lay, for there is something ludicrous in the stupidity of fate which never fits the fortune to the desert and blunts our pain in wonder. The tragedy lies in making promises, and seeing possibilities, and in the sense of failure. There at least the pain is without mixture. But one does not fail so long as one sees possibilities still, and the judgment on our failure is that which Byron murmured when he heard that Sheridan was dead, and praised his gifts and greatness—"But alas, poor human nature!"

Thomas Hood[1]

AT the same time that Keats and Lamb were writing there flour-ished—so thick that even men like these showed little higher than the rest—a whole forest of strenuous and lusty human beings, journalists, artists, or people simply who happened to live then and rear their children. What profuse clamour, what multitudinous swarms of life a wise biographer can call up for us from fields long since shorn and flat if he will take for his subject one of these mortals it is really bewildering for a moment to consider. A student of letters is so much in the habit of striding through the centuries from one pinnacle of accomplishment to the next that he forgets all the hub-bub that once surged round the base; how Keats lived in a street and had a neighbour and his neighbour had a family—the rings widen infinitely; how Oxford-street ran turbulent with men and women while de Quincey talked with Ann. And such considerations are not trivial if only because they had their effect upon things that we are wont to look upon as isolated births, and to judge, therefore, in a spirit that is more than necessarily dry. Mr Jerrold's life of Thomas Hood gives rise to a number of such reflections, both because he has written with delightful good taste and discrimina-tion and because his subject, after all, belonged almost the whole of him to the race of the mortals. If it had not been for his two or three poems perhaps he would have sunk with the rest of them, with the load of albums and annuals and their makers, or would have survived as some half mythical comic figure, the father of a few good stories and the author of innumerable puns. There is even some-thing nugatory about the facts of his life; they suggest, in the easy ordinary way in which they fit and succeed each other, that there were hundreds of Thomas Hoods, sons of middle-class parents, apprenticed to engravers, with a turn for writing verse or prose; kindly domestic young men, who if they did take to letters—their parents were well advised in dissuading them—would make no mark there, but fill endless columns satisfactorily. Such, to a great extent, was the life of Hood; but there was just that exaggeration of

[1] *Thomas Hood: his Life and Times* by Walter Jerrold. *Poems* by Thomas Hood, edited by F. C. Burnand. *The Times Literary Supplement*, January 30, 1908.

temper or fortune in it that made him, while he was one of a class, typical of it also. He was impelled by his gifts and his feelings to travel the whole course that slighter men trod partly, until he achieved something significant and completed his symbol.

As a boy he showed an abnormal facility; if he went away on a holiday he sent home profuse letters full of descriptions. Already the surface show of life tickled him with its incongruities; and at a time when most boys are aping some older writer he was simply observing with a lively eye what went on round him and scribbling it down in sheets of fresh easy prose. He laughed at his fellow lodgers, or stood at the window and took off the people whom he saw passing on their way to church. "The study of character (I mean of amusing ones) I enjoy exceedingly," he wrote when he was sixteen, and in the same spirit he dashed off a long poem on the town of Dundee, in imitation of the "New Bath Guide." No one could doubt where his gift would lead him, in spite of the engraving; and when he was twenty-two some papers, accepted by the *London Magazine*, definitely determined him, as Mr Jerrold thinks, to trust entirely to his pen. From that time onward his life was the complex life of a busy journalist. There was no respite, scarcely any partition; for where are we to seek the events of his life but in his writings? And when we read him we must remember his wife and children, his ill-health, the ceaseless pressure of money cares. If a particular style pleased the public he must continue it, though the mood was spent; and as his first success was made in the "Whims and Oddities" he had still, as he says, to "breathe his comic vein." "Could Hood at this moment have taken some editorial appointment [writes Mr Jerrold] we might have had more of his best and less of that journeyman work." That is a very moderate statement of the regret that bursts from our lips at many stages of this panting, hard-driven career: but in our desire to round the picture, to possess our tragedy, are we not inclined to fall into the fallacy to which Thackeray gave shape in his paper "On a joke I once heard from the late Thomas Hood"? He speaks of the grinning and tumbling, "through sorrow, through exile, poverty, fever, depression," "the sad marvellous picture of courage, of honesty, of patient endurance, of duty struggling against pain"—until in our compassion we forget very likely the true spirit of the man, his exuberance and brilliancy, the odd vulgar humour of a cockney life, the practical jokes and the supper parties. "O Hood, Hood, you do run on so!" exclaimed poor Mrs Hood, half inarticulate, at one of these feasts. The very fact that he gave himself with such pliancy to the drudgery of a journalist's life proves that there was something in the nature of his gift and temperament akin to it.

And when we turn to his writing we can surely discover there signs, not only of work "pumped out," but of ideas springing gladly to the surface at the cheerful command of throbbing presses and fast falling sheets. No other invitation could have sounded quite so aptly to a man with a brain full of puns. But it is largely on account of these puns, we are told, that Hood is now so little read. Indeed, the portent is one that strikes the attention directly, and it must be held to typify something fundamental in the constitution of his mind. For his puns divide themselves into two classes or degrees; the greater part of them are simply happy matchings of sound in which there is so thin a burden of meaning that the contrast is almost purely verbal.

> *Alas; they've taken my beau Ben*
> *To sail with old Benbow*

But there are others in which the pun is the result of some strange association in Hood's mind of two remote ideas, which it is his singular gift to illustrate by a corresponding coincidence of language.

> *Even the bright extremes of joy*
> *Bring on conclusions of disgust;*
> *Like the sweet blossoms of the May,*
> *Whose fragrance ends in must.*

These lines are taken from one of his most serious poems, that on Melancholy, and serve to illustrate, compactly, a remarkable tendency—perhaps it is the remarkable tendency—of his thought. They show how the original leaning of his mind was really to wild and incongruous associations, grotesque and monstrous conceits, not in words only, but in human life, such as those we see so strikingly displayed in poems like "Eugene Aram," "The Haunted House," and "The Last Man." And also we may discover a certain superficiality of conception, which suffers him to find such contrasts as the verbal one of "may" and "must" adequate, and makes him so supersensitive to the surface inflections of language as he was

sensitive to the influence of contemporary writers. The influence of
Lamb is clear in his prose, of Keats in his verse, and Coleridge one
may guess affected his thought more deeply than either.

From these poems Sir Francis Burnand has lately published in
the Red Letter Library a selection which gives a fair representation
of the different moods in which Hood sang. They are broadly
farcical, or romantic, or satirical or wildly fantastical; and there are
the two famous poems which admirers of Hood will scarcely classify
at all except by calling them inspired. The "Song of the Shirt" in
particular makes Sir Francis "positively disinclined to dwell upon
any other serious poems of Hood's be it even the "Bridge of Sighs'";
and he has some quarrel with Thackeray for the way in which he
dwelt upon Hood's perverse love of "comicalities." He points out
that it was the jesting that paid, and that Hood was forced to make
an income. But what perhaps is overlooked is the necessary relationship between Hood's fun and Hood's tragedy; you could not have
the one without the other—if he laughed in this way he must cry in
that—and the faults which we find in his light verse surely reproduce themselves in his serious poems. Thus, the reason why we
cannot, with deference to Sir Francis Burnand, accept the "Song of
the Shirt" as an enduring masterpiece is because of the slight
cheapness of effect, tending to the melodramatic, which has something in common with the verbal dexterity, the supersensitive
surface of mind already noticed. Such lines as

> *Sewing at once, with a double thread,*
> *A shroud as well as a shirt.*

or,

> *A little weeping would ease my heart,*
> *But in their briny bed*
> *My tears must stop, for every drop*
> *Hinders needle and thread!*

go straight, as he says, to our hearts; but not to the noblest part of
them. "Ruth" or "The Death Bed" touches a higher note. You
must honour and pity so fine a nature, so honest and brilliant a
mind, stung now to impulsive and passionate utterance by the
sorrows of the world, now to irrepressible showers of merriment by
its oddities. But in the most solid of his work the sharp blade of his
own circumstance is always wearing through. You do not find all of

him in his work; you rise from it unsatisfied, to ask what were the accidents of his life that made him write so. Mr Jerrold's book, then, is a valuable addition to our knowledge of Hood, and any one who has had occasion to consult the Memorials by his son and daughter will perceive at once how much all readers in the future must be indebted to Mr Jerrold's laborious research and good judgment. A life was needed, and he has provided it.

Praeterita[1]

THAT an abridgement of "Modern Painters" should lately have been published may be held to prove that while people still want to read Ruskin, they have no longer the leisure to read him in the mass. Happily, for it would be hard to let so great a writer recede from us, there is another and much slighter book of Ruskin's, which contains as in a teaspoon the essence of those waters from which the many-coloured fountains of eloquence and exhortation sprang. "Praeterita"—"outlines of scenes and thoughts perhaps worthy of memory in my past life" as he called it—is a fragmentary book, written in a season of great stress toward the end of his life, and left unfinished. It is, for these reasons perhaps, less known than it should be; yet if anybody should wish to understand what sort of man Ruskin was, how he was brought up, how he came to hold the views he did, he will find it all indicated here; and if he wishes to feel for himself the true temper of his genius, these pages, though much less eloquent and elaborate than many others, preserve it with exquisite simplicity and spirit.

Ruskin's father was "an entirely honest" wine merchant, and his mother was the daughter of the landlady of the Old King's Head at Croydon. The obscurity of his birth is worth notice because he paid some attention to it himself, and it influenced him much. His natural inclination was to love the splendour of noble birth and the glamour of great possessions. Sitting between his father and mother when they drove about England in their chariot taking orders for sherry, he loved best to explore the parks and castles of the aristocracy. But he owned manfully, if with a tinge of regret, that his uncle was a tanner and his aunt a baker's wife. Indeed, if he reverenced aristocracy and what it stood, or should stand for, he reverenced still more the labours and virtues of the poor. To work hard and honestly, to be truthful in speech and thought, to make one's watch or one's table as well as tables and watches can be made, to keep one's house clean and pay one's bills punctually were

[1] *The New Republic*, December 28, 1927.

qualities that won his enthusiastic respect. The two strains are to be found conflicting in his life and produce much contradiction and violence in his work. His passion for the great French cathedrals conflicted with his respect for the suburban chapel. The colour and warmth of Italy fought with his English puritanical love of order, method and cleanliness. Though to travel abroad was a necessity to him, he was always delighted to return to Herne Hill and home. Again, the contrast finds expression in the marked varieties of his style. He is opulent in his eloquence, and at the same time meticulous in his accuracy. He revels in the description of changing clouds and falling waters, and yet fastens his eye to the petals of a daisy with the minute tenacity of a microscope. He combined, or at least there fought in him, the austerity of the puritan and the sensuous susceptibility of the artist. Unluckily for his own peace of mind, if nature gave him more than the usual measure of gifts and mixed them with more than her usual perversity, his parents brought him up to have far less than the usual power of self-control. Mr and Mrs Ruskin were both convinced that their son John was to become a great man, and in order to insure it they kept him like any other precious object, in a cardboard box wrapped in cotton wool. Shut up in a large house with very few friends and very few toys, perfectly clothed, wholesomely nourished and sedulously looked after, he learned, he said, "Peace, obedience, faith," but on the other hand, "I had nothing to love. . . I had nothing to endure. . . I was taught no precision nor etiquette of manners. . . Lastly and chief of evils, my judgment of right and wrong, and power of independent action, were entirely undeveloped; because the bridle and blinkers were never taken off me." He was not taught to swim, that is to say, but only to keep away from the water.

He grew up, therefore, a shy, awkward boy, who was intellectually so highly precocious that he could write the first volume of "Modern Painters" before he was twenty-four, but was emotionally so stunted that, desperately susceptible as he was, he did not know how to amuse a lady for an evening. His efforts to ingratiate himself with the first of those enchanting girls who made havoc of his life reminded him, he said, of the efforts of a skate in an aquarium to get up the glass. Adèle was Spanish-born, Paris-bred and Catholic-hearted, he notes, yet he talked to her of the Spanish Armada, the Battle of Waterloo and the doctrine of Transubstantiation. Some such pane of glass or other impediment was always to lie between him and the freedom of ordinary intercourse. Partly the boyish days of anxious supervision were to blame. He had much rather go away alone and look at things, he said, than stay at home and be looked at. He did not want friends; he marvelled that anyone should be fond of a creature as impersonal and self-contained as a *camera lucida* or an ivory foot-rule. And then he was still further withdrawn from the ordinary traffic of life by Nature who, to most people only the background, lovely or sympathetic to their own activities, was to him a presence mystic, formidable, sublime, dominating the little human figures in the foreground. But though she thus rapt him from his fellows, Nature did not console him. The cataract and the mountain did not take the place of the hearth and lamplight and children playing on the rug; the beauty of the landscape only made more terrible to him the wickedness of man. The rant and fury and bitterness of his books seem to spring, not merely from the prophetic vision, but from a sense of his own frustration. More eloquent they could hardly be; but we cannot help guessing that had little John cut his knees and run wild like the rest of us, not only would he have been a happier man, but instead of the arrogant scolding and preaching of the big books, we should have had more of the clarity and simplicity of "Praeterita."

For in "Praeterita," happily, there is little left of these old rancours. At last Ruskin was at peace; his pain was no longer his own, but everbody's pain; and when Ruskin is at peace with the world, it is surprising how humorously, kindly, and observantly he writes of it. Never were portraits more vividly drawn than those of his father and mother; the father, upright, able, sensitive, yet vain, too, and glad that his clerk's incompetence should prove his own capacity; the mother, austere and indomitably correct, but with a dash of "the Smollettesque" in her, so that when a maid toppled backward over a railing in full view of a monastery, she laughed for a full quarter of an hour. Never was there a clearer picture of English middle-class life when merchants were still princes and suburbs still sanctuaries. Never did any autobiographer admit us more hospitably and generously into the privacy of his own experience. That he should go on for ever talking, and that we should still listen, is all we ask, but in vain. Before the book is finished the beautiful stream wanders out of his control and loses itself in the sands. Limpid as it looks, that pure water was distilled from turmoil; and serenely as the pages run, they resound with the echoes of thunder and are lit with the reflections of lightning. For the old man who sits now babbling of his past was a prophet once and had suffered greatly.

Mr Kipling's Notebook[1]

BETWEEN the ages of sixteen and twenty-one, speaking roughly, every writer keeps a large notebook devoted entirely to landscape. Words must be found for a moon-lit sky, for a stream, for plane-trees after rain. They "must" be found. For the plane-tree dries very quickly, and if the look as of a sea-lion sleek from a plunge is gone, and nothing found to record it better than those words, the wet plane-tree does not properly exist. Nothing can exist unless it is properly described. Therefore the young writer is perpetually on the stretch to get the thing expressed before it is over and the end of the day finds him with a larder full of maimed objects—half-realized trees, streams that are paralytic in their flow, and leaves that obstinately refuse to have that particular—what was the look of them against the sky, or, more difficult still to express, how did the tree erect its tent of green layers above you as you lay flat on the ground beneath? Early in the twenties this incessant matching and scrutiny of nature is relaxed, perhaps in despair, more probably because the attention has been captured by the usual thing—the human being. He wanders into the maze. When once more he can look at a tree it seems to him quite unnecessary to consider whether the bark is like a wet seal, or the leaves are jagged emeralds. The truth of the tree is not in that kind of precision at all. Indeed the old notebooks, with their trees, streams, sunsets, Piccadilly at dawn, Thames at midday, waves on the beach, are quite unreadable. And for the same reason so is much of Mr Kipling—quite unreadable.

A fat carp in a pond sucks at a fallen leaf with just the sound of a wicked little worldly kiss. Then the earth steams and steams in silence, and a gorgeous butterfly, full six inches from wing to wing, cuts through the steam in a zigzag of colour and flickers up to the forehead of the god.

That is a perfect note. Every word of it has been matched with the object with such amazing skill that no one could be expected to bury it in a notebook. But when it is printed in a book meant to be read consecutively, and on to it are stitched all the notes that Mr

¹ *Letters of Travel* 1892-1913, by Rudyard Kipling. *The Athenæum*, July 16, 1920.

Kipling has made with unfaltering eye, and even increasing skill, it becomes, literally, unreadable. One has to shut the eyes, shut the book, and do the writing over again. Mr Kipling has given us the raw material; but where is this to go, and where that, and what about the distance, and who, after all, is seeing this temple, or God, or desert? All notebook literature produces the same effect of fatigue and obstacle, as if there dropped across the path of the mind some block of alien matter which must be removed or assimilated before one can go on with the true process of reading. The more vivid the note the greater the obstruction. The malady can be traced to Lord Tennyson, who brought the art of taking notes to the highest perfection, and displayed the utmost skill in letting them, almost imperceptibly, into the texture of his poetry. Here is an example:

> *Crisp foam-flakes scud along the level sand,*
> *Torn from the fringe of spray.*

That must have been seen one day on the beach at Freshwater, and preserved for future use; and when we come upon it we detect its bottled origin, and say, "Yes, that is exactly like a foam-flake, and I wonder whether Tennyson's foam-flakes were yellowish, and had that porous look which I myself have thought of comparing to the texture of cork? 'Crisp' he calls it. But surely cork . . ." and so on through all the old business of word-matching, while the "Dream of Fair Women" wastes in air. But when Keats wanted to describe autumn, he said that he had seen her "sitting careless on a granary floor"; which does all the work for us, whether innumerable notes were the basis of it or none at all. Indeed, if we want to describe a summer evening, the way to do it is to set people talking in a room with their backs to the window, and then, as they talk about something else, let someone half turn her head and say, "A fine evening," when (if they have been talking about the right things) the summer evening is visible to anyone who reads the page, and is for ever remembered as of quite exceptional beauty.

To return to Mr Kipling. Is he then directing us to nothing, and are these brilliant scenes merely pages torn from the copy-book of a prodigy among pupils? No; it is not so simple as that. Just as the railway companies have a motive in hanging their stations with seductive pictures of Ilfracombe and Blackpool Bay, so MrKipling's pictures of places are painted to display the splendours of Empire and to induce young men to lay down their lives on her behalf. And again, it is not so simple as that. It is true that Mr Kipling shouts, "Hurrah for the Empire!" and puts out his tongue at her enemies. But praise as crude as this, abuse as shallow, can be nothing but a disguise rigged up to justify some passion or other of which Mr Kipling is a little ashamed. He has a feeling, perhaps, that a grown man should not enjoy making bridges, and using tools, and camping out as much as he does. But if these activities are pursued in the service of Empire, they are not only licensed, but glorified. Hence the excuse. Yet it is the passion that gives his writing its merit, and the excuse that vitiates it:

> I wonder sometimes whether any eminent novelist, philosopher, dramatist, or divine of to-day has to exercise half the imagination, not to mention insight, endurance, and self-restraint, which is accepted without comment in what is called "the material exploitation" of a new country . . . The mere drama of it, the play of the human virtues, would fill a book.

It has, indeed, filled many books, from the travels of Hakluyt to the novels of Mr Conrad, and if Mr Kipling would concentrate upon "the mere drama of it, the play of the human virtues," there would be no fault to find with him. Even as it is, there are pages in the "Letters of Travel" in the contemplation of which the most lily-livered Socialist forgets to brand the labouring and adventuring men with the curse of Empire. There is, for example, an account of a bank failure in Japan. All Mr Kipling's sympathy with men who work is there displayed, and there, too, much more vividly than by means of direct description, is expressed the excitement and strangeness of the East. Up to a point that is perfectly true; Mr Kipling is a man of sympathy and imagination. But the more closely you watch the more puzzled you become. Why do these men, in the first shock of loss, step there, turn their backs just there, and say precisely that? There is something mechanical about it, as if they were acting; or is it that they are carefully observing the rules of a game?

> A man passed stiffly, and some one of a group turned to ask lightly, "Hit, old man?" "Like Hell," he said, and went on biting his unlit cigar. . . "We're doing ourselves well this year," said a wit grimly. "One free-shooting case, one thundering libel

case, and a bank smash. Showing off pretty before the globe trotters, aren't we?"

It is as if they were afraid to be natural. But Mr Kipling ought to have insisted that with him at least they should drop this pose, instead of which the effect of his presence is to make them talk more by rule than ever. Whether grown-up people really play this game, or whether, as we suspect, Mr Kipling makes up the whole British Empire to amuse the solitude of his nursery, the result is curiously sterile and depressing.

Emerson's Journals[1]

EMERSON'S Journals have little in common with other journals. They might have been written by starlight in a cave if the sides of the rock had been lined with books. In reality they cover twelve most important years—when he was at college, when he was a clergyman, and when he was married for the first time. But circumstances as well as nature made him peculiar. The Emerson family was now threadbare, but it had noble traditions in the past. His widowed mother and his eccentric aunt were possessed with the fierce Puritan pride of family which insisted upon intellectual distinction and coveted with a pride that was not wholly of the other world a high place for their name among the select families of Boston. They stinted themselves and stinted the boys that they might afford learning. The creed of the enthusiastic women was but too acceptable to children "born to be educated." They chopped the firewood, read classics in their spare time, and lay bare in all their sensitiveness to the "pressure of I know not how many literary influences" with which the Emerson household was charged. The influence of Aunt Mary, their father's sister, was clearly the most powerful. There are general rough sketches of men of genius in the family, and Miss Emerson rudely represented her nephew. She possessed the intense faith of the first Americans, together with a poetic imagination which made her doubt it. Her soul was always in conflict. She did not know whether she could suffer her nephews to reform the precious fabric, and yet was so full of new ideas herself that she could not help imparting them. But, unlike them, she was only self-taught, and her fervour boiled within her, scalding those she loved best. "I love to be a vessel of cumbersomeness to society," she remarked. But the strange correspondence which she kept up with Ralph, although it is but half intelligible from difficulty of thought and inadequacy of language, shows us what an intense and crabbed business life was to a serious American.

With such voices urging him on Emerson went to school fully impressed with the importance of the intellect. But his journals do not show vanity so much as a painful desire to get the most out of

[1] *Journals of Ralph Waldo Emerson*, edited by E. W. Emerson and W. Emerson Forbes, 1820-32. Two vols. *The Times Literary Supplement*, March 3, 1910.

himself and a precocious recognition of ends to be aimed at. His
first object was to learn how to write. The early pages are written to
the echo of great prose long before he could fit words that gave his
meaning into the rhythm. "He studied nature with a classical
enthusiasm, and the constant activity of his mind endowed him
with an energy of thought little short of inspiration." Then he
began to collect rare words out of the books he read:—"Ill con-
ditioned, Cameleon, Zeal, Whortleberry." The frigid exercises
upon "The Drama," "Death," "Providence" were useful also to
decide the anxious question whether he belonged to the society of
distinguished men or not. But it was the responsibility and the
labour of being great and not the joy that impressed him. His
upbringing had early made him conscious that he was exceptional,
and school no doubt confirmed him. At any rate he could not share
his thoughts with friends. Their arguments and views are never
quoted beside his own in the diary. The face of one Freshman
attracted him, but "it would seem that this was an imaginary
friendship. There is no evidence that the elder student ever brought
himself to risk disenchantment by active advances." To make up
for the absence of human interest we have the annals of the
Pythologian Club. But although they show that Emerson occasionally read and listened to papers comparing love and ambition,
marriage and celibacy, town-life and country life, they give no
impression of intimacy. Compared with the contemporary life of an
Englishman at Oxford or Cambridge, the life of an American
undergraduate seems unfortunately raw. Shelley took the world
seriously enough, but Oxford was so full of prejudices that he could
never settle into complacent self-improvement; Cambridge made
even Wordsworth drunk. But the great bare building at Harvard,
which looks (in an engraving of 1823) like a reformatory in the
middle of a desert, had no such traditions; its pupils were profoundly conscious that they had to make them. Several volumes of
the Journals are dedicated to "America," as though to a cause.

A weaker mind, shut up with its finger on its pulse, would have
used a diary to revile its own unworthiness. But Emerson's diary
merely confirms the impression he made on his friends; he appeared
"kindly, affable, but self-contained . . . apart, as if in a tower"; nor
was he more emotional writing at midnight for his own eye; but
we can guess the reason. It was because he had convictions. His

indefatigable brain raised a problem out of every sight and incident; but they could be solved if he applied his intellect. Safe in this knowledge, which time assured, he could live alone, registering the development, relying more and more on his sufficiency, and coming to believe that by close scrutiny he could devise a system. Life at twenty-one made him ponder thoughts like these: "Books and Men; Civilization; Society and Solitude; Time; God within." Novels, romances, and plays seemed for the most part written for "coxcombs and deficient persons." The only voice that reached him from without was the voice of his Aunt Mary, tumultuous in fear lest he should lose his belief in original sin. Before he had developed his theory of compensation, he was sometimes harassed by the existence of evil; occasionally he accused himself of wasting time. But his composure is best proved by an elaborate essay headed "Myself." There one quality is weighed with another, so that the character seems to balance scrupulously. Yet he was conscious of a "signal defect," which troubled him because it could destroy this balance more completely than its importance seemed to justify. Either he was without "address," or there was a "levity of the understanding" or there was an "absence of common sympathies." At any rate, he felt a "sore uneasiness in the company of most men and women . . . even before women and children I am compelled to remember the poor boy who cried, 'I told you, Father, they would find me out'." To be a sage in one's study, and a stumbling schoolboy out of it—that was the irony he had to face.

Instead, however, of slipping into easier views, he went on with his speculations; nor was he bitter against the world because it puzzled him. What he did was to assert that he could not be rejected because he held the universe within him. Each man, by finding out what he feels, discovers the laws of the universe; the essential thing, therefore, is to be as conscious of yourself as possible.

He that explores the principles of architecture and detects the beauty of the proportions of a column, what doth he but ascertain one of the laws of his own mind? . . . The Kingdom of God is within you . . . I hold fast to my old faith: that to each soul is a solitary law, a several universe.

Every man is a new creation: can do something best, has some intellectual modes or forms, or a character the general result of all, such as no other in the universe has.

But this is different from selfishness; praise or blame or a reflection in the face of society—anything that made him remember himself discomfited him; a solitude as empty as possible, in which he could feel most acutely his contact with the universe, rejoiced him. "The more exclusively idiosyncratic a man is, the more general and infinite he is"—that was the justification of solitude, but the fruits depend upon the worth of the man. Small minds, imbibing this doctrine, turn their possessors into cranks and egoists, and a delicate mind is strained until it is too pure to act: there was Mr Bradford, for example, who, "too modest and sensitive" to be a clergyman, became a "teacher of classes for young ladies," and was a "devoted gardener." In Emerson the reason was strong enough to lift him beyond the temptation of purifiying his own soul. Yet it did not free him, in youth at least, from an interest in the distempers of his spirit which is unpleasantly professional. Often in company and in solitude he was absorbed in regulating his sensations. "When I stamp through the mud in dirty boots, I hug myself with the feeling of my immortality." Only the bland and impersonal spirit which never left him makes such reflections other than smug; they are often dismal enough. But the wonder is that, treating as he does of platitudes and expounding them for our good, he yet contrives to make them glow so frequently, as if, next minute, they would illumine the world. He had the poet's gift of turning far, abstract thoughts, if not into flesh and blood, at least into something firm and glittering. In the pages of his diary one can see how his style slowly emerged from its wrappings, and became more definite and so strong that we can still read it even when the thought is too remote to hold us. He discovered that "No man can write well who thinks there is any choice of words for him. . . . In good writing, every word means something. In good writing, words become one with things." But the theory has something priggish about it. All good writing is honest in the sense that it says what the writer means; but Emerson did not see that one can write with phrases as well as with words. His sentences are made up of hard fragments each of which has been matched separately with the vision in his head. It is far rarer to find sentences which, lacking emphasis because the joins are perfect and the words common, yet grow together so that you cannot dismember them, and are steeped in meaning and suggestion.

But what is true of his style is true of his mind. An austere life, spent in generalizing from one's own emotions and in keeping their edges sharp, will not yield rich romantic pages, so deep that the more you gaze into them the more you see. Isolated, one loses the power of understanding why men and women do not live by rule, and the confusion of their feelings merely distresses one. Emerson, born among half-taught people, in a new land, kept always the immature habit of conceiving that a man is made up of separate qualities, which can be separately developed and praised. It is a belief necessary to schoolmasters; and to some extent Emerson is always a schoolmaster, making the world very simple for his scholars, a place of discipline and reward. But this simplicity, which is in his diaries as well as in his finished works—for he was not to be "found out"—is the result not only of ignoring so much, but of such concentration upon a few things. By means of it he can produce an extraordinary effect of exaltation, as though the disembodied mind were staring at the truth. He takes us to a peak above the world, and all familiar things have shrunk into pinheads and faint greys and pinks upon the flat. There, with beating hearts, we enjoy the sensation of our own dizziness; there he is natural and benign. But these exaltations are not practicable; they will not stand interruption. Where shall we lay the blame? Is he too simple, or are we too worn? But the beauty of his view is great, because it can rebuke us, even while we feel that he does not understand.

Thoreau[1]

A HUNDRED years ago, on July 12, 1817, was born Henry
David Thoreau, the son of a pencil maker in Concord, Massa-
chusetts. He has been lucky in his biographers, who have been
attracted to him not by his fame so much as by their sympathy with
his views, but they have not been able to tell us a great deal about
him that we shall not find in the books themselves. His life was not
eventful; he had, as he says, "a real genius for staying at home." His
mother was quick and voluble, and so fond of solitary rambling that
one of her children narrowly escaped coming into the world in an
open field. The father, on the other hand, was a "small, quiet,
plodding man," with a faculty for making the best lead pencils in
America, thanks to a secret of his own for mixing levigated plum-
bago with fuller's earth and water, rolling it into sheets, cutting it
into strips, and burning it. He could at any rate afford, with much
economy and a little help, to send his son to Harvard, although
Thoreau himself did not attach much importance to this expensive
opportunity. It is at Harvard, however, that he first becomes visible
to us. A class mate saw much in him as a boy that we recognize later
in the grown man, so that instead of a portrait we will quote what
was visible about the year 1837 to the penetrating eye of the Rev.
John Weiss:

> He was cold and unimpressible. The touch of his hand was
> moist and indifferent, as if he had taken up something when he
> saw your hand coming, and caught your grasp on it. How the
> prominent grey-blue eyes seemed to rove down the path, just in
> advance of his feet, as his grave Indian stride carried him down to
> University Hall. He did not care for people; his class-mates
> seemed very remote. This reverie hung always about him, and
> not so loosely as the odd garments which the pious household care
> furnished. Thought had not yet awakened his countenance; it
> was serene, but rather dull, rather plodding. The lips were not
> yet firm; there was almost a look of smug satisfaction lurking
> round their corners. It is plain now that he was preparing to hold
> his future views with great setness and personal appreciation of
> their importance. The nose was prominent, but its curve fell
> forward without firmness over the upper lip, and we remember

[1] *The Times Literary Supplement*, July 12, 1917.

him as looking very much like some Egyptian sculpture of faces, large-featured, but brooding, immobile, fixed in a mystic egoism. Yet his eyes were sometimes searching, as if he had dropped, or expected to find, something. In fact his eyes seldom left the ground, even in his most earnest conversations with you. . . .

He goes on to speak of the "reserve and inaptness" of Thoreau's life at college.

Clearly the young man thus depicted, whose physical pleasures took the form of walking and camping out, who smoked nothing but "dried lily stems," who venerated Indian relics as much as Greek classics, who in early youth had formed the habit of "settling accounts" with his own mind in a diary, where his thoughts, feelings, studies, and experiences had daily to be passed under review by that Egyptian face and searching eye—clearly this young man was destined to disappoint both parents and teachers and all who wished him to cut a figure in the world and become a person of importance. His first attempt to earn his living in the ordinary way by becoming a schoolmaster was brought to an end by the necessity of flogging his pupils. He proposed to talk morals to them instead. When the committee pointed out that the school would suffer from this "undue leniency" Thoreau solemnly beat six pupils and then resigned, saying that school-keeping "interfered with his arrangements." The arrangements that the penniless young man wished to carry out were probably assignations with certain pine trees, pools, wild animals, and Indian arrowheads in the neighbourhood, which had already laid their commands upon him.

But for a time he was to live in the world of men, at least in that very remarkable section of the world of which Emerson was the centre and which professed the Transcendentalist doctrines. Thoreau took up his lodgings in Emerson's house and very soon became, so his friends said, almost indistinguishable from the prophet himself. If you listened to them both talking with your eyes shut you could not be certain where Emerson left off and Thoreau began " . . . in his manners, in the tones of his voice, in his modes of expression, even in the hesitations and pauses of his speech, he had become the counterpart of Mr Emerson." This may well have been so. The strongest natures, when they are influenced, submit the most unreservedly: it is perhaps a sign of their strength. But that Thoreau lost any of his own force in the process, or took on permanently any colours not natural to himself the readers of his books will certainly deny.

The Transcendentalist movement, like most movements of vigour, represented the effort of one or two remarkable people to shake off the old clothes which had become uncomfortable to them and fit themselves more closely to what now appeared to them to be the realities. The desire for readjustment had, as Lowell has recorded and the Memoirs of Margaret Fuller bear witness, its ridiculous symptoms and its grotesque disciples. But of all the men and women who lived in an age when thought was remoulded in common, we feel that Thoreau was the one who had least to adapt himself, who was by nature most in harmony with the new spirit. He was by birth among those people, as Emerson expresses it, who have "silently given in their several adherence to a new hope, and in all companies do signify a greater trust in the nature and resources of man than the laws of the popular opinion will well allow." There were two ways of life which seemed to the leaders of the movement to give scope for the attainment of these new hopes; one in some cooperative community, such as Brook Farm; the other in solitude with nature. When the time came to make his choice Thoreau decided emphatically in favour of the second. "As for the communities," he wrote in his journal, "I think I had rather keep bachelor's quarters in hell than go to board in heaven." Whatever the theory might be, there was deep in his nature "a singular yearning to all wildness" which would have led him to some such experiment as that recorded in "Walden," whether it seemed good to others or not. In truth he was to put in practice the doctrines of the Transcendentalists more thoroughly than any one of them, and to prove what the resources of man are by putting his entire trust in them. Thus, having reached the age of 27, he chose a piece of land in a wood on the brink of the clear deep green waters of Walden Pond, built a hut with his own hands, reluctantly borrowing an axe for some part of the work, and settled down, as he puts it, "to front only the essential facts of life, and see if I could not learn what it had to teach, and not, when I came to die, discover that I had not lived."

And now we have a chance of getting to know Thoreau as few people are known, even by their friends. Few people, it is safe to say, take such an interest in themselves as Thoreau took in himself; for if we are gifted with an intense egoism we do our best to suffocate it in order to live on decent terms with our neighbours. We are not sufficiently sure of ourselves to break completely with the established order. This was Thoreau's adventure; his books are the record of that experiment and its results. He did everything he could to intensify his own understanding of himself, to foster whatever was peculiar, to isolate himself from contact with any force that might interfere with his immensely valuable gift of personality. It was his sacred duty, not to himself alone but to the world; and a man is scarcely an egoist who is an egoist on so grand a scale. When we read "Walden," the record of his two years in the woods, we have a sense of beholding life through a very powerful magnifying glass. To walk, to eat, to cut up logs, to read a little, to watch the bird on the bough, to cook one's dinner—all these occupations when scraped clean and felt afresh prove wonderfully large and bright. The common things are so strange, the usual sensations so astonishing that to confuse or waste them by living with the herd and adopting habits that suit the greater number is a sin—an act of sacrilege. What has civilization to give, how can luxury improve upon these simple facts? "Simplicity, simplicity, simplicity!" is his cry. "Instead of three meals a day, if it be necessary eat but one; instead of a hundred dishes, five; and reduce other things in proportion."

But the reader may ask, what is the value of simplicity? Is Thoreau's simplicity simplicity for its own sake, and not rather a method of intensification, a way of setting free the delicate and complicated machinery of the soul, so that its results are the reverse of simple? The most remarkable men tend to discard luxury because they find that it hampers the play of what is much more valuable to them. Thoreau himself was an extremely complex human being, and he certainly did not achieve simplicity by living for two years in a hut and cooking his own dinner. His achievement was rather to lay bare what was within him—to let life take its own way unfettered by artificial constraints. "I did not wish to live what was not life, living is so dear; nor did I wish to practice resignation, unless it was quite necessary. I wanted to live deep and suck out all the marrow of life. . . ." "Walden"—all his books, indeed—are packed with subtle, conflicting, and very fruitful discoveries. They are not written to prove something in the end. They are written as the Indians turn down twigs to mark their path through the forest.

He cuts his way through life as if no one had ever taken that road before, leaving these signs for those who come after, should they care to see which way he went. But he did not wish to leave ruts behind him, and to follow is not an easy process. We can never lull our attention asleep in reading Thoreau by the certainty that we have now grasped his theme and can trust our guide to be consistent. We must always be ready to try something fresh; we must always be prepared for the shock of facing one of those thoughts in the original which we have known all our lives in reproductions. "All health and success does me good, however far off and withdrawn it may appear; all disease and failure helps to make me sad and do me evil, however much sympathy it may have with me or I with it." "Distrust all enterprises that require new clothes." "You must have a genius for charity as well as for anything else." That is a handful, plucked almost at random, and of course there are plenty of wholesome platitudes.

As he walked his woods, or sat for hours almost motionless like the sphinx of college days upon a rock watching the birds, Thoreau defined his own position to the world not only with unflinching honesty, but with a glow of rapture at his heart. He seems to hug his own happiness. Those years were full of revelations—so independent of other men did he find himself, so perfectly equipped by nature not only to keep himself housed, fed, and clothed, but also superbly entertained without any help from society. Society suffered a good many blows from his hand. He sets down his complaints so squarely that we cannot help suspecting that society might one of these days have come to terms with so noble a rebel. He did not want churches or armies, post-offices or newspapers, and very consistently he refused to pay his tithes and went into prison rather than pay his poll tax. All getting together in crowds for doing good or procuring pleasure was an intolerable infliction to him. Philanthropy was one of the sacrifices, he said, that he had made to a sense of duty. Politics seemed to him "unreal, incredible, insignificant," and most revolutions not so important as the drying up of a river or the death of a pine. He wanted only to be left alone tramping the woods in his suit of Vermont grey, unhampered even by those two pieces of limestone which lay upon his desk until they proved guilty of collecting the dust, and were at once thrown out of the window.

76

And yet this egoist was the man who sheltered runaway slaves in his hut; this hermit was the first man to speak out in public in defence of John Brown; this self-centred solitary could neither sleep nor think when Brown lay in prison. The truth is that anyone who reflects as much and as deeply as Thoreau reflected about life and conduct is possessed of an abnormal sense of responsibility to his kind, whether he chooses to live in a wood or to become President of the Republic. Thirty volumes of diaries which he would condense from time to time with infinite care into little books prove, moreover, that the independent man who professed to care so little for his fellows was possessed with an intense desire to communicate with them. "I would fain," he writes, "communicate the wealth of my life to men, would really give them what is most precious in my gift. . . . I have no private good unless it be my peculiar ability to serve the public. . . . I wish to communicate those parts of my life which I would gladly live again." No one can read him and remain unaware of this wish. And yet it is a question whether he ever succeeded in imparting his wealth, in sharing his life. When we have read his strong and noble books, in which every word is sincere, every sentence wrought as well as the writer knows how, we are left with a strange feeling of distance; here is a man who is trying to communicate but who cannot do it. His eyes are on the ground or perhaps on the horizon. He is never speaking directly to us; he is speaking partly to himself and partly to something mystic beyond our sight. "Says I to myself," he writes, "should be the motto to my journal," and all his books are journals. Other men and women were wonderful and very beautiful, but they were distant; they were different; he found it very hard to understand their ways. They were as "curious to him as if they had been prairie dogs." All human intercourse was infinitely difficult; the distance between one friend and another was unfathomable; human relationships were very precarious and terribly apt to end in disappointment. But, although concerned and willing to do what he could short of lowering his ideals, Thoreau was aware that the difficulty was one that could not be overcome by taking pains. He was made differently from other people. "If a man does not keep pace with his companions, perhaps it is because he hears a different drummer. Let him step to the music which he hears, however measured or far away." He was a wild man, and he would never submit to be a tame one. And for us here lies his peculiar charm. He hears a different drummer. He is a man into whom nature has breathed other instincts than ours, to whom she has whispered, one may guess, some of her secrets.

"It appears to be a law," he says, "that you cannot have a deep sympathy with both man and nature. Those qualities which bring you near to the one estrange you from the other." Perhaps that is true. The greatest passion of his life was his passion for nature. It was more than a passion, indeed; it was an affinity; and in this he differs from men like White and Jefferies. He was gifted, we are told, with an extraordinary keenness of the senses; he could see and hear what other men could not; his touch was so delicate that he could pick up a dozen pencils accurately from a box holding a bushel; he could find his way alone through thick woods at night. He could lift a fish out of the stream with his hands; he could charm a wild squirrel to nestle in his coat; he could sit so still that the animals went on with their play round him. He knew the look of the country so intimately that if he had waked in a meadow he could have told the time of year within a day or two from the flowers at his feet. Nature had made it easy for him to pick up a living without effort. He was so skilled with his hands that by labouring forty days he could live at leisure for the rest of the year. We scarcely know whether to call him the last of an older race of men, or the first of one that is to come. He had the toughness, the stoicism, the unspoilt senses of an Indian, combined with the self-consciousness, the exacting discontent, the susceptibility of the most modern. At times he seems to reach beyond our human powers in what he perceives upon the horizon of humanity. No philanthropist ever hoped more of mankind, or set higher and nobler tasks before him, and those whose ideal of passion and of service is the loftiest are those who have the greatest capacities for giving, although life may not ask of them all that they can give, and forces them to hold in reserve rather than to lavish. However much Thoreau had been able to do, he would still have seen possibilities beyond; he would always have remained, in one sense, unsatisfied. That is one of the reasons why he is able to be the companion of a younger generation.

He died when he was in the full tide of life, and had to endure long illness within doors. But from nature he had learnt both silence and stoicism. He had never spoken of the things that had moved him most in his private fortunes. But from nature, too, he had learnt to be content, not thoughtlessly or selfishly content, and certainly not with resignation, but with a healthy trust in the wisdom of nature, and in nature, as he says, there is no sadness. "I am enjoying existence as much as ever," he wrote from his deathbed, "and regret nothing." He was talking to himself of moose and Indian when, without a struggle, he died.

Herman Melville[1]

SOMEWHERE upon the horizon of the mind, not recognizable yet in existence, "Typee" and "Omoo" together with the name of Herman Melville, float in company. But since Herman Melville is apt to become Whyte Melville or Herman Merivale and "Omoo" for some less obvious reason connects itself with the adventures of an imaginary bushranger who is liable to turn jockey and then play a part in the drama of "Uncle Tom's Cabin," it is evident that a mist, due to ignorance or the lapse of time, must have descended upon those far distant regions. Ignorance we do not scruple to admit; the lapse of time, since the first of August marks the centenary of Melville's birth, is undeniable; but this haziness may spring in part from a little seed dropped years ago by the books themselves. Was not some one talking about the South Seas? "Typee," they said, was in their opinion the best account ever written of—something or other. Memory has dropped that half of the sentence, and then, as memory will, has drawn a great blue line and a yellow beach. Waves are breaking; there is a rough white frill of surf; and how to describe it one does not know, but there is, simultaneously, a sense of palm trees, yellow limbs, and coral beneath clear water. This blundering brushwork of memory has been corrected since by Stevenson, Gauguin, Rupert Brooke and many others. Yet, in some important respects, Herman Melville, with his "Typee" and "Omoo" and his ineradicable air of the early forties, has done the business better than the more sophisticated artists of our own day.

He was not sophisticated; perhaps it would be wrong to call him an artist. He came, indeed, to the Marquesas Islands as an ordinary seaman on board a whaling ship in the year 1842. Nor was it a love of the picturesque, but rather a hatred of salt beef, stale water, hard bread, and the cruelty of a captain that led him, in company with another sailor, to try his fortunes inland. They deserted, and, with as much food and calico as they could stow in the front of their frocks, made off into the interior of Nukuheva. But at what point their marvellous adventures in reaching the valley of the Typees

---

[1] *The Times Literary Supplement*, August 7, 1919.

cease to be authentic and become, for the sake of an American public, of the heroic order we have no means of saying. The number of days that two strong men, going through incredible exertions meanwhile, can support themselves upon a hunk of bread soaked in sweat and ingrained with shreds of tobacco must be fewer than Melville makes out; and then the cliff down which they lowered themselves by swinging from creeper to creeper with horrid gaps between them—was it as steep as he says, and the creepers as far apart? And did they, on another occasion, as he asserts, break a second gigantic fall by pitching on to the topmost branches of a very high palm tree? It matters little; whatever the proportions of art and truth, each obstacle, and that is all we ask of it, seems impassable. There can be no way out of this, one says for the tenth time, a little grimly, for one has come to feel a kind of comradeship for the poor wretches in their struggles; and then, at the last moment, the incredible sagacity of Toby and the manful endurance of Melville find an outlet, as they deserve to do; and we have just drawn breath and judged them warranted in breaking off another precious crumb of the dwindling loaf when Toby, who has run on a little ahead, gives a shout, and behold, the summit on which they stand is not the end of their journey, but a ravine of immense depth and steepness still separates them from the valley of their desire; the bread must be put back uneaten and, with Melville's leg getting more and more painful, and nothing to cheer us but the conviction that it is better to die of starvation here than in the hold of a whaling ship, off again we must start. Even when the valley is reached there is a terrible moment while Melville hesitates whether to reply "Typee" or "Happar" to the demand of the native chief, and only by a fluke saves them from instant death; nor need one be a boy in an Eton jacket to skip half a dozen chapters in a frenzy to make sure that the reason of Toby's disappearance was neither tragic nor in any way to his discredit as a friend.

But then, when they are settled as the guests, or rather as the idolized prisoners, of the Typees, Melville appears to change his mind, as an artist is not generally supposed to do. Dropping his adventures, at which, as Stevenson said, he has proved himself "a howling cheese," he becomes engrossed in the lives and customs of the natives. However much the first half of the book owed to his imagination, the second we should guess to be literally true. This

random American sailor having done his best to excite our interest
in the usual way, now has to confess that what he found when he
blundered into the midst of this tribe of South Sea islanders was—a
little puzzling. They were savages, they were idolaters, they were
inhuman beasts who licked their lips over the tender thighs of their
kindred; and at the same time they were crowned with flowers,
exquisite in beauty, courteous in manner, and engaged all day long
in doing not only what they enjoyed doing but what, so far as he
could judge, they had every right to enjoy doing. Of course, he had
his suspicions. A dish of meat was not to be tasted until he had
ascertained that it was pig slaughtered hospitably for him and not
human flesh. The almost universal indolence of the natives was
another remarkable and not altogether reassuring characteristic.
Save for one old lady who busied herself "rummaging over bundles
of old tappa, or making a prodigious clatter among the calabashes,"
no one was ever seen to do anything in the way of work. Nature, of
course, abetted them in their indolence. The bread fruit tree, with
very little effort on their part, would give them all the food they
wanted; the cloth tree, with the same gentle solicitation, provided
them with tappa for their clothing. But the work needed for these
processes was light; the climate divine; and the only intimations of
industry were the clear musical sounds of the different mallets, one
here, one there, beating out the cloth, which rang charmingly in
unison throughout the valley.

Being puzzled, Melville, very naturally, did his best to make a
joke of it. He has a good laugh at Marheyo for instance, who
accepted a pair of mouldy old boots with profound gratitude, and
hung them round his neck for an ornament. The ancient naked
women who leapt into the air "like so many sticks bobbing to the
surface, after being pressed perpendicularly into the water," might
be widows mourning their husbands slain in battle, but they did
not seem to him decorous; he could not take his eyes off them. And
then there were no laws, human or divine, except the queer business
of the taboo. Yet what puzzled Herman Melville, as it puzzled Lord
Pembroke twenty years later, was that this simple, idle, savage
existence was after all remarkably pleasant. There must be something wrong about happiness granted on such easy terms. The earl,
being the better educated of the two, puzzled out the reason. He
had been smothered with flowers and hung with mats until he

looked like a cross between a Roman Catholic priest and a youthful Bacchus. He had enjoyed it immensely.

> I was so happy there, that I verily believe I should have been content to dream away my life, without care or ambition. . . . It could not be, and it was best for me as it was. . . . Peace, and quiet, and perfect freedom, are useful medicines, but not wholesome diet. Their charm lies in contrast; there is no spark without the concussion of the flint and steel; there is no fine thought, even no perfect happiness, that is not born of toil, sorrow, and vexation of spirit.

So the earl and the doctor sailed back to Wilton, and Providence saw to it that they were shipwrecked on the way. But Melville only made his escape with the greatest difficulty. He was almost drugged into acquiescence by those useful medicines, peace, quiet and perfect freedom. If there had been no resistance to his going he might have succumbed for ever. Laughter no longer did its office. It is significant that in the preface to his next book he is careful to insist that "should a little jocoseness be shown upon some curious traits of the Tahitians, it proceeds from no intention to ridicule." Did his account of some curious traits of European sailors, which directly follows, proceed from no intention to satirize? It is difficult to say. Melville reports very vividly and vigorously, but he seldom allows himself to comment. He found the whaling vessel that took him off in "a state of the greatest uproar"; the food was rotten; the men riotous; rather than land and lose his crew, who would certainly desert and thus cost him a cargo of whale oil, the captain kept them cruising out at sea. Discipline was maintained by a daily allowance of rum and the kicks and cuffs of the chief mate. When at last the sailors laid their case before the English Consul at Tahiti the fountain of justice seemed to them impure. At any rate, Melville and others who had insisted upon their legal rights found themselves given into the charge of an old native who was directed to keep their legs in the stocks. But his notion of discipline was vague, and somehow or other, what with the beauty of the place and the kindness of the natives, Melville began once more, curiously and perhaps dangerously, to feel content. Again there was freedom and indolence; torches brandished in the woods at night; dances under the moon, rainbow fish sparkling in the water, and women stuck about with variegated flowers. But something was wrong. Listening, Melville heard the aged Tahitians singing in a low, sad tone a song which ran: "The palm trees shall grow, the coral shall spread, but man shall cease"; and statistics bore them out. The population had sunk from two hundred thousand to nine thousand in less than a century. The Europeans had brought the diseases of civilization along with its benefits. The missionaries followed, but Melville did not like the missionaries. "There is, perhaps, no race on earth," he wrote, "less disposed, by nature, to the monitions of Christianity" than the Tahitians, and to teach them any useful trade is an impossibility. Civilization and savagery blended in the strangest way in the palace of Queen Pomaree. The great leaf-hung hall, with its mats and screens and groups of natives, was furnished with rosewood writing desks, cut-glass decanters, and gilded candelabras. A coconut kept open the pages of a volume of Hogarth's prints. And in the evenings the Queen herself would put on a crown which Queen Victoria had good-naturedly sent her from London, and walk up and down the road raising her hand as people passed her to the symbol of majesty in what she thought a military salute. So Marheyo had been profoundly grateful for the present of a pair of old boots. But this time, somehow, Melville did not laugh.

Rupert Brooke[1]

THIS memoir of Rupert Brooke has been delayed, in Mrs Brooke's words, because of "my great desire to obtain the collaboration of some of his contemporaries at Cambridge and during his young manhood, for I strongly believe that they knew the largest part of him." But his contemporaries are for the most part scattered or dead; and though Mr Marsh has done all that ability or care can do, the memoir which now appears is "of necessity incomplete." It is inevitably incomplete, as Mr Marsh, we are sure, would be the first to agree, if for no other reason because it is the work of an older man. A single sentence brings this clearly before us. No undergraduate of Rupert Brooke's own age would have seen "his radiant youthful figure in gold and vivid red and blue, like a page in the Riccardi Chapel"; that is the impression of an older man. The contemporary version would have been less pictorial and lacking in the half-humorous tenderness which is so natural an element in the mature vision of beautiful and gifted youth. There would have been less of the vivid red and blue and gold, more that was mixed, parti-coloured, and matter for serious debate. In addition Mr Marsh has had to face the enormous difficulties which beset the biographers of those who have died with undeveloped powers, tragically, and in the glory of public gratitude. They leave so little behind them that can serve to recall them with any exactitude. A few letters, written from school and college, a fragment of a diary—that is all. The power of expressing oneself naturally in letters comes to most people late in life. Rupert Brooke wrote freely, but not altogether without self-consciousness, and it is evident that his friends have not cared to publish the more intimate passages in his letters to them. Inevitably, too, they have not been willing to tell the public the informal things by which they remember him best. With these serious and necessary drawbacks Mr Marsh has done his best to present a general survey of Rupert Brooke's life which those who knew him will be able to fill in here and there more fully, perhaps a little to the detriment of the com-

[1] *The Collected Poems of Rupert Brooke. The Times Literary Supplement*, August 8, 1918.

position as a whole. But they will be left, we believe, to reflect rather sadly upon the incomplete version which must in future represent Rupert Brooke to those who never knew him.

Nothing, it is true, but his own life prolonged to the usual term, and the work that he would have done, could have expressed all that was latent in the crowded years of his youth—years crowded beyond the measure that is usual even with the young. To have seen a little of him at that time was to have seen enough to be made sceptical of the possibility of any biography of a man dying, as he died, at the age of twenty-eight. The remembrance of a week spent in his company, of a few meetings in London and the country, offers a tantalizing fund of memories at once very definite, very little related to the Rupert Brooke of legend, presenting each one an extremely clear sense of his presence, but depending so much upon that presence and upon other circumstances inextricably involved with it, that one may well despair of rendering a clear account to a third person, let alone to a multiple of many people such as the general public.

But the outline at least is clear enough. So much has been written of his personal beauty that to state one's own first impression of him in that respect needs some audacity, since the first impression was of a type so conventionally handsome and English as to make it inexpressive or expressive only of something that one might be inclined half-humorously to disparage. He was the type of English young manhood at its healthiest and most vigorous. Perhaps at the particular stage he had then reached, following upon the decadent phase of his first Cambridge days, he emphasized this purposely; he was consciously and defiantly pagan. He was living at Grantchester; his feet were permanently bare; he disdained tobacco and butcher's meat; and he lived all day, and perhaps slept all night, in the open air. You might judge him extreme, and from the pinnacle of superior age assure him that the return to Nature was as sophisticated as any other pose, but you could not from the first moment of speech with him doubt that, whatever he might do, he was an originator, one of those leaders who spring up from time to time and show their power most clearly by subjugating their own generation. Under his influence the country near Cambridge was full of young men and women walking barefoot, sharing his passion for bathing and fish diet, disdaining book learning, and proclaiming that there was something deep and wonderful in the man who brought the milk and in the woman who watched the cows. One may trace some of the effects of this belief in the tone of his letters at this time; their slap-dash method, their hasty scrawled appearance upon the paper, the exclamations and abbreviations were all, in part at least, a means of exorcising the devils of the literary and the cultured. But there was too much vigour in his attitude in this respect, as in all others, to lend it the appearance of affectation. It was an amusing disguise; it was in part, like many of his attitudes, a game played for the fun of it, an experiment in living by one keenly inquisitive and incessantly fastidious; and in part it was the expression of a profound and true sympathy which had to live side by side with highly sophisticated tastes and to be reported upon by a nature that was self-conscious in the highest degree. Analyse it as one may, the whole effect of Rupert Brooke in those days was a compound of vigour and of great sensitiveness. Like most sensitive people, he had his methods of self-protection; his pretence now to be this and now to be that. But, however sunburnt and slap-dash he might choose to appear at any particular moment, no one could know him even slightly without seeing that he was not only very sincere, but passionately in earnest about the things he cared for. In particular, he cared for literature and the art of writing as seriously as it is possible to care for them. He had read everything and he had read it from the point of view of a working writer. As Mrs Cornford says, "I can't imagine him using a word of that emotional jargon in which people usually talk or write of poetry. He made it feel more like carpentering." In discussing the work of living writers he gave you the impression that he had the poem or the story before his eyes in a concrete shape, and his judgments were not only very definite but had a freedom and a reality which mark the criticism of those who are themselves working in the same art. You felt that to him literature was not dead nor of the past, but a thing now in process of construction by people many of whom were his friends; and that knowledge, skill, and, above all, unceasing hard work were required of those who attempt to make it. To work hard, much harder than most writers think it necessary, was an injunction of his that remains in memory from a chaos of such discussions.

The proofs of his first book of poems were lying about that summer on the grass. There were also the manuscripts of poems that were in process of composition. It seemed natural to turn his poetry over and say nothing about it, save perhaps to remark upon his habit of leaving spaces for unforthcoming words which gave his manuscript the look of a puzzle with a number of pieces missing. On one occasion he wished to know what was the brightest thing in nature? and then, deciding with a glance round him that the brightest thing was a leaf in the sun, a blank space towards the end of "Town and Country" was filled in immediately.

Cloud-like we lean and stare as bright leaves stare.

But instead of framing any opinion as to the merit of his verses we recall merely the curiosity of watching him finding his adjective, and a vague conception that he was somehow a mixture of scholar and man of action, and that his poetry was the brilliant by-product of energies not yet turned upon their object. It may seem strange, now that he is famous as a poet, how little it seemed to matter in those days whether he wrote poetry or not. It is proof perhaps of the exciting variety of his gifts and of the immediate impression he made of a being so complete and remarkable in himself that it was sufficient to think of him merely as Rupert Brooke. It was not necessary to imagine him dedicated to any particular pursuit. If one traced a career for him many different paths seemed the proper channels for his store of vitality; but clearly he must find scope for his extraordinary gift of being on good terms with his fellow-creatures. For though it is true to say that "he never 'put himself forward' and seldom took the lead in conversation," his manner shed a friendliness wherever he happened to be that fell upon all kinds of different people, and seemed to foretell that he would find his outlet in leading varieties of men as he had led his own circle of Cambridge friends. His practical ability, which was often a support to his friends, was one of the gifts that seemed to mark him for success in active life. He was keenly aware of the state of public affairs, and if you chanced to meet him when there was talk of a strike or an industrial dispute he was evidently as well versed in the complications of social questions as in the obscurities of the poetry of Donne. There, too, he showed his power of being in sympathy with the present. Nothing of this is in the least destructive of his possession of poetic power. No breadth of sympathy or keenness of susceptibility could come amiss to the writer; but perhaps if one feared for him at all it was lest the pull of all his gifts in their different directions might somehow rend him asunder. He was, as he said of himself, "forty times as sensitive as anybody else," and apt, as he wrote, to begin "poking at his own soul, examining it, cutting the soft and rotten parts away." It needed no special intimacy to guess that beneath "an appearance almost of placidity" he was the most restless, complex, and analytic of human beings. It was impossible to think of him withdrawn, abstracted, or indifferent. Whether or not it was for the good of his poetry he would be in the thick of things, and one fancies that he would in the end have framed a speech that came very close to the modern point of view—a subtle analytic poetry, or prose perhaps, full of intellect, and full of his keen unsentimental curiosity.

No one could have doubted that as soon as war broke out he would go without hesitation to enlist. His death and burial on the Greek island, which "must ever be shining with his glory that we buried there," was in harmony with his physical splendour and with the generous warmth of his spirit. But to imagine him entombed, however nobly and fitly, apart from our interests and passions still seems impossibly incongruous with what we remember of his inquisitive eagerness about life, his response to every side of it, and his complex power, at once so appreciative and so sceptical, of testing and enjoying, of suffering and taking with the utmost sharpness the impression of everything that came his way. One turns from the thought of him not with a sense of completeness and finality, but rather to wonder and to question still: what would he have been, what would he have done?

The Intellectual Imagination[1]

"IS not life both a dream and an awakening?" Mr de la Mare asks in his study of Rupert Brooke. The greatest poets, having both the visionary imagination and the intellectual imagination, deal with both sides of life; in the lesser poets either the one kind of imagination or the other predominates. Blake and Shelley are obvious instances of the visionary; Donne and Meredith of the intellectual. The distinction is finely and subtly elaborated by Mr de la Mare; and when he affirms that Rupert Brooke possessed the intellectual imagination in a rare degree we assent with a conviction which shows that the problem of Rupert Brooke's poetry has, for us, come nearer solution.

A poet of one's own time and acquaintance is inevitably much of a problem. We hear so many strains in his voice that will be silent in a hundred years' time. Nor do we know what allowance to make for our personal attachment, nor what for old arguments and theories once taken in such good part and such high spirit by an unknown and eager boy. There is in existence a copy of his first volume, in which a pencil has underlined each adjective judged wrong or unnecessary. The lines still stand, though the poet is dead and famous. He would not have had it otherwise. But, do what we will, it is idle to read "The Fish," where a great number of those marks occur, without finding them the signposts of memories and dreams. Rupert Brooke was certainly fond of adjectives. But was not his passion for loading his lines, like the fingers of some South American beauty, with gem after gem, part of his boldness and brilliancy and strength? So he went to the South Seas, turned Socialist, made friend after friend, and passed from one extreme to another of dress and diet—better preparation, surely, for the choice of the right adjective than to sit dreaming over the fire with a book. But all this time one is not reading "The Fish"; one is thinking of Rupert Brooke, one is dreaming of what he would have done. When we turn again to Mr de la Mare, he helps us to define what was, and still is, our case against the adjectives. Magic, he says, "is all but

---

[1] *Rupert Brooke and the Intellectual Imagination*, by Walter de la Mare. *The Times Literary Supplement*, December 11, 1919.

absent from his verse." The words remain separate, however well assorted. Though he has described most of the English country sights, it has never happened to us, walking the woods, to hum over a line or two and, waking, to find them his. The test is personal and, of course, imperfect. Yet perhaps the same is generally true of those poets in whom the intellectual imagination predominates. The supreme felicities of Keats or Shelley seem to come when the engine of the brain is shut off and the mind glides serene but unconscious, or, more truly, perhaps, is exalted to a different sphere of consciousness. Like Meredith and like Donne, Rupert Brooke was never for a second unconscious. The brain was always there, working steadily, strenuously, and without stopping.

There can be no question that his brain was both a fine instrument and a strong one; but there are other questions, for is it not true that the intellectual poet, unlike the visionary poet, improves and develops with age? Though Keats died younger, and Shelley only a year or two older, than Rupert Brooke, both left behind them unmistakable proof not merely that they were great poets, but that their greatness was of a particular character. If we cannot call Rupert Brooke a great poet, that is to some extent the result of feeling that, compared with the others, he has left us only sketches and premonitions of what was to come. He was of the type that reacts sharply to experience, and life would have taught him much, perhaps changed him greatly. Like Dryden, like Meredith, like Donne himself, as Mr Pearsall Smith has lately shown us, it might have been in prose and not in poetry that he achieved his best. It might have been in scholarship; it might have been in action. But if we seem to disparage what he left, there again we trace the effect of friendship. We do not want our friend rapt away into the circle of the good and the great. We want still to cherish the illusion that the poems will be bettered, the adjectives discussed, the arguments resumed, the convictions altered. The actual achievement must always have for those who knew him a ghostly rival in the greatness which he did not live to achieve. But he was of the few who seem to exist in themselves, apart from what they accomplish, apart from length of life. Again and again Mr de la Mare turns from the poetry, greatly though he admires it, to bathe and warm himself in the memory of the man. One sort of magic may have been absent from his verse, but "above all Brooke's poems are charged with and surrender the magic of what we call personality. What, if he had lived, he would have *done* in this world is a fascinating but an unanswerable question. This only can be said: that he would have gone on being his wonderful self." One might add that he still goes on being his self, since none of those who knew him can forget him; and it must be a wonderful self when no two people remember the same thing, but all are agreed that he was wonderful.

These are the Plans[1]

SO far as we can read Charles Sorley's character between the lines of his book, nothing would have annoyed him more than to find himself acclaimed either a poet or a hero. He was far too genuine a writer not to be disgusted by any praise implying that his work, at the stage it had reached, was more than a promise and an experiment. It is indeed largely because Charles Sorley was experimental, here trying his hand at narrative, here at description, always making an effort to shed the conventional style and press more closely to his conception, that one is convinced that he was destined, whether in prose or in verse, to be a writer of considerable power. The writer's problem presented itself very early in his life. Here at Marlborough, where he was at school, the downs showed themselves not, as other poets have seen them, soft, flowery, seductive, but stony, rain-beaten, wind-blown beneath a clay-coloured sky. He tried to put down in verse his delight in that aspect of nature and his corresponding notion of a race of men

> *Stern, sterile, senseless, mute, unknown,*
> *But bold, O, bolder far than we!*

He tried to say how much had been revealed to him when he wandered, as he was fond of doing, alone among the downs:

> *I who have walked along her downs in dreams,*
> *And known her tenderness, and felt her might,*
> *And sometimes by her meadows and her streams*
> *Have drunk deep-storied secrets of delight,*
>
> * * *
>
> *Have had my times, when, though the earth did wear*
> *Her selfsame trees and grasses, I could see*
> *The revelation that is always there,*
> *But somehow is not always clear to me.*

Succeeding these schoolboy attempts at landscape comes the natural mood of feeling that beauty is better not expressed, and

---

[1] *Marlborough and Other Poems* by Charles Hamilton Sorley. *The Athenæum,* August 1, 1919.

that his spirit, compared with the spirits of the poets, is dumb. Running alongside of them, also, is his characteristic view—or the view that was characteristic of that stage of his life—of our modern sin of inactivity. The rain beats and the wind blows, but we are sluggish and quiescent—

> *We do not see the vital point*
> *That 'tis the eighth, most deadly, sin*
> *To wail, "The world is out of joint"—*
> *And not attempt to put it in.*

> *We question, answer, make defence,*
> *We sneer, we scoff, we criticize,*
> *We wail and moan our decadence,*
> *Enquire, investigate, surmise—*

We might of course cap these verses with a stanza to prove that Sorley found satisfaction in the outbreak of war, and died bidding men

> *On, marching men, on*
> *To the gates of death with song.*
> *Sow your gladness for earth's reaping,*
> *So you may be glad though sleeping,*
> *Strew your gladness on earth's bed.*
> *So be merry, so be dead.*

And yet from the evidence of his poetry, and still more from the evidence of his remarkable prose, it is clear that Sorley was as far from trumping up a precocious solution, as ready to upset all his convictions and be off on a fresh track, as any other boy with a mind awakening daily more widely to the complexity of things, and naturally incapable of a dishonest or sentimental conclusion. "A Call to Action," from which we have quoted, was written when Sorley, at the age of seventeen, was going through a phase of admiration for the work of Mr Masefield. And then came a time, in Germany, of "setting up and smashing of deities," Masefield and Hardy and Goethe being the gods to suffer, while Ibsen and the Odyssey and Robert Browning inherited the vacant pedestals. Almost at once the war broke out.

94

I'm sure the German nature is the nicest in the world, as far as it is not warped by the German Empire [he wrote]. I regard the war as one between sisters . . . the efficient and intolerant against the casual and sympathetic . . . but I think that tolerance is the larger virtue of the two, and efficiency must be her servant. So I am quite glad to fight against the rebellious servant. . . . Now you know what Sorley thinks about it.

"What Sorley thinks about it" appears to us of extreme interest, because, as our quotations have tried to show, Sorley thought for himself, and fate contrived that the young men of his generation should have opportunities for doing the thinking of a lifetime in a very few years. Such opportunities for changing his mind and moving on Sorley used to the full. There was, directly he joined the army, the problem of what he called "the poorer classes." "The public school boy," he said, "should live among them to learn a little Christianity; for they are so extraordinarily nice to one another." After that reflection there comes, a page or two later, the remark: "I have had a conventional education: Oxford would have corked it." So his dream for next year is to be perhaps in Mexico, selling cloth.

Or in Russia, doing Lord knows what: in Serbia or the Balkans: in England never. England remains the dream, the background: at once the memory, and the ideal. . . . Details can wait—perhaps for ever. These are the plans.

It is upon the plans rather than upon the details that one is inclined to dwell, asking oneself to what goal this generation, captained by men of such vigour and clear-sightedness as Sorley, was making its way.

> *We know not whom we trust,*
> *Nor whitherward we fare,*
> *But we run because we must*
> *Through the great wide air,*

are lines from an early poem that seem to express a force yet undirected seeking a new channel. But the poems are more than scattered details to be used to illustrate an imaginary career. They have often enough literary merit to stand upon their own feet independently of any personal considerations. They have the still rarer merit of suggesting that the writer is so well aware of his own purpose that he is content to leave a roughness here, a jingle there, for the sake of getting on quickly to the next stage. What the finished work, the final aim, would have been we can only guess, for Charles Sorley at the age of twenty was killed near Hulluch.

Mr Sassoon's Poems[1]

AS it is the poet's gift to give expression to the moments of insight or experience that come to him now and then, so in following him we have to sketch for ourselves a map of those submerged lands which lie between one pinnacle and the next. If he is a true poet, at least we fill up in thought the space between one poem and another with speculations that are half guesses and half anticipations of what is to come next. He offers us a new vision of the world; how is the light about to fall? What ranges, what horizons will it reveal? At least if he is a sincere artist this is so, and to us Mr Sassoon seems undoubtedly sincere. He is a poet, we believe, meaning by that that we cannot fancy him putting down these thoughts in any form save the one he has chosen. His vision comes to him directly; he seems almost always, before he began to get his words into order, to have had one of those puzzling shocks of emotion which the world deals by such incongruous methods, to the poet often, to the rest of us too seldom for our soul's good. It follows that this one slim volume is full of incongruities; but the moments of vision are interesting enough to make us wish to follow them up very carefully.

There are the poems about the war, to begin with. If you chance to read one of them by itself you may be inclined to think that it is a very clever poem, chiefly designed with its realism and its surface cynicism to shock the prosperous and sentimental. Naturally the critical senses rise in alarm to protect their owner from such insinuations. But read them continuously, read in particular "The Hero" and "The Tomb-Stone Maker," and you will drop the idea of being shocked in that sense altogether.

> *"Jack fell as he'd have wished," the Mother said,*
> *And folded up the letter that she'd read.*
> *"The Colonel writes so nicely." Something broke*
> *In the tired voice that quavered to a choke.*
> *She half looked up. "We mothers are so proud*
> *Of our dead soldiers." Then her face was bowed.*

[1] *The Old Huntsman and Other Poems* and *Counter-Attack and Other Poems*, by Siegfried Sassoon. *The Times Literary Supplement*, May 31, 1917 and July 11, 1918.

97

Quietly the Brother Officer went out. . . . .
He thought how "Jack," cold-footed, useless swine,
Had panicked down the trench that night the mine
Went up at Wicked Corner; how he'd tried
To get sent home; and how at last he died,
Blown to small bits. And no one seemed to care
Except that lonely woman with white hair.

What Mr Sassoon has felt to be the most sordid and horrible experiences in the world he makes us feel to be so in a measure which no other poet of the war has achieved. As these jaunty matter-of-fact statements succeed each other such loathing, such hatred accumulates behind them that we say to ourselves "Yes, this is going on; and we are sitting here watching it," with a new shock of surprise, with an uneasy desire to leave our place in the audience, which is a tribute to Mr Sassoon's power as a realist. It is realism of the right, of the poetic kind. The real things are put in not merely because they are real, but because at a certain moment of emotion the poet happened to be struck by them and is not afraid of spoiling his effect by calling them by their right names. The wounded soldier looking out of the train window sees the English country again—

There shines the blue serene, the prosperous land,
Trees, cows, and hedges; skipping these, he scanned
Large friendly names that change not with the year,
Lung Tonic, Mustard, Liver Pills, and Beer.

To call back any moment of emotion is to call back with it the strangest odds and ends that have become somehow part of it, and it is the weeds pulled up by mistake with the flowers that bring back the extraordinary moment as a whole. With this straight, courageous method Mr Sassoon can produce such a solid and in its way beautiful catalogue of facts as that of the train leaving the station— "The Morning Express."

But we might hazard the guess that the war broke in and called out this vein of realism before its season; for side by side with these pieces there are others very different, not so effective perhaps, not particularly accomplished, but full of a rarer kind of interest, full of promise for the future. For the beauty in them, though fitful, is of the individual, indefinable kind which comes, we know not how, to make lines such as we read over each time with a renewed delight that after one comes the other.

> *Where have you been, South Wind, this May-day morning,*
> *With larks aloft, or skimming with the swallow,*
> *Or with blackbirds in a green, sun-glinted thicket?*
>
> *Oh, I heard you like a tyrant in the valley;*
> *Your ruffian haste shook the young, blossoming orchards;*
> *You clapped rude hands, hallooing round the chimney,*
> *And white your pennons streamed along the river.*
>
> *You have robbed the bee, South Wind, in your adventure,*
> *Blustering with gentle flowers; but I forgave you*
> *When you stole to me shyly with scent of hawthorn.*

Here we have evidence not of accomplishment, indeed, but of a gift much more valuable than that, the gift of being a poet, we must call it; and we shall look with interest to see what Mr Sassoon does with his gift.

Counter-Attack

It is natural to feel an impulse of charity towards the poems written by young men who have fought or are still fighting; but in the case of Mr Sassoon there is no temptation to indulge in this form of leniency, because he is so evidently able-bodied in his poetic capacity and requires no excuses to be made for him. At the same time, it is difficult to judge him dispassionately as a poet, because it is impossible to overlook the fact that he writes as a soldier. It is a fact, indeed, that he forces upon you, as if it were a matter of indifference to him whether you called him a poet or not. We know no other writer who has shown us as effectually as Mr Sassoon the terrible pictures which lie behind the colourless phrases of the newspapers. From the thousand horrors which in their sum compose one day of warfare he selects, as if by chance, now this of the counter-attack, now that of mending the front-line wires, or this again of suicide in the trenches. "The General" is as good an example of his method as another:

> *"Good-morning; good-morning!" the General said*
> *When we met him last week on our way to the line.*
> *Now the soldiers he smiled at are most of 'em dead,*
> *And we're cursing his staff for incompetent swine.*
> *"He's a cheery old card," grunted Harry to Jack,*
> *As they slogged up to Arras with rifle and pack.*

*   *   *

> *But he did for them both by his plan of attack.*

The vision of that "hell where youth and laughter go" has been branded upon him too deeply to allow him to tolerate consolation or explanation. He can only state a little of what he has seen, a very little one guesses, and turn away with a stoical shrug as if a superficial cynicism were the best mask to wear in the face of such incredible experiences. His farewell to the dead is spoken in this fashion:

> *Good-bye, old lad! Remember me to God,*
> *And tell him that our polititians swear*
> *They won't give in till Prussian Rule's been trod*
> *Under the heel of England. . . . Are you there? . . .*
> *Yes . . . and the war won't end for at least two years;*
> *But we've got stacks of men. . . . I'm blind with tears,*
> *Staring into the dark. Cheero!*
> *I wish they'd killed you in a decent show.*

There is a stage of suffering, so these poems seem to show us, where any expression save the barest is intolerable; where beauty and art have something too universal about them to meet our particular case. Mr Sassoon sums up that point of view in his "Dead Musicians." Not Bach or Beethoven or Mozart brings back the memory of his friends, but the gramophone does it bawling out "Another little drink won't do us any harm." Mr Sassoon's poems are too much in the key of the gramophone at present, too fiercely suspicious of any comfort or compromise, to be read as poetry; but his contempt for palliative or subterfuge gives us the raw stuff of poetry.

A Russian Schoolboy[1]

THE previous volumes of this chronicle, "Years of Childhood" and "A Russian Gentleman," left us with a feeling of personal friendship for Serge Aksakoff; we had come to know him and his family as we know people with whom we have stayed easily for weeks at a time in the country. The figure of Aksakoff himself has taken a place in our minds which is more like that of a real person than a person whom we have merely known in a book. Since reading the first volume of Mr Duff's translation we have read many new books; many clear, sharp characters have passed before our eyes, but in most cases they have left nothing behind them but a sense of more or less brilliant activity. But Aksakoff has remained— a man of extraordinary freshness and substance, a man with a rich nature, moving in the sun and shadow of real life so that it is possible, as we have found during the past year or two, to settle down placidly and involuntarily to think about him. Such words as these would not apply truthfully perhaps to some very great works of art; but nothing that produces this impression of fullness and intimacy can be without some of the rarest qualities and, in our opinion, some of the most delightful. We have spoken of Aksakoff as a man, but unfortunately we have no right to do that for we have known him only as a boy, and the last volume of the three leaves him when he has but reached the age of fifteen. With this volume, Mr Duff tells us, the chronicle is finished; and our regret and desire to read another three, at least, is the best thanks we can offer him for his labour of translation. When we consider the rare merit of these books we can scarcely thank the translator sufficiently. We can only hope that he will look round and find another treasure of the same importance.

Ignorant as we are of the works of Aksakoff, it would be rash to say that this autobiography is the most characteristic of them; and yet one feels certain that there was something especially congenial to him in the recollection of childhood. When he was still a small boy he could plunge into "the inexhaustible treasury of recollec-

[1] *A Russian Schoolboy* by Serge Aksakoff. Translated by J. D. Duff. *The Times Literary Supplement*, November 8, 1917.

tion." He is not, we think, quite so happy in the present volume because he passes a little beyond the scope of childhood. It deals less with the country; and the magic, which consists so much in being very small among people of immeasurable size so that one's parents are far more romantic than one's brothers and sisters, was departing. When he was at school the boys were on an equality with him; the figures were contracting and becoming more like the people whom we see when we are grown up. Aksakoff's peculiar gift lay in his power of living back into the childish soul. He can give to perfection the sense of the nearness, the largeness, the absolute dominance of the detail before the prospect has arranged itself so that details are only part of a well-known order. He makes us consider that for unreflecting passion and for amazement the life of a grown person cannot compare with the life of a child. He makes us remember, and this is perhaps more difficult, how curiously the child's mind is taken up with what we call childish things together with premonitions of another kind of life, and with moments of extreme insight into its surroundings. He is thus able to give us a very clear notion of his father and mother, although we see them always as they appeared to a child. The effect of truth and vividness which is so remarkable in each of his volumes is the result of writing not from the man's point of view, but by becoming a child again; for it is impossible that the most tenacious memory should have been able to store the millions of details from which these books are fashioned. We have to suppose that Aksakoff kept to the end of his life a power of changing back into a different stage of growth at the touch of recollection, so that the process is more one of living over again than of remembering. From a psychological point of view this is a curious condition—to view the pond or the tree as it is now without emotion, but to receive intense emotion from the same sight by remembering the emotion which it roused fifty years ago. It is clear that Aksakoff, with his abundant and impressionable nature, was precisely the man to feel his childhood to the full, and to keep the joy of reviving it fresh to the end.

The happiness of childhood, he writes, is the Golden Age, and the recollection of it has power to move the old man's heart with pleasure and with pain. Happy is the man who once possessed it and is able to recall the memory of it in later years! With many the time passes by unnoticed or unenjoyed; and all that remains in the ripeness of age is the recollection of the coldness or even cruelty of men.

He was no doubt peculiar in the strength of his feelings, and singular compared with English boys in the absence of discipline at school and at college. As Mr Duff says. "His university studies are remarkable; he learnt no Greek, no Latin, no mathematics, and very little science—hardly anything but Russian and French." For this reason, perhaps, he remained conscious of all those little impressions which in most cases fade and are forgotten before the power of expressing them is full grown. Who is there, for example, who will not feel his early memories of coming back to a home in the country wonderfully renewed by the description of the return to Aksakovo:

> As before I took to bed with me my cat, which was so attached that she followed me everywhere like a dog; and I snared small birds or trapped them and kept them in a small room which was practically converted into a spacious coop. I admired my pigeons with double tufts and feathered legs . . . which had been kept warm in my absence under the stoves or in the houses of the outdoor servants. . . . To the island I ran several times a day, hardly knowing myself why I went; and there I stood motionless as if under a spell, while my heart beat hard, and my breath came unevenly.

Nor is it possible to read his account of butterfly collecting without recalling some such period of fanatical excitement. Indeed, we have read no description to compare with this one for its exact, prosaic, and yet most stirring reproduction of the succeeding stages of a child's passion. It begins almost by accident; it becomes in a moment the only thing in the world; of a sudden it dies down and is over for no perceptible reason. One can verify, as if from an old diary, every step that he takes with his butterfly net in his hand down that grassy valley in the burning heat until he sees within two yards of him "fluttering from flower to flower a splendid *swallow-tail*!" And then follows the journey home, where the small sister has begun collecting on her brother's account, and has turned all the jugs and tumblers in her room upside down, and even opened the lid of the piano and put butterflies alive inside of it. Nevertheless, in a few months the passion is over, and "we devoted all our leisure to literature, producing a manuscript magazine. . . . I became deeply interested in acting also."

All childhood is passionate, but if we compare the childhood of Aksakoff with our memories and observations of English childhood we shall be struck with the number and the violence of his enthusiasms. When his mother left him at school he sat on his bed with his eyes staring wildly, unable to think or to cry, and had to be put to bed, rubbed with flannels, and restored to consciousness by a violent fit of shivering. His sensitiveness to any recollection of childhood was such, even as a child, that the sound of a voice, a patch of sunlight on the wall, a fly buzzing on the pane, which reminded him of his past, threw him into a fit. His health became so bad that he had to be taken home. These fits and ecstasies in which his mother often joined him, will hardly fail to remind the reader of many similar scenes which are charged against Dostoevsky as a fault. The fault, if it is a fault, appears to be more in the Russian nature than in the novelist's version of it. From the evidence supplied by Aksakoff we realize how little discipline enters into their education; and we also realize, what we do not gather from Dostoevsky, how sane, natural and happy such a life can be. Partly because of his love of nature, that unconscious perception of beauty which lay at the back of his shooting and fishing and butterfly catching, partly because of the largeness and generosity of his character, the impression produced by these volumes is an impression of abundance and of happiness. As Aksakoff says in a beautiful description of an uncle and aunt of his, "The atmosphere seemed to have something calming and life-giving in it, something suited to beast and plant." At the same time we have only to compare him, as he has been compared, with Gilbert White to realize the Russian element in him, the element of self-consciousness and introspection. No one is very simple who realizes so fully what is happening to him, or who can trace, as he traces it, the moment when "the radiance" fades and the "peculiar feeling of sadness" begins. His power of registering these changes shows that he was qualified to write also an incomparable account of maturity.

He gives in this book a description of the process of letting water out of a pond. A crowd of peasants collected upon the banks. "All Russians love to watch moving water. . . . The people saluted with shouts of joy the element they loved, as it tore its way to freedom from its winter prison." The shouts of joy and the love of watching both seem the peculiar property of the Russian people. From such a combination one would expect to find one of these days that they have produced the greatest of autobiographies, as they have produced perhaps the greatest of novels. But Aksakoff is more than a prelude; his work in its individuality and its beauty stands by itself.

A Glance at Turgenev[1]

IF this were not the sixteenth volume of a classic—if it were the first volume by an unknown writer—what should we find to say? To begin with we should say that Turgenev is an observant young man, who, if he can restrain his faculty for observing detail may in time have something to offer us. "She had the habit of turning her head to the right while she lifted a morsel to her mouth with the left hand, as if she were playing with it." ". . . . They pacified the infuriated curs, but a maidservant was obliged to drag one of them . . . into a bedroom, getting bitten on her right hand in the process." In themselves both those facts are admirably noted; but we should not fail to point out that it is dangerous to observe like that—dangerous to stress little facts because one happens to have a store of them in readiness. All round us are strewn the melancholy relics of those who have insisted upon telling us that she was bitten on the right hand, but raised her fork with the left. And then, even as we are making this observation, the details dissolve and disappear. There is nothing left but the scene itself. It lives unsupported, unvouched for. The father and mother; the two girls; the visitors; the very sheep dogs and the food on the table are all contributing spontaneously to the final impression which makes us positive, when the door shuts and the two young men drive off, that nothing will induce Boris Andreyitch to marry Emerentsiya. That is the principal thing we know; but we also know, as the house recedes in the distance, that in the drawing-room Emerentsiya is simpering over her conquest; while the plain sister Polinka has run upstairs and is crying to the maid that she hates visitors; they will talk to her about music; and then her mother scolds her.

That scene is not the work of a prentice hand. It is not the result of keen eyesight and notebooks crammed with facts. But it would be impossible if we had only that scene before us to say that we detect a master's hand and are already certain that this unknown Russian writer is the famous novelist Turgenev. The story goes on, however. Greatly to the surprise of his friend, Boris marries a simple country girl. They settle down; life is perfect, but perhaps a trifle dull. Boris

[1] *The Two Friends and Other Stories* by Ivan Turgenev. Translated by Constance Garnett. *The Times Literary Supplement*, December 8, 1921.

travels. He goes to Paris, and there drifting vaguely into an affair
with a young woman he is challenged by her lover and killed. Far
away in Russia his widow mourns for him sincerely. But after all
Boris did not "belong to the number of people who are irreplace-
able. (And indeed are there such people?)" Nor was his widow
"capable of devoting herself for ever to one feeling. (And indeed are
there such feelings?)" So she marries her husband's old friend, and
they live peacefully in the country, and have children and are
happy, "for there is no other happiness on earth." Thus, that first
scene which was so lively and suggestive has led to other scenes;
they add themselves to it; they bring in contrast, distance, solidity.
In the end everything seems to be there. Here is a world able to
exist by itself. Now perhaps we can talk with some certainty of a
master; for now we have not a single brilliant episode which is gone
the moment after, but a succession of scenes attached one to another
by the feelings which are common to humanity. Space forbids us to
inquire more minutely by what means this is achieved. Besides,
there are other books by Turgenev which illustrate his powers
more clearly. The stories in this volume are not equal to his best
work. But they have this characteristic of greatness—they exist by
themselves. We can judge from them what sort of world Turgenev
created. We can see in what respects his vision was different from
other people's.

Like most Russian writers, he was melancholy. Beyond the circle
of his scene seems to lie a great space, which flows in at the window,
presses upon people, isolates them, makes them incapable of action,
indifferent to effect, sincere, and open-minded. Some background
of that sort is common to much of Russian literature. But Turgenev
adds to this scene a quality which we find nowhere else. They are
sitting as usual talking round the samovar, talking gently, sadly,
charmingly, as Turgenev's people always do talk, when one of them
ceases, gets up, and looks out of the window. "But the moon must
have risen," she says, "that's moonlight on the tops of the poplars."
And we look up and there it is—the moonlight on the poplars. Or
take, as an example of the same power, the description of the garden
in "Three Meetings":

Everything was slumbering. The air, warm and fragrant, did
not stir; only from time to time it quivered as water quivers at the

fall of a twig. There was a feeling of languor, of yearning in it.
. . . I bent over the fence; a red field poppy lifted its stalk above
the rank grass, . . .

and so on. Then the woman sings, and her voice sounds straight into
an atmosphere which has been prepared to wrap it up, to enhance
it, and float it away. No quotation can convey the impression, for
the description is part of the story as a whole. What is more, we feel
again and again that Turgenev evades his translator. It is not Mrs
Garnett's fault. The English language is not the Russian. But the
original description of the garden in the moonlight must be written,
not with this inevitable careful exactness, but flowingly; there must
be melody, variety, transparency. But the general effect is there even
if we miss the beauty with which it is rendered. Turgenev, then, has
a remarkable emotional power; he draws together the moon and the
group round the samovar, the voice and the flowers and the warmth
of the garden—he fuses them in one moment of great intensity,
though all round are the silent spaces, and he turns away, in the
end, with a little shrug of his shoulders.

A Giant with Very Small Thumbs[1]

IN this substantial book Mr Yarmolinsky has collected an immense amount of information about Turgenev, but the value is seriously diminished by the fact that the statements are taken from books which are not accessible to Western readers and no references are given. Mr Yarmolinsky is, if not a disillusioned, still a highly critical biographer. The faults of his subject are very clear to him. But we must be grateful to him for raising the whole question of Turgenev again, and for giving us a profusion of material on which to found our own judgment. Of all the great Russian writers, Turgenev is, perhaps, the one who has had least justice done him in England. It is easy to guess the reason; here is a new country, people said, and therefore its literature must be different, if it is true literature, from any other. They sought out and relished in Chekhov and Dostoevsky those qualities which they supposed to be peculiarly Russian and therefore of peculiar excellence. They welcomed joyously an abandonment to emotion and introspection, a formlessness which they would have detested in the French or in the English. People drank tea endlessly and discussed the soul without stopping in a room where nothing could be seen distinctly; such was our supposition.

But Turgenev was different altogether. In the first place he was a cosmopolitan, who hunted in England and lived, rather ambiguously, in France. His domestic circumstances indeed were not such as to attach him to his native land. His mother was a woman of extraordinary character. In the heart of Russia she tried to mimic the ceremonies and splendour of the French aristocracy before the Revolution. She was despotic to the verge of mania. She banished serfs for neglecting to bow to her. She had her porridge brought hot by relays of horsemen from a village where they made it to her liking ten miles away. A waterfall was turned from its course because it disturbed her sleep. Whether or not these stories are true, it is certain that she drove her sons from the house. The novelist, in particular, with his democratic sympathies, detested his mother's

---

[1] *Turgenev: The Man, his Art, and his Age* by Avrahm Yarmolinsky. *The Nation and Athenæum* April 2, 1927.

behaviour, and being, as he was fond of saying, a man with very small thumbs, he found it simpler to withdraw. Pauline Viardot received him. He had a seat allotted to him on one of the gilt paws of the bear skin on which her admirers sat and talked to her between the acts of the play. Nor was he ever to find another lodging. At the end of his life he advised young men with melancholy humour to find a home of their own and not to sit "on the edge of another man's nest." Madame Viardot, it is said, never asked him to come inside. There he sat, "a large man with a weak mouth and a skull padded with fat, who gave the impression of being as soft as butter," until he died in her presence. But for all his melancholy and his loneliness, it was probable that the arrangement, with its mixture of freedom and intimacy, was the one that suited him best. The rigours of domesticity would have thwarted him. He was always late for meals; he was extremely generous, but very untidy; and he had, after all, a passion for art.

It is this passion of his that makes him so unlike the English idea of what a Russian should be. For Turgenev novels might well be the late ripe fruit on a very old tree. Such restraint, such selection one attributes to ages of endeavour. All his books are so small in bulk that one can slip them into one's pocket. Yet they leave behind them the impression that they contain a large world in which there is ample room for men and women of full size and the sky above and the fields around. He is the most economical of writers. One of his economies is at once obvious. He takes up no room with his own person. He makes no comments upon his characters. He places them before the reader and leaves them to their fate. The contact between ourselves and Bazarov, for instance, is peculiarly direct. No saying is underlined, no conclusion is forced upon us. But the reader's imagination is perpetually stimulated to work for itself, and hence each scene and each character has a peculiar vitality. Hence, too, another peculiarity; we are never able to say that the point lies here or the point lies there. Return to a definite page, and the meaning, the power, seems to have fled. For in this highly suggestive art the effect has been produced by a thousand small touches which accumulate, but cannot be pinned down in one emphatic passage or isolated in one great scene. For this reason Turgenev can handle, with a sweetness and wholeness which put our English novelists to shame, such burning questions as the relations of fathers and sons, of the new order and the old. The treatment is of such width and dispassionateness that we are not coerced in our sympathies, and so do not harbour a grudge against the writer which we shall liberate when opportunity serves. After all these years "Fathers and Sons" still keeps its hold on our emotions. In this clarity lie profound depths; its brevity holds in it a large world. For though Turgenev was, according to his present biographer, full of weaknesses and obsessed with a sense of the futility of all things, he held strangely rigorous views on the subject of literature. Be truthful to your own sensations, he counselled; deepen your experience with study; be free to doubt everything; above all, do not let yourself be caught in the trap of dogmatism. Sitting on the edge of another man's nest, he practised these difficult counsels to perfection. Untidy in his habits, a giant with very small thumbs, he was nevertheless a great artist.

Dostoevsky the Father[1]

I T would be a mistake to read this book as if it were a biography. Mlle Dostoevsky expressly calls it a study, and to this the reader must add that it is a study by a daughter. The letters, the facts, the testimonies of friends, even to a great extent the dates which support the orthodox biography are here absent or are introduced as they happen to suit the writer's purpose. And what is a daughter's purpose in writing a study of her father? We need not judge her very severely if she wishes us to see him as she saw him— upright, affectionate, infallible, or, if he had his failings, she is to be excused if she represents them as the foibles of greatness. He was extravagant perhaps. He gambled sometimes. There were seasons when, misled by the wiles of women, he strayed from the paths of virtue. We can make allowance for these filial euphemisms; and if we come to feel, as this book makes us feel, that the daughter was fond as well as proud of her father, that is a real addition to our knowledge. At the same time we should have listened more sympathetically if Mlle Dostoevsky had suppressed her version of the quarrel between Dostoevsky and Turgenev. To make out that your father is a hero is one thing; to insist that his enemies are villains is another. Yet she must have it that all the blame was on Turgenev's side; that he was jealous, a snob, "even more cruel and malicious than the others." She neglects the testimony supplied by Turgenev's own works, and, what is more serious, makes no mention of the evidence on the other side which must be known to her. The effect is naturally to make the reader scrutinize Dostoevsky's character more closely than he would otherwise have done. He asks himself inevitably what there was in the man to cause this shrill and excited partisanship on the part of his daughter. The search for an answer among the baffling yet illuminating materials which Mlle Dostoevsky supplies is the true interest of this book.

If we were to be guided by her we should base our inquiry upon the fact that Dostoevsky was of Lithuanian descent on his father's side. Mlle Dostoevsky has read Gobineau, and shows a perverse

[1] *Fyodor Dostoevsky* by Aimée Dostoevsky. *The Times Literary Supplement*, January 12, 1922.

ingenuity and considerable industry in attributing almost every mental and moral characteristic to race heredity. Dostoevsky was a Lithuanian and thus loved purity; he was a Lithuanian and thus paid his brother's debts; he was a Lithuanian and thus wrote bad Russian; he was a Lithuanian and thus a devout Catholic. When he complained that he had a strange and evil character he did not realize that it was neither strange nor evil, but simply Lithuanian. As Dostoevsky himself never attached much importance to his descent, we may be allowed to follow his example. We shall not come much closer to him by pursuing that track. But Mlle Dostoevsky increases our knowledge by more indirect methods. A clever little girl cannot run about her father's house without picking up many things which she is not expected to know. She knows whether the cook is grumbling; which of the guests bores her parents; whether her father is in a good temper, or whether there has been some mysterious grown-up catastrophe. Considering that Aimée was very young when her father died, she could scarcely be expected to observe anything of much greater importance than this. But then she is a Russian. She has that apparently involuntary candour which must make family life so disconcerting in Russia. Her father's greatness subdues her to a dutiful attitude, which, if reverent, is also a little colourless. But no one else has that power over her. "Her self-esteem was always excessive, almost morbid; a trifle would offend her, and she easily fell a victim to those who flattered her." Thus she describes her mother, and her mother is still alive. As for her uncles and aunts, her step-brother, her father's first wife, his mistress, she is completely outspoken about them all and—were it not that she qualifies her blame by detecting strains of Slav, Norman, Ukrainian, Negro, Mongol, and Swedish blood— equally severe. That, indeed, is her contribution to our knowledge of Dostoevsky. No doubt she exaggerates; but there can also be no doubt that her bitterness is the legacy of old family quarrels— sordid, degrading, patched-up, but bursting out afresh and pursuing Dostoevsky to the verge of his death-chamber. The pages seem to ring with scoldings and complainings and recriminations; with demands for more money and with replies that all the money has been spent. Such, or something like it, we conclude, was the atmosphere in which Dostoevsky wrote his books.

His father was a doctor who had to resign his appointment owing to drunkenness; and it was on account of his drunken savagery that his serfs smothered him one day beneath the cushions of his carriage as he was driving on his estate. The disease was inherited by his children. Two of Dostoevsky's brothers were drunkards; his sister was miserly to the verge of insanity, and was also murdered for her money. Her son was "so stupid that his folly verged on idiocy. My uncle Andrey's son, a young and brilliant savant, died of creeping paralysis. The whole Dostoevsky family suffered from neurasthenia." And to the family eccentricity one must add what appears to the English reader the national eccentricity—the likelihood, that is to say, that if Dostoevsky escapes death on the scaffold and survives imprisonment in Siberia he will marry a wife who has a handsome young tutor for her lover, and will take for his mistress a girl who arrives at his bedside at seven in the morning brandishing an enormous knife with which she proposes to kill a Frenchman. Dostoevsky dissuades her, and off they go to Wiesbaden where "my father played roulette with passionate absorption, was delighted when he won, and experienced a despair hardly less delicious when he lost." It is all violent and extreme, later, even, when Dostoevsky was happily married, there was still a worthless stepson who expected to be supported; still the brothers' debts to pay; still the sisters trying to make mischief between him and his wife; and then the rich aunt Kumanin must needs die and leave her property to stir up the last flames of hatred among the embittered relations. "Dostoevsky lost patience and, refusing to continue the painful discussion, left the table before the meal was finished." Three days later he was dead. One thinks of Farringford flourishing not so very far away. One wonders what Matthew Arnold, who deplored the irregularities of the Shelley set, would have said to this one.

And yet, has it anything to do with Dostoevsky? One feels rather as if one had been admitted to the kitchen where the cook is smashing the china, or to the drawing-room where the relations are gossiping in corners, while Dostoevsky sits upstairs alone in his study. He had, it is clear, an extraordinary power of absenting his mind from his body. The money troubles alone, one would think, were enough to drive him distracted. On the contrary, it was his wife who worried, and it was Dostoevsky, says his daughter, who remained serene, saying, "in tones of conviction,'We shall never be without money.'" We catch sight of his body plainly enough, but it is rather as if we passed him taking his afternoon walk, always at four o'clock, always along the same road, so absorbed in his own thoughts that "he never recognized the acquaintance he met on the way." They travelled in Italy, visited the galleries, strolled in the Boboli gardens, and "the roses blooming there struck their Northern imaginations." But after working at "The Idiot" all the morning how much did he see of the roses in the afternoon? It is the waste of his day that is gathered up and given us in place of his life. But now and then, when Mlle Dostoevsky forgets the political rancours of the moment and the complex effect of the Norman strain upon the Lithuanian temperament, she opens the study door and lets us see her father as she saw him. He could not write if he had a spot of candle-grease on his coat. He liked dried figs and kept a box of them in a cupboard from which he helped his children. He liked eau-de-Cologne to wash with. He liked little girls to wear pale green. He would dance with them and read aloud Dickens and Scott. But he never spoke to them about his own childhood. She thinks that he dreaded discovering signs of his father's vices in himself; and she believes that he "wished intensely to be like others." At any rate, it was the greatest pleasure of her day to be allowed to breakfast with him and to talk to him about books. And then it is all over. There is her father laid out in his evening dress in his coffin; a painter is sketching him; grand dukes and peasants crowd the staircase; while she and her brother distribute flowers to unknown people and enjoy very much the drive to the cemetery.

More Dostoevsky[1]

EACH time that Mrs Garnett adds another red volume to her admirable translations of the works of Dostoevsky we feel a little better able to measure what the existence of this great genius who is beginning to permeate our lives so curiously means to us. His books are now to be found on the shelves of the humblest English libraries; they have become an indestructible part of the furniture of our rooms, as they belong for good to the furniture of our minds. The latest addition to Mrs Garnett's translation, "The Eternal Husband," including also "The Double" and "The Gentle Spirit," is not one of the greatest of his works, although it was produced in what may be held to be the greatest period of his genius, between "The Idiot" and "The Possessed." If one had never read anything else by Dostoevsky, one might lay the book down with a feeling that the man who wrote it was bound to write a very great novel some day; but with a feeling also that something strange and important had happened. This strangeness and this sense that something important has happened persist, however, although we are familiar with his books and have had time to arrange the impression that they make on us.

Of all great writers there is, so it seems to us, none quite so surprising, or so bewildering, as Dostoevsky. And although "The Eternal Husband" is nothing more than a long short story which we need not compare with the great novels, it too has this extraordinary power; nor while we are reading it can we liberate ourselves sufficiently to feel certain that in this or that respect there is a failure of power, or insight, or craftsmanship; nor does it occur to us to compare it with other works either by the same writer or by other writers. It is very difficult to analyse the impression it has made even when we have finished it. It is the story of one Velchaninov, who, many years before the story opens, has seduced the wife of a certain Pavel Pavlovitch in the town of T——. Velchaninov has almost forgotten her and is living in Petersburg. But now as he walks about Petersburg he is constantly running into a man who

[1] *The Eternal Husband and Other Stories.* Translated by Constance Garnett. *The Times Literary Supplement*, February 22, 1917.

wears a crape hat-band and reminds him of someone he cannot put a name to. At last, after repeated meetings which bring him to a state bordering on delirium, Velchaninov is visited at two o'clock in the morning by the stranger, who explains that he is the husband of Velchaninov's old love, and that she is dead. When Velchaninov visits him the next day he finds him maltreating a little girl, who is, he instantly perceives, his own child. He manages to take her away from Pavel, who is a drunkard and in every way disreputable, and give her lodging with friends, but almost immediately she dies. After her death Pavel announces that he is engaged to marry a girl of sixteen, but when, as he insists, Velchaninov visits her, she confides to him that she detests Pavel and is already engaged to a youth of nineteen. Between them they contrive to pack Pavel off to the country; and he turns up finally at the end of the story as the husband of a provincial beauty, and the lady, of course, has a lover.

These, at least, are the little bits of cork which mark a circle upon the top of the waves while the net drags the floor of the sea and encloses stranger monsters than have ever been brought to the light of day before. The substance of the book is made out of the relationship between Velchaninov and Pavel. Pavel is a type of what Velchaninov calls "the eternal husband." "Such a man is born and grows up only to be a husband, and, having married, is promptly transformed into a supplement of his wife, even when he happens to have an unmistakable character of his own. . . . [Pavel] could only as long as his wife was alive have remained all that he used to be, but, as it was, he was only a fraction of a whole, suddenly cut off and set free, that is something wonderful and unique." One of the peculiarities of the eternal husband is that he is always half in love with the lovers of his wife, and at the same time wishes to kill them. Impelled by this mixture of almost amorous affection and hatred, he cannot keep away from Velchaninov, in whom he breeds a kind of reflection of his own sensations of attraction and repulsion. He can never bring himself to make any direct charge against Velchaninov; and Velchaninov is never able to confess or to deny his misconduct. Sometimes, from the stealthy way in which he approaches, Velchaninov feels certain that he has an impulse to kill him; but then he insists upon kissing him and cries out, "So, you understand, you're the one friend left me now!" One night when Velchaninov is ill and Pavel has shown the most enthusiastic devotion Velchaninov wakes from a nightmare to find Pavel standing over him and attempting to murder him with a razor. Pavel is easily mastered and slinks away shamefaced in the morning. But did he mean to murder him, Velchaninov muses, or did he want it without knowing that he wanted it?

> But did he love me yesterday when he declared his feeling and said "Let us settle our account"? Yes, it was from hatred that he loved me; that's the strongest of all loves. . . . It would be interesting to know by what I impressed him. Perhaps by my clean gloves and my knowing how to put them on. . . . He comes here "to embrace me and weep," as he expressed it in the most abject way—that is, he came here to murder me and thought he came "to embrace me and to weep." But who knows? If I had wept with him, perhaps, really, he would have forgiven me, for he had a terrible longing to forgive me! . . . Ough! wasn't he pleased, too, when he made me kiss him! Only he didn't know then whether he would end by embracing me or murdering me. . . . The most monstrous monster is the monster with noble feelings. . . . But it was not your fault, Pavel Pavlovitch, it was not your fault: you're a monster, so everything about you is bound to be monstrous, your dreams and your hopes.

Perhaps this quotation may give some idea of the labyrinth of the soul through which we have to grope our way. But being only a quotation it makes the different thoughts appear too much isolated; for in the context Velchaninov, as he broods over the blood-stained razor, passes over his involved and crowded train of thought without a single hitch, just, in fact, as we ourselves are conscious of thinking when some startling fact has dropped into the pool of our consciousness. From the crowd of objects pressing upon our attention we select now this one, now that one, weaving them inconsequently into our thought; the associations of a word perhaps make another loop in the line, from which we spring back again to a different section of our main thought, and the whole process seems both inevitable and perfectly lucid. But if we try to construct our mental processes later, we find that the links between one thought and another are submerged. The chain is sunk out of sight and only the leading points emerge to mark the course. Alone among writers Dostoevsky has the power of reconstructing these most swift and complicated states of mind, of rethinking the whole train of thought in all its speed, now as it flashes into light, now as it lapses into darkness; for he is able to follow not only the vivid streak of achieved thought but to suggest the dim and populous underworld of the mind's consciousness where desires and impulses are moving blindly beneath the sod. Just as we awaken ourselves from a trance of this kind by striking a chair or a table to assure ourselves of an external reality, so Dostoevsky suddenly makes us behold, for an instant, the face of his hero, or some object in the room.

This is the exact opposite of the method adopted, perforce, by most of our novelists. They reproduce all the external appearances —tricks of manner, landscape, dress, and the effect of the hero upon his friends—but very rarely, and only for an instant, penetrate to the tumult of thought which rages within his own mind. But the whole fabric of a book by Dostoevsky is made out of such material. To him a child or a beggar is as full of violent and subtle emotions as a poet or a sophisticated woman of the world; and it is from the intricate maze of their emotions that Dostoevsky constructs his version of life. In reading him, therefore, we are often bewildered because we find ourselves observing men and women from a different point of view from that to which we are accustomed. We have to get rid of the old tune which runs so persistently in our ears, and to realize how little of our humanity is expressed in that old tune. Again and again we are thrown off the scent in following Dostoevsky's psychology; we constantly find ourselves wondering whether we recognize the feeling that he shows us, and we realize constantly and with a start of surprise that we have met it before in ourselves, or in some moment of intuition have suspected it in others. But we have never spoken of it, and that is why we are surprised. Intuition is the term which we should apply to Dostoevsky's genius at its best. When he is fully possessed by it he is able to read the most inscrutable writing at the depths of the darkest souls; but when it deserts him the whole of his amazing machinery seems to spin fruitlessly in the air. In the present volume, "The Double," with all its brilliancy and astonishing ingenuity, is an example of this kind of elaborate failure; "The Gentle Spirit," on the other hand, is written from start to finish with a power which for the time being turns everything we can put beside it into the palest commonplace.

Dostoevsky in Cranford[1]

IT is amusing sometimes to freshen one's notion of a great, and thus semi-mythical, character by transplanting him in imagination to one's own age, shore, or country village. How, one asks, would Dostoevsky have behaved himself upon the vicarage lawn? In "Uncle's Dream," the longest story in Mrs Garnett's new volume, he enables one to fancy him in those incongruous surroundings. Mordasov bears at any rate a superficial resemblance to Cranford. All the ladies in that small country town spend their time in drinking tea and talking scandal. A newcomer, such as Prince K., is instantly torn to pieces like a fish tossed to a circle of frenzied and ravenous seagulls. Mordasov cannot be altogether like Cranford, then. No such figure of speech could be used with propriety to describe the demure activities and bright-eyed curiosities of the English circle of ladies. After sending our imaginary Dostoevsky, therefore, pacing up and down the lawn, there can be no doubt that he suddenly stamps his foot, exclaims something unintelligible, and rushes off in despair. "The instinct of provincial newsmongers sometimes approaches the miraculous. . . . They know you by heart, they know even what you don't know about yourself. The provincial ought, one would think, by his very nature to be a psychologist and a specialist in human nature. That is why I have been sometimes genuinely amazed at meeting in the provinces not psychologists and specialists in human nature, but a very great number of asses. But that is aside; that is a superfluous reflection." His patience is already exhausted; it is idle to expect that he will linger in the High-street or hang in a rapture of observation round the draper's shop. The delightful shades and subtleties of English provincial life are lost upon him.

But Mordasov is a very different place from Cranford. The ladies do not confine themselves to tea, as their condition after dinner sometimes testifies. Their tongues wag with a fury that is rather that of the open market-place than of the closed drawing-room. Though they indulge in petty vices such as listening at keyholes and stealing

[1] *An Honest Thief and Other Stories.* Translated by Constance Garnett. *The Times Literary Supplement*, October 23, 1919.

the sugar when the hostess is out of the room, they act with the brazen boldness of viragoes. One would be alarmed to find oneself left alone with one of them. Nevertheless, in his big rough way, Dostoevsky is neither savagely contemptuous nor sadly compassionate; he is genuinely amused by the spectacle of Mordasov. It roused, as human life so seldom did, his sense of comedy. He tries even to adapt his dialogue to the little humours of a gossiping conversation.

"Call that a dance! I've danced myself, the shawl dance, at the breaking-up party at Madame Jarnis's select boarding-school —and it really was a distinguished performance. I was applauded by senators! The daughters of princes and counts were educated there! . . . Only fancy" [she runs on, as if she were imitating the patter of Miss Bates] "chocolate was handed round to everyone, but not offered to me, and they did not say a word to me all the time. . . . The tub of a woman, I'll pay her out!"

But Dostoevsky cannot keep to that tripping measure for long. The language becomes abusive, and the temper violent. His comedy has far more in common with the comedy of Wycherly than with the comedy of Jane Austen. It rapidly runs to seed, and becomes a helter-skelter, extravagant farce. The restraint and aloofness of the great comic writers are impossible to him. It is probable, for one reason, that he could not allow himself the time. "Uncle's Dream," "The Crocodile," and "An Unpleasant Predicament" read as if they were the improvisations of a gigantic talent reeling off its wild imaginations at breathless speed. They have the diffuseness of a mind too tired to concentrate, and too fully charged to stop short. Slack and ungirt as it is, it tumbles out rubbish and splendour pell-mell.

Yet we are perpetually conscious that, if Dostoevsky fails to keep within the proper limits, it is because the fervour of his genius goads him across the boundary. Because of his sympathy his laughter passes beyond merriment into a strange violent amusement which is not merry at all. He is incapable, even when his story is hampered by the digression, of passing by anything so important and loveable as a man or a woman without stopping to consider their case and explain it. Thus at one moment it occurs to him that there must be a reason why an unfortunate clerk could not afford to pay for a bottle of wine. Immediately, as if recalling a story which is known to him down to its most minute detail, he describes how the clerk had been born and brought up; it is then necessary to bring in the career of his brutal father-in-law, and that leads him to describe the peculiarities of the five unfortunate women whom the father-in-law bullies. In short, once you are alive, there is no end to the complexity of your connexions, and sorrow and misery are so rubbed into the texture of life that the more you examine it the more cloudy and confused it becomes. Perhaps it is because we know so little about the family history of the ladies of Cranford that we can put the book down with a smile. Still, we need not underrate the value of comedy because Dostoevsky makes the perfection of the English product appear to be the result of leaving out all the most important things. It is the old, unnecessary quarrel between the inch of smooth ivory and the six feet of canvas with its strong coarse grains.

The Russian Background[1]

THANKS chiefly to the labours of Mrs Garnett we are now not so much at sea when a new translation from the Russian novelists comes our way. Since "The Bishop" is the seventh volume of the tales of Tchehov, this comparative degree of enlightenment does not say much perhaps for our perspicacity. We ought not, as we read, to be still drawing a rough plan, with the left hand, of this strange Russian temperament; we ought not to feel any warmth of self-approbation when the sketch rapidly fills itself in and wears a momentary air of completeness.

Yet the seventh volume finds us not quite so ill-prepared as its predecessors. No one now is going to be so foolish as to complain that the story of "The Bishop" is not a story at all but only a rather vague and inconclusive account of a bishop who was distressed because his mother treated him with respect, and soon after died of typhoid. We are by this time alive to the fact that inconclusive stories are legitimate; that is to say, though they leave us feeling melancholy and perhaps uncertain, yet somehow or other they provide a resting point for the mind—a solid object casting its shade of reflection and speculation. The fragments of which it is composed may have the air of having come together by chance. Certainly it often seems as if Tchehov made up his stories rather in the way that a hen picks up grain. Why should she pick here and there, from side to side, when, so far as we can see, there is no reason to prefer one grain to another? His choice is strange, and yet there is no longer any doubt that whatever Tchehov chooses he chooses with the finest insight. He is like the peasant in his story "The Steppe," who could see the fox lying on her back playing like a dog far in the distance, where no one else could see her. Like Vassya, Tchehov's sight is so keen that he has, "besides the world seen by everyone, another world of his own, accessible to no one else, and probably a very beautiful one."

All these doubts and false starts are now powerless to disturb our enjoyment of Tchehov. We may, therefore, attempt to press on a

---

[1] *The Bishop and Other Stories* by Anton Tchehov. Translated by Constance Garnett. *The Times Literary Supplement*, August 14, 1919.

step further. Is it possible to adopt with Tchehov the position that comes so easily in the case of writers of one's own tongue? We want to understand the great sum of things which a writer takes for granted, which is the background of his thought; for if we can imagine that, the figures in the foreground, the pattern he has wrought upon it, will be more easily intelligible. Our own background, so far as we can detach ourselves from it, is presumably a very complex and yet very orderly civilization. The peasant, even in the depths of the country, has his station assigned to him, and is in a thousand ways controlled by London; and there must be very few windows in England from which it is not possible to see the smoke of a town by day or its lamps by night. We become more aware of the detail and of the intricacy of all that we hold in our minds when Tchehov describes "the things that come back to your mind," "the things one has seen and treasured"—the things, that is, which form his background.

> . . . of the unfathomable depth and infinity of the sky one can only form a conception at sea and on the steppes by night when the moon is shining. It is terribly lonely and caressing. . . . Everything looks different from what it is. . . . You drive on and suddenly see standing before you right in the roadway a dark figure like a monk . . . the figure comes closer, grows bigger; now it is on a level with the chaise, and you see it is not a man, but a solitary bush, or a great stone. . . . You drive on for one hour, for a second. . . . You meet upon the way a silent old barrow or a stone figure put up God knows when and by whom . . . the soul responds to the call of the lovely austere fatherland, and longs to fly over the steppes with the nightbird.

Tchehov is here describing, very beautifully we can guess even through the coarse mesh of a foreign tongue, the effect of the steppe upon a little company of travellers. The steppe is the background for that particular story. Yet, as the travellers move slowly over the immense space, now stopping at an inn, now overtaking some shepherd or waggon, it seems to be the journey of the Russian soul, and the empty space, so sad and so passionate, becomes the background of his thought. The stories themselves in their inconclusiveness and intimacy, appear to be the result of a chance meeting on a lonely road. Fate has sent these travellers across our path; whoever they may be, it is natural to stop and talk, and as they will never come our way again it is possible to say all kinds of things that we do not say to friends. The English reader may have had something of the same experience when isolated on board ship on a sea voyage. From the surrounding emptiness, from the knowledge that they will soon be over, those meetings have an intensity, as if shaped by the hand of an artist, which long preserves their significance in memory. "All this," says Tchehov, describing a camp by the wayside where the men sit gathered together over the camp fire— "all this was of itself so marvellous and terrible that the fantastic colours of legend and fairy tale were pale and blended with life." Take away the orderly civilization: look from your window upon nothing but the empty steppe, feel towards each human being that he is a traveller who will be seen once and never again, and then life "of itself" is so terrible and marvellous that no fantastic colouring is necessary. Almost all the stories in the present volume are stories of peasants; and whether or not it is the effect of this solitude and emptiness, each obscure and brutish mind has had rubbed in it a little transparency through which the light of the spirit shines amazingly. Thus the convict Yakov, as he walks in chains, comes by this means to the conviction that "at last he had learned the true faith. . . . He knew it all now and understood where God was." But this is not merely the end of a Tchehov story; it is also the light which, falling fitfully here and there, marks out their conformity and form. Without metaphor, the feelings of his characters are related to something more important and far more remote than personal success or happiness.

A Scribbling Dame[1]

THERE are in the Natural History Museum certain little insects so small that they have to be gummed to the cardboard with the lightest of fingers, but each of them, as one observes with constant surprise, has its fine Latin name spreading far to the right and left of the miniature body. We have often speculated upon the capture of these insects and the christening of them, and marvelled at the labours of the humble, indefatigable men who thus extend our knowledge. But their toil, though comparable in its nature, seems light and certainly agreeable compared with that of Mr Whicher in the book before us. It was not for him to wander through airy forests with a butterfly net in his hand; he had to search out dusty books from desolate museums, and in the end to pin down this faded and antique specimen of the domestic house fly with all her seventy volumes in orderly array around her. But it appears to the Department of English and Comparative Literature in Columbia University that Mrs Haywood has never been classified, and they approve therefore of the publication of this book on her as "a contribution to knowledge worthy of publication." It does not matter, presumably, that she was a writer of no importance, that no one reads her for pleasure, and that nothing is known of her life. She is dead, she is old, she wrote books, and nobody has yet written a book about her.

Mr Whicher accordingly has supplied not merely an article, or a few lines in a history of literature, but a careful, studious, detailed account of all her works regarded from every possible point of view, together with a bibliography which occupies 204 pages of print. It is but fair to him to add that he has few illusions as to the merits of his authoress, and only claims for her that her "domestic novels" foreshadowed the work of Miss Burney and Miss Austen, and that she helped to open a new profession for her sex. Whatever help he can afford us by calling Pope "Mr" Pope or Pope Alexander, and alluding to Mrs Haywood as "the scribbling dame," he proffers generously enough. But it is scarcely sufficient. If he had been able

[1] *The Life and Romances of Mrs Eliza Haywood*, by George F. Whicher. *The Times Literary Supplement*, February 17, 1916.

126

to throw any light upon the circumstances of her life we should make no complaint. A woman who married a clergyman and ran away from him, who supported herself and possibly two children, it is thought without gallantry, entirely by her pen in the early years of the eighteenth century, was striking out a new line of life and must have been a person of character. But nobody knows anything about her, save that she was born in 1693 and died in 1756; it is not known where she lived or how she got her work; what friends she had, or even, which is strange in the case of a woman, whether she was plain or handsome. "The apprehensive dame," as Mr Whicher calls her, warned, we can imagine, by the disgusting stanzas in the "Dunciad," took care that the facts of her life should be concealed, and, withdrawing silently, left behind her a mass of unreadable journalism which both by its form and by the inferiority of the writer's talent throws no light upon her age or upon herself. Anyone who has looked into the works of the Duchess of Newcastle and Mrs Behn knows how easily the rich prose style of the Restoration tends to fall languid and suffocate even writers of considerable force and originality. The names alone of Mrs Haywood's romances make us droop, and in the mazes of her plots we swoon away. We have to imagine how Emilia wandering in Andalusia meets Berinthus in a masquerade. Now Berinthus was really Henriquez her brother. . . . Don Jaque di Morella determines to marry his daughter Clementine to a certain cardinal. . . . In Montelupe Clementina meets the funeral of a young woman who has been torn to pieces by wolves. . . . The young and gay Dorante is tempted to expose himself to the charms of the beautiful Kesiah. . . . The doting Baron de Tortillés marries the extravagant and lascivious Mademoiselle la Motte. . . Melliora, Placentia, Montrano, Miramillia, and a thousand more swarm over all the countries of the South and of the East, climbing ropes, dropping letters, overhearing secrets, plunging daggers, languishing and dying, fighting and conquering, but loving, always loving, for, as Mr Whicher puts it, to Mrs Haywood "love was the force that motivated all the world."

These stories found certain idle people very ready to read them, and were generally successful. Mrs Haywood was evidently a born journalist. As long as romances of the heart were in fashion she turned out romance after romance; when Richardson and

Fielding brought the novel into closer touch with life she followed suit with her "Miss Betsy Thoughtless" and her "Jemmy and Jenny Jessamy." In the interval she turned publisher, edited a newspaper called *The Parrot*, and produced secret histories and scandal novels rather in the style of our gossip in the illustrated papers about the aristocracy. In none of these departments was she a pioneer, or even a very distinguished disciple; and it is more for her steady industry with the pen than for the product of it that she is remarkable. Reading when Mrs Haywood wrote was beginning to come into fashion, and readers demanded books which they could read "with a tea-cup in one hand without danger of spilling the tea." But that class, as Mr Gosse indicates when he compares Mrs Haywood to Ouida, has not been improved away nor lessened in numbers. There is the same desire to escape from the familiar look of life by the easiest way, and the difference is really that we find our romance in accumulated motor-cars and marquises rather than in foreign parts and strange-sounding names. But the heart which suffered in the pages of the early romancers beats to-day upon the railway bookstall beneath the shiny coloured cover which depicts Lord Belcour parting from the Lady Belinda Fitzurse, or the Duchess of Ormonde clasping the family diamonds and bathed in her own blood at the bottom of the marble staircase.

In what sense Mr Whicher can claim that Mrs Haywood "prepared the way for . . . quiet Jane Austen" it is difficult to see, save that one lady was undeniably born some eighty years in advance of the other. For it would be hard to imagine a less professional woman of letters than the lady who wrote on little slips of paper, hid them when anyone was near, and kept her novels shut up in her desk, and refused to write a romance about the august House of Coburg at the suggestion of Prince Leopold's librarian—behaviour that must have made Mrs Haywood lift her hands in amazement in the grave. And in that long and very intricate process of living and reading and writing which so mysteriously alters the form of literature, so that Jane Austen, born in 1775, wrote novels, while Jane Austen born a hundred years earlier would probably have written not novels but a few exquisite lost letters, Mrs Haywood plays no perceptible part, save that of swelling the chorus of sound. For people who write books do not necessarily add anything to the history of literature, even when those books are little old volumes, stained with age, that have crossed the Atlantic; nor can we see that the students of Columbia University will love English literature the better for knowing how very dull it can be, although the University may claim that this is a "contribution to knowledge."

Maria Edgeworth and Her Circle[1]

S O far as we can remember, Miss Hill does not ask herself once
in the volume before us whether people now read Miss
Edgeworth's novels. Perhaps she takes it for granted that they do,
or perhaps she thinks that it does not matter. The past has an
immense charm of its own; and if one can show how people lived
a hundred years ago—one means by that, how they powdered
their hair, and drove in yellow chariots, and passed Lord Byron in
the street—one need not trouble oneself with minds and emotions.
Indeed, we can know very little of the dead; when we talk of the
different ages of the past we are really thinking of different fashions
of dress and different styles of architecture. We have an enormous
supply of such properties in our minds, deposited there by a library
of books like this book of Miss Hill's. She stamps the figure of a
chariot in gold upon her boards, as though it helped us to understand Miss Edgeworth. We persuade ourselves that it does, and
yet we should think it strange if the future biographer of "Mrs
Humphry Ward and her Circle" illustrated his meaning by a
hansom cab. To Miss Edgeworth herself, we may be sure, Miss
Hill's account of her would seem a little irrelevant and perhaps not
very amusing; nevertheless, we are under the illusion that this
enumeration of trifles and names helps us somehow to see her more
clearly than before, as certainly it produces in us a mild feeling of
benevolence and pleasure. To Miss Hill undoubtedly belongs the
credit of choosing her illustrations happily, so that they excite in
us the curious illusion that we are peopling the past. For the
moment it seems very much alive, and yet it is nothing like the life
we know. The chief difference is that it makes us laugh much more
consistently than the present does, and that it is composed to a
much greater extent of visual impressions—of turbans and chariots
with nothing inside them.

Miss Edgeworth, although she lived in Ireland, sometimes
visited London and Paris. She crossed the Channel for the first time
in 1802, the voyage taking three hours and a half, "a comparatively

[1] *Maria Edgeworth and Her Circle*, by Constance Hill. *The Times Literary
Supplement*, December 9, 1909.

quick passage for those days of sailing packets," Miss Hill points out, invoking the spell of the past. Something, after all, must be invoked when one has a heroine who, brought face to face with Mme Récamier, merely remarks, "Mme Récamier is of quite an opposite sort, though in the first fashion a graceful and *decent* beauty of excellent character." To solidify the chapter one can also quote at length what the poet Rogers said about the famous bath and how Miss Berry admired the famous bed. At the same time, we cannot believe that Maria would have included Mme Récamier among her circle. In common with all the women writers of the eighteenth century, Miss Edgeworth was strikingly modest. Her habits were such that no one would have taken her for a remarkable person, but it is scarcely necessary to be at such pains to prove it. She was diminutive in figure, plain in feature, and wrote demurely at her desk in the family living room. Nevertheless, she observed everything, and in congenial company talked well upon "old French classic literature" and listened sympathetically to stories of the Revolution. Moreover, she was so sprightly and sensible that young men of fashion both of "the light, easy, enjoying-the-world style" and of the "melancholy and Byronic" were fascinated and let her twit them with impunity. She turned the conversation adroitly from politics to wit, and ridiculed the fashion for the "triste" in manner and "le vague" in poetry. One love affair she had with a Swedish gentleman called Edelcrantz, whose understanding was superior and whose manners were mild. But, on ascertaining that she would have to leave her family and live in Sweden if she married him, she refused, although, "being exceedingly in love with him," she suffered much at the time and long afterwards. In May, 1813, Maria Edgeworth, with her father and stepmother, spent some weeks in London. The town ran mad to see her; at parties the crowd turned and twisted to discover her, and as she was very small, almost closed above her head. She bore it with composure and amusement; the general verdict seems to have been Lord Byron's:—"One would never have guessed that she could write *her name*; whereas her father talked, *not* as if he could write nothing else, but as if nothing else was worth writing." On the other hand, we have Miss Edgeworth:—"Of Lord Byron I can tell you only that his appearance is nothing that you would remark."

The obvious thing happened; people stared, were disappointed, laughed good-humouredly, and began to talk of other things. Her biographer is in the same predicament. She has recourse, with the rest of the world, to Mme de Staël. That lady was lavishing her eloquence upon London; report said that when she was silent— that is while her hair was dressed and while she breakfasted—she continued to scribble. She extorted four words from that Duke of Marlborough, who was scarcely known to speak. "Let me go away," he cried, on hearing her announced. Unfortunately, Napoleon escaped from Elba and Miss Edgeworth withdrew to Ireland, and for some reason we hear much more of Mme d'Arblay's impressions of the battle of Waterloo than of a much more interesting subject—Miss Edgeworth herself. Maria took no part in the campaign, save that she describes (from hearsay) a banquet given at Drogheda by the Lord Mayor, at which the victorious generals were represented in sugared paste. Perverse although it may seem, Drogheda and the opinion of Drogheda upon the victory interests us far more than the account of Wellington's reception in Paris; possibly if we were told what Miss Edgeworth saw among the peasants on her estate we should realize far better what Waterloo meant than by reading the faded exclamations of Mme d'Arblay upon the spot.

Europe settled down again, however, and Maria was able to visit Hampstead in 1818, and to stay with Miss Joanna Baillie, the author of "Plays on the Passions," and the lyric,

The chough and crow to roost are gone,

admired by Scott. In spite of her fame she, too, was modest:—"No one could have taken her for a married woman. An innocent maiden grace hovered over her to the end of old age." She walked discreetly behind her elder sister when the two old ladies, dressed in grey silk and lace caps alike, were present at the reading of one of Joanna's "Plays on the Passions" in the assembly rooms. On hearing of it some of her friends were shocked and wrote, "Have ye heard that Jocky Baillie has taken to the *public line?*" There was Mrs Barbauld also, who sometimes stayed at Hampstead, and was severely reproved by the *Quarterly Review* for her Ode, "1811," by which she depressed the spirits of the nation. There was Lady Breadalbane, who fell asleep in her carriage and was locked up in the coachhouse; nobody missing her for a considerable time, several carriages were rolled in after hers, and then, "she wakened" —but what she said Maria has no time to report. There was Mr Standish, "the tip-top dandy," who stayed at Trentham and displayed such a toilet-table that all the ladies' maids were invited to a private view of his dressing-case, "which, I assure you, my lady, is the thing best worth seeing in this house, all of gilt plate, and I wish, my lady, you had such a dressing box." How charming our ancestors were!—so simple in their manners, so humorous in their behaviour, so strange in their expressions! Thus, as we run through Miss Hill's book, we pick up straws everywhere, and dull must be our fancy if we fail in the end to furnish all the Georgian houses in existence with tables and chairs and ladies and gentlemen. There is no need to tease ourselves with the suspicion that they were quite different in the flesh, and as ugly, as complex, and as emotional as we are, for their simplicity is more amusing to believe in and much easier to write about. Nevertheless, there are moments when we bewail the opportunity that Miss Hill seems to have missed—the opportunity of getting at the truth at the risk of being dull.

Jane Austen and the Geese[1]

O F all writers Jane Austen is the one, so we should have thought, who has had the least cause to complain of her critics. Her chief admirers have always been those who write novels themselves, and from the time of Sir Walter Scott to the time of George Moore she has been praised with unusual discrimination.

So we should have thought. But Miss Austen-Leigh's book shows that we were far too sanguine. Never have we had before us such certain proof of the incorrigible stupidity of reviewers. Ever since Jane Austen became famous they have been hissing inanities in chorus. She did not like dogs; she was not fond of children; she did not care for England; she was indifferent to public affairs; she had no book learning; she was irreligious; she was alternately cold and coarse; she knew no one outside her family circle; she derived her pessimistic view of family life from observing the differences between her father and mother. Miss Austen-Leigh, whose piety is natural but whose concern we cannot help thinking excessive, is persuaded that there is some "misapprehension" about Jane Austen, and is determined to right it by taking each of the geese separately and wringing his neck. Some one, properly anonymous and we can scarcely help thinking fabulous, has expressed his opinion that Jane Austen was not qualified to write about the English gentry. The fact is, says Miss Austen-Leigh, that she was descended on her father's side from the Austens, who sprang, "like other county families, from the powerful Clan of the Clothiers"; on her mother's from the Leighs of Addlestrop, who entertained King Charles. Moreover, she went to dances. She moved in good society. "Jane Austen was in every way well fitted to write of the lives and feelings of English gentle people." In that conclusion we entirely concur. Still the fact that you are well fitted to write about one set of people may be taken to prove that you are not well fitted to write about another. That profound observation is to the credit of a second anonymous fowl. Nor, to be candid, does Miss Austen-Leigh altogether succeed in silencing him. Jane

[1] *Personal Aspects of Jane Austen,* by Mary Augusta Austen-Leigh. *The Times Literary Supplement,* October 28, 1920.

Austen had, she assures us, opportunities for a wider knowledge of life than falls to the lot of most clergymen's daughters. An uncle by marriage lived in India and was a friend of Warren Hastings. He must have written home about the trial and the climate. A cousin married a French nobleman whose head was cut off in the Revolution. She must have had something to say about Paris and the guillotine. One of her brothers made the grand tour, and two were in the Navy. It is, therefore, undeniable that Jane Austen might have "indulged in romantic flights of fancy with India or France for a background," but it is equally undeniable that Jane Austen never did. Yet it is difficult to deny that had she been not only Jane Austen but Lord Byron and Captain Marryat into the bargain her works might have possessed merits which, as it is, we cannot truthfully say that we find in them.

Leaving these exalted regions of literary criticism the reviewers now attack her character. She was cold they say, and "turned away from whatever was sad, unpleasant, or painful." That is easily disposed of. The family archives contain proof that she nursed a cousin through the measles, and "attended her brother Henry, in London, in an illness of which he nearly died." It is as easy from the same source to dispose of the malevolent assertion that she was the illiterate daughter of an illiterate father. When the Rev. George Austen left Steventon he sold five hundred books. The number that he must have kept is quite enough to prove that Jane Austen was a well read woman. As for the slander that her family life was unhappy, it is sufficient to quote the words of a cousin who was in the habit of staying with the Austens. "When among this Liberal Society, the simplicity, hospitality, and taste which commonly prevail in different families among the delightful vallies of Switzerland ever occurs to my memory." The malignant and persistent critic still remains who says that Jane Austen was without morality. Indeed, it is a difficult charge to meet. It is not enough to quote her own statement, "I am very fond of Sherlock's sermons." The testimony of Archbishop Whately does not convince us. Nor can we personally subscribe to Miss Austen-Leigh's opinion that in all her works "one line of thought, one grace, or quality, or necessity . . . is apparent. It's name is Repentance." The truth appears to us to be much more complicated than that.

If Miss Austen-Leigh does not throw much light upon that

problem, she does one thing for which we are grateful to her. She prints some notes made by Jane at the age of twelve or thirteen upon the margin of Goldsmith's History of England. They are slight and childish, useless, we should have thought, to confute the critics who hold that she was unemotional, unsentimental and passionless. "My dear Mr. G——, I have lived long enough in the world to know that it is always so." She corrects her author amusingly. "Oh! Oh! The wretches!" she exclaims against the Puritans. "Dear Balmerino I cannot express what I feel for you!" she cries when Balmerino is executed. There is nothing more in them than that. Only to hear Jane Austen saying nothing in her natural voice when the critics have been debating whether she was a lady, whether she told the truth, whether she could read, and whether she had personal experience of hunting a fox is positively upsetting. We remember that Jane Austen wrote novels. It might be worth while for her critics to read them.

Mrs Gaskell[1]

FROM what one can gather of Mrs Gaskell's nature, she would not have liked Mrs Chadwick's book. A cultivated woman, for whom publicity had no glamour, with a keen sense of humour and a quick temper, she would have opened it with a shiver and dropped it with a laugh. It is delightful to see how cleverly she vanishes. There are no letters to be had; no gossip; people remember her, but they seem to have forgotten what she was like. At least, cries Mrs Chadwick, she must have lived somewhere; houses can be described. "There is a long, glass-covered porch, forming a conservatory, which is the main entrance. . . . On the ground-floor, to the right, is a large drawing room. On the left are a billiard room . . . a large kitchen . . . and a scullery. . . . There are ten bed rooms . . . and a kitchen garden sufficiently large to supply vegetables for a large family." The ghost would feel grateful to the houses; it might give her a twinge to hear that she had "got into the best literary set of the day," but on the other hand it would please her to read of how Charles Darwin was "the well-known naturalist."

The surprising thing is that there should be a public who wishes to know where Mrs Gaskell lived. Curiosity about the houses, the coats, and the pens of Shelley, Peacock, Charlotte Brontë, and George Meredith seems lawful. One imagines that these people did everything in a way of their own; and in such cases a trifle will start the imagination when the whole body of their published writings fails to thrill. But Mrs Gaskell would be the last person to have that peculiarity. One can believe that she prided herself upon doing things as other women did them, only better—that she swept manuscripts off the table lest a visitor should think her odd. She was, we know, the best of housekeepers, "her standard of comfort," writes Mrs Chadwick, being "expensive, but her tastes were always refined"; and she kept a cow in her back garden to remind her of the country.

For a moment it seems surprising that we should still be reading

[1] *Mrs Gaskell*, by Ellis H. Chadwick. *The Times Literary Supplement*, September 29, 1910.

her books. The novels of to-day are so much terser, intenser, and more scientific. Compare the strike in "North and South," for example, with the *Strife* of Mr Galsworthy. She seems a sympathetic amateur beside a professional in earnest. But this is partly due to a kind of irritation with the methods of mid-Victorian novelists. Nothing would persuade them to concentrate. Able by nature to spin sentence after sentence melodiously, they seem to have left out nothing that they knew how to say. Our ambition, on the other hand, is to put in nothing that need not be there. What we want to be there is the brain and the view of life; the autumnal woods, the history of the whale fishery, and the decline of stage coaching we omit entirely. But by means of comment, dialogues that depart from truth by their wit and not by their pomposity, descriptions fused into a metaphor, we get a world carved out arbitrarily enough by one dominant brain. Every page supplies a little heap of reflections, which, so to speak, we sweep aside from the story and keep to build a philosophy with. There is really nothing to stimulate such industry in the pages of Thackeray, Dickens, Trollope, and Mrs Gaskell. A further deficiency (in modern eyes) is that they lack "personality." Cut out a passage and set it apart and it lies unclaimed, unless a trick of rhythm mark it. Yet it may be a merit that personality, the effect not of depth of thought but of the manner of it, should be absent. The tuft of heather that Charlotte Brontë saw was her tuft; Mrs Gaskell's world was a large place, but it was everybody's world.

She waited to begin her first novel until she was thirty-four, driven to write by the death of her baby. A mother, a woman who had seen much of life, her instinct in writing was to sympathize with others. Loving men and women, she seems to have done her best, like a wise parent, to keep her own eccentricities in the background. She would devote the whole of her large mind to understanding. That is why, when one begins to read her, one is dismayed by the lack of cleverness.

> Carriages still roll along the streets, concerts are still crowded by subscribers, the shops for expensive luxuries still find daily customers, while the workman loiters away his unemployed time in watching these things, and thinking of the pale, uncomplaining wife at home, and the wailing children

asking in vain for enough of food—of the sinking health, of the dying life of those near and dear to him. The contrast is too great. Why should he alone suffer from bad times? I know that this is not really the case; and I know what is the truth in such matters; but what I wish to impress is what the workman feels and thinks.

So she misses the contrast. But by adding detail after detail in this profuse impersonal way she nearly achieves what has not been achieved by all our science. Because they are strange and terrible to us, we always see the poor in stress of some kind, so that the violence of their feeling may break through conventions, and, bringing them rudely into touch with us, do away with the need of subtle understanding. But Mrs Gaskell knows how the poor enjoy themselves; how they visit and gossip and fry bacon and lend each other bits of finery and show off their sores. This is the more remarkable because she was hampered by a refined upbringing and traditions of culture. Her working men and women, her outspoken and crabbed old family domestics, are generally more vigorous than her ladies and gentlemen, as though a touch of coarseness did her good. How admirable, for instance, is the scene when Mrs Boucher is told of her husband's death.

"Hoo mun be told because of th' inquest. See! hoo's coming round; shall you or I do it? Or mappen your father would be best?"

"No; you, you," said Margaret.

They awaited her perfect recovery in silence. Then the neighbour woman sat down on the floor, and took Mrs Boucher's head and shoulders on her lap.

"Neighbour," said she, "your man is ded. Guess yo' how he died?"

"He were drowned," said Mrs Boucher feebly, beginning to cry for the first time at this rough probing of her sorrow.

"He were found drowned. He were coming home very hopeless o' aught on earth. . . . I'm not saying he did right, and I'm not saying he did wrong. All I say is, may neither me nor mine ever have his sore heart, or we may do like things."

"He has left me alone wi' a' these children!" moaned the widow, less distressed at the manner of the death than Margaret expected; but it was of a piece with her helpless character to feel his loss as principally affecting herself and her children.

Too great a refinement gives "Cranford" that prettiness which is the weakest thing about it, making it, superficially at least, the favourite copy for gentle writers who have hired rooms over the village post-office.

When she was a girl, Mrs Gaskell was famous for her ghost stories. A great story-teller she remained to the end, able always in the middle of the thickest book to make us ask "What happens next?" Keeping a diary to catch the overflow of life, observing clouds and trees, moving about among numbers of very articulate men and women, high-spirited, observant, and free from bitterness and bigotry, it seems as though the art of writing came to her as easily as an instinct. She had only to let her pen run to shape a novel. When we look at her work in the mass we remember her world, not her individuals. In spite of Lady Ritchie, who hails Molly Gibson "dearest of heroines, a born lady, unconsciously noble and generous in every thought," in spite of the critic's praise of her "psychological subtlety," her heroes and heroines remain solid rather than interesting. With all her humour she was seldom witty, and the lack of wit in her character-drawing leaves the edges blunt. These pure heroines, having no such foibles as she loved to draw, no coarseness and no violent passions, depress one like an old acquaintance. One will never get to know them; and that is profoundly sad. One reads her most perhaps because one wishes to have the run of her world. Melt them together, and her books compose a large, bright, country town, widely paved, with a great stir of life in the streets and a decorous row of old Georgian houses standing back from the road. "Leaving behind your husband, children, and civilization, you must come out to barbarism, loneliness, and liberty." Thus Charlotte Brontë, inviting her to Haworth, compared their lives, and Mrs Gaskell's comment was "Poor Miss Brontë." We who never saw her, with her manner "gay but definite," her beautiful face, and her "almost perfect arm," find something of the same delight in her books. What a pleasure it is to read them!

The Compromise[1]

NONE of the great Victorian reputations has sunk lower than that of Mrs Humphry Ward. Her novels, already strangely out of date, hang in the lumber-room of letters like the mantles of our aunts, and produce in us the same desire that they do to smash the window and let in the air, to light the fire and pile the rubbish on top. Some books fade into a gentle picturesqueness with age. But there is a quality, perhaps a lack of quality, about the novels of Mrs Ward which makes it improbable that, however much they fade, they will ever become picturesque. Their large bunches of jet, their intricate festoons of ribbon, skilfully and firmly fabricated as they are, obstinately resist the endearments of time. But Mrs Trevelyan's life of her mother makes us consider all this from a different angle. It is an able and serious book, and like all good biographies so permeates us with the sense of the presence of a human being that by the time we have finished it we are more disposed to ask questions than to pass judgments. Let us attempt, in a few words, to hand on the dilemma to our readers.

Of Mrs Ward's descent there is no need to speak. She had by birth and temperament all those qualities which fitted her, before she was twenty, to be the friend of Mark Pattison, and "the best person," in the opinion of J. R. Green, to be asked to contribute a volume to a history of Spain. There was little, even at the age of twenty, that this ardent girl did not know about the Visigothic Invasion or the reign of Alfonso el Sabio. One of her first pieces of writing, A Morning in the Bodleian, records in priggish but burning words her scholar's enthusiasm: ". . . let not the young man reading for his pass, the London copyist, or the British Museum illuminator," hope to enjoy the delights of literature; that deity will only yield her gifts to "the silent ardour, the thirst, the disinterestedness of the true learner." With such an inscription above the portal, her fate seems already decided. She will marry a Don, she will rear a small family; she will circulate Plain Facts on Infant Feeding in the Oxford slums; she will help

[1] *The Life of Mrs Humphry Ward*, by Janet Penrose Trevelyan. *The New Republic*, January 9, 1924.

to found Somerville College; she will sit up writing learned articles for the Dictionary of Christian Biography; and at last, after a hard life of unremunerative toil, she will finish the book which fired her fancy as a girl and will go down to posterity as the author of a standard work upon the origins of modern Spain. But, as every one knows, the career which seemed so likely, and would have been so honorable, was interrupted by the melodramatic success of Robert Elsmere. History was entirely forsaken for fiction, and the Origins of Modern Spain became transmuted into the Origins of Modern France, a phantom book which the unfortunate Robert Elsmere never succeeded in writing.

It is here that we begin to scribble in the margin of Mrs Ward's life those endless notes of interrogation. After Robert Elsmere—which we may grant to have been inevitable—we can never cease to ask ourselves, why? Why desert the charming old house in Russell Square for the splendour and expenses of Grosvenor Place? Why wear beautiful dresses, why keep butlers and carriages, why give luncheon parties and week-end parties, why buy a house in the country and pull it down and build it up again, when all this can only be achieved by writing at breathless speed novels which filial piety calls autumnal, but the critic, unfortunately, must call bad? Mrs Ward might have replied that the compromise, if she agreed to call it so, was entirely justified. Who but a coward would refuse, when cheques for £7,000 dropped out of George Smith's pocket before breakfast, to spend the money as the great ladies of the Renaissance would have spent it, upon society and entertainment and philanthropy? Without her novel-writing there would have been no centre for good talk in the pretty room overlooking the grounds of Buckingham Palace. Without her novel-writing thousands of poor children would have ranged the streets unsheltered. It is impossible to remain a schoolgirl in the Bodleian for ever, and, once you breast the complicated currents of modern life at their strongest, there is little time to ask questions, and none to answer them. One thing merges in another; one thing leads to another. After an exhausting At Home in Grosvenor Place, she would snatch a meal and drive off to fight the cause of play centres in Bloomsbury. Her success in that undertaking involved her, against her will, in the anti-suffrage campaign. Then, when the war came, this elderly lady of weak health was selected by the highest authorities to peer into shell-holes, and be taken over men-of-war by admirals. Sometimes, says Mrs Trevelyan, eighty letters were dispatched from Stocks in a single day; five hats were bought in the course of one drive to town—"on spec., darling"; and what with grandchildren and cousins and friends; what with being kind and being un-methodical and being energetic; what with caring more and more passionately for politics, and finding the meetings of liberal churchmen "desperately, perhaps disproportionately" interesting, there was only one half-hour in the whole day left for reading Greek.

It is tempting to imagine what the schoolgirl in the Bodleian would have said to her famous successor. "Literature has no guerdon for bread-students, to quote the expressive German phrase . . . only to the silent ardour, the thirst, the disinterested-ness of the true learner, is she prodigal of all good gifts." But Mrs Humphry Ward, the famous novelist, might have rounded up her critic of twenty. "It is all very well," she might have said, "to accuse me of having wasted my gifts; but the fault lay with you. Yours was the age for seeing visions; and you spent it in dreaming how you stopped the Princess of Wales's runaway horses, and were rewarded by 'a command' to appear at Buckingham Palace. It was you who starved my imagination and condemned it to the fatal compromise." And here the elder lady undoubtedly lays her finger upon the weakness of her own work. For the depressing effects of her books must be attributed to the fact that while her imagination always attempts to soar, it always agrees to perch. That is why we never wish to open them again.

In Mrs Trevelyan's biography these startling discrepancies between youth and age, between ideal and accomplishment, are successfully welded together, as they are in life, by an infinite series of details. She makes it apparent that Mrs Ward was beloved, famous, and prosperous in the highest degree. And if to achieve all this implies some compromise, still—but here we reach the dilemma which we intend to pass on to our readers.

Wilcoxiana[1]

HOW can one begin? Where can one leave off? There never was a more difficult book to review. If one puts in the Madame de Staël of Milwaukee, there will be no room for the tea-leaves; if one concentrates upon Helen Pitkin, Raley Husted Bell must be done without. Then all the time there are at least three worlds spinning in and out, and as for Ella Wheeler Wilcox—Mrs Wilcox is indeed the chief problem. It would be easy to make fun of her; equally easy to condescend to her; but it is not at all easy to express what one does feel for her. There is a hint of this complexity in her personal appearance. We write with forty photographs of Mrs Wilcox in front of us. If you omit those with the cats in her arms and the crescent moons in her hair, those stretched on a couch with a book, and those seated on a balustrade between Theodosia Garrison and Rhoda Hero Dunn, all primarily a tribute to the Muse, there remain a number which represent a plump, personable, determined young woman, vain, extremely vivacious, arch, but at the same time sensible, and always in splendid health. She was never a frump at any stage of her career. Rather than look like a bluestocking, she would have forsaken literature altogether. She stuck a rod between her arms to keep her back straight; she galloped over the country on an old farm horse; she defied her mother and bathed naked; at the height of her fame "a new stroke in swimming or a new high dive gave me more of a thrill than a new style of verse, great as my devotion to the Muses was, and ever has been." In short, if one had the pleasure of meeting Mrs Wilcox, one would find her a very well-dressed, vivacious woman of the world. But, alas for the simplicity of the problem! there is not one world but three.

The pre-natal world is indicated rather sketchily. One is given to understand that Mrs Wilcox is appearing for by no means the first time. There have been Ella Wheeler Wilcoxes in Athens and Florence, Rome and Byzantium. She is a recurring, but an improving phenomenon. "Being an old soul myself," she says, "reincarnated many more times than any other member of my

[1] *The Worlds and I* by Ella Wheeler Wilcox. *The Athenæum*, September 19, 1919.

144

family, I knew the truth of spiritual things not revealed to them."
One gift, at least, of supreme importance she brought with her
from the shades—"I was born with unquenchable hope ... I
always expected wonderful things to happen to me." Without
hope, what could she have done? Everything was against her.
Her father was an unsuccessful farmer; her mother an embittered
woman worn down by a life of child-bearing and hard work; the
atmosphere of the home was one of "discontent and fatigue and
irritability." They lived far out in the country, five miles from a
post office, uncomfortably remote even from the dissipations of
Milwaukee. Yet Ella Wheeler never lost her belief in an amazing
future before her; she was probably never dull for five minutes
together. Although acutely aware that her father's taste in hats
was distressing, and that the farmhouse walls were without
creepers, she had the power within her to transform everything
to an object of beauty. The buttercups and daisies of the fields
looked to her like rare orchids and hothouse roses. When she was
galloping to the post on her farm horse, she expected to be
thrown at the feet of a knight, or perhaps the miracle would be
reversed and it was into her bosom that the knight would be
pitched instead. After a day of domestic drudgery, she would
climb a little hill and sit in the sunset and dream. Fame was to
come from the East, and love and wealth. (As a matter of fact,
she notes, they came from the West.) At any rate something
wonderful was bound to happen. "And I would awaken happy in
spite of myself, and put all my previous melancholy into verses—
and dollars." The young woman with the determined mouth
never forgot her dollars, and one respects her for saying so. But
often Miss Wheeler suggested that in return for what he called her
"heart wails" the editor should send her some object from his prize
list—bric-à-brac, tableware, pictures—anything to make the farmhouse more like the house of her dreams. Among the rest came six
silver forks, and judge of her emotion! conceive the immeasurable
romance of the world!—years later she discovered that the silver
forks were made by the firm in which her husband was employed.
But it is time to say something of the poetic gift which brought
silver forks from Milwaukee, and letters and visits from complete
strangers, so that she cannot remember "any period of my
existence when I have not been before the public eye." She was

taught very little; there were odd volumes of Shakespeare, Ouida, and Gauthier scattered about the house, but no complete sets. She did not wish to read, however. Her passion for writing seems to have been a natural instinct—a gift handed down mature from Heaven, and manifesting itself whenever it chose, without much control or direction from Mrs Wilcox herself. Sometimes the Muse would rise to meet an emergency. "Fetch me a pencil and pad!" she would say, and in the midst of a crowd, to the amazement of the beholders, and to the universal applause, she would dash off precisely the verse required to celebrate the unexpected arrival of General Sherman. Yet sometimes the Muse would obstinately forsake her. What could have been more vexatious than its behaviour in the Hotel Cecil, when Mrs Wilcox wished to write a poem about Queen Victoria's funeral? She had been sent across the Atlantic for that very purpose. Not a word could she write. The newspaper-man was coming for her copy at nine the next morning. She had not put pen to paper when she went to bed. She was in despair. And then at the inconvenient hour of three a.m. the Muse relented. Mrs Wilcox woke with four verses running in her head. "I felt an immense sense of relief. I knew I could write something the editor would like; something England would like." And, indeed, "The Queen's Last Ride" was set to music by a friend of King Edward's, and sung in the presence of the entire Royal family, one of whom afterwards graciously sent her a message of thanks.

Capricious and fanciful, nevertheless the Muse has a heart of gold; she never does desert Mrs Wilcox. Every experience turns, almost of its own accord and at the most unexpected moments, to verse. She goes to stay with friends; she sits next a young widow in the omnibus. She forgets all about it. But as she stands before the looking-glass fastening her white dress in the evening, something whispers to her:

> *Laugh and the world laughs with you,*
> *Weep and you weep alone,*
> *For the sad old earth must borrow its mirth,*
> *It has trouble enough of its own.*

The following morning at the breakfast table I recited the quatrain to the Judge and his wife . . . and the Judge, who was a great Shakespearean scholar said, "Ella, if you keep the remainder of the poem up to that epigrammatic standard, you will have a literary gem."

She did keep the poem up to that standard, and two days later he said, "Ella, that is one of the biggest things you ever did, and you are mistaken in thinking it uneven in merit, it is all good and up to the mark." Such is the depravity of mankind, however, that a wretched creature called Joyce, belonging to "the poison-insect order of humanity," as Mrs Wilcox says, afterwards claimed that he had written "Solitude" himself—written it, too, upon the head of a whisky barrel in a wine-room.

A poetess also was very trying. Mrs Wilcox, who is generosity itself, detected unusual genius in her verse, and fell in love with the idea of playing Fairy Godmother to the provincial poetess. She invited her to stay at an hotel, and gave a party in her honour. Mrs Croly, Mrs Leslie, Robert Ingersoll, Nym Crinkle, and Harriet Webb all came in person. The carriages extended many blocks down the street. Several of the young woman's poems were recited; "there was some good music and a tasteful supper." Moreover, each guest, on leaving, was given a piece of ribbon upon which was printed the verse that Mrs Wilcox so much admired. What more could she have done? And yet the ungrateful creature went off with the barest words of thanks; scarcely answered letters; refused to explain her motives, and stayed in New York with an eminent literary man without letting Mrs Wilcox know.

> To this day when I see the occasional gems of beauty which still fall from this poet's pen I feel the old wound ache in my heart. . . . Life, however, always supplies a balm after it has wounded us. . . . The spring following this experience my husband selected a larger apartment.

For by this time Ella Wheeler was Wilcox.

She first met Mr Wilcox in a jeweller's shop in Milwaukee. He was engaged in the sterling-silver business, and she had run in to ask the time. Ironically enough, she never noticed him. There was Mr Wilcox, a large, handsome man with a Jewish face and a deep bass voice, doing business with the jeweller, and she never noticed his presence. Out she went again, anxious only to be in time for dinner, and thought no more about it. A few days later a very distinguished-looking letter arrived in a blue envelope. Might Mr Wilcox be presented to her? "I knew it was, according to established ideas, bordering on impropriety, yet I so greatly admired the penmanship and stationery of my would-be acquaintance that I was curious to know more of him." They corresponded. Mr Wilcox's letters were "sometimes a bit daring," but never sentimental; and they were always enclosed in envelopes "of a very beautiful shade," while "the crest on the paper seemed to lead me away from everything banal and common." And then the Oriental paper-knife arrived. This had an extraordinary effect upon her such as had hitherto been produced only by reading "a rare poem, or hearing lovely music, or in the presence of some of Ouida's exotic descriptions." She went to Chicago and met Mr Wilcox in the flesh. He seemed to her—correctly dressed and very cultured in manner as he was—"like a man from Mars." Soon afterwards they were married, and almost immediately Mr Wilcox, to the profound joy of his wife, expressed his belief in the immortality of the soul.

Mrs Wilcox was now established in New York, the admired centre of a circle of "very worth-while people." Her dreams in the sunset were very nearly realized. The Bungalow walls were covered with autographs of brilliant writers and the sketches of gifted artists. Universal brotherhood was attempted. It was the rule of the house "to treat mendicants with sympathy and peddlers with respect." No one left without "some little feeling of uplift." What was wanting? In the first place, "the highbrows have never had any use for me." The highbrows could be dispatched with a phrase. "May you grow at least a sage bush of a heart to embellish your desert of intellect!"

All the same, in her next incarnation she will have nothing to do with genius. "To be a gifted poet is a glory; to be a worth-while woman is a greater glory." There are moments when she wishes that the Muse would leave her at peace. To be the involuntary mouthpiece of Songs of Purpose, Passion, and Power, greet the war with *Hello, Boys*, and death with Sonnets of Sorrow and Triumph, to feel that at any moment a new gem may form or a fresh cameo compose itself, what fate could be more appalling? Yet such has been the past, and such must be the future, of Ella Wheeler Wilcox.

The Genius of Boswell[1]

THE letters which are here reprinted have had an adventurous history. It was in the year 1850 that a gentleman making a purchase at Boulogne found that his parcel was wrapped in sheets of old manuscript. The sheets proved to be letters written by Boswell to the Rev. W. J. Temple, an ancestor of the archbishop, and when the rest of the series had been recovered from the paper merchant they were published in 1857 by Richard Bentley, with an introduction from the hand of an anonymous editor. Mr Seccombe, who introduces the present edition, conjectures that his predecessor was Sir Philip Francis, of the Supreme Consular Court of the Levant. If, as there is reason to think, Boswell never wrote without some thought of posterity, his ghost must have gone through a long time of suspense. The edition of 1857 was greeted with applause by the critics; "*The Times* devoted six entire columns to a review of the book"; but it was sold out in under two years (a fire, it is thought, helping to destroy it), and there has been no reprint of the book until the present time. There must be many, then, who love their Boswell, but have never read his letters—many, therefore, who will thank Messrs Sidgwick and Jackson for the handsome shape of the volume and Mr Seccombe for the skill and humour with which he has introduced his subject. When a man has had the eyes of Carlyle and Macaulay fixed upon him it may well seem that there is nothing fresh to be said. And yet each of these observers came to a very different conclusion; Carlyle, although he called Boswell "an ill-assorted, glaring mixture of the highest and the lowest" contrived to make him glow with much of the splendour of the true hero-worshipper; and Macaulay indulged in the famous paradox, which, like the twisted mirror in the fair, shows us the human body with corkscrew legs and an undulating face. Mr Seccombe is not so amusing, but he is far more judicious. He has no theory to parade, and he has had the advantage of studying the letters; he can talk thus of "a tender-hearted man" in spite of "ludicrous immoralities"; he can see

[1] *Letters of James Boswell to the Rev. W. J. Temple. The Times Literary Supplement,* January 21, 1909.

149

that Boswell was a "great artist" as well as a "freak." The letters certainly tend to make the usual discrepancies less marked, because they show that Boswell existed independently of Johnson, and had many qualities besides those that we are wont to allow him. To read a man's letters after reading his works has much the same effect as staying with him in his own house after meeting him in full dress at dinner parties.

The letters begin in 1758, when Boswell was a boy of eighteen; they end a few months only before his death, and though they are scattered with wide gaps over a great many years, the story is continuous—there is a glimpse of Boswell on every page. The Rev. W. J. Temple met Boswell in the Greek class at Edinburgh University; he held the living of Mamhead and then the living of St Gluvias in Cornwall, and Mr Seccombe describes him, judging from published correspondence (unluckily it is not to Boswell), as a "dissatisfied atrabilious man." But there is no doubt that he provided Boswell with a perfect audience. He was neither illustrious, like Johnson, nor a humorous correspondent, like the Hon. Andrew Erskine, but he was a contemporary, a man with literary ambitions, and a cleric. They shared their loves and their "hopes of future greatness"; and it was under "the solemn yew" at Mamhead that Boswell made one of his vows. Temple, who had received the earliest of Boswell's confidences, who had reflected the image of what Boswell would like to be, was used ever after as the person who had a right to know what became of Boswell. During the first years of the correspondence he acted the part of the brilliant but irresponsible young man, whose follies are a proof of his spirit. He was a Newmarket courser yoked to a dung-cart; he was "a sad dupe—a perfect Don Quixote"; his life was "one of the most romantic that I believe either you or I really know of"; his scenes with his "charmers" were incredible. In short, with such a turmoil of gifts and failings buzzing through his brain, he was often really at a loss to account for himself. There were so many attitudes, and they were all so striking; should he be a Don Juan, or the friend of Johnson and Paoli, or the "great man at Adamtown"? And then, because he finds himself writing "in a library forty feet long," these visions fade, and he determines to live like "the most privileged spirits of antiquity." He imagines himself with his folios before him the head of a great family and an erudite country gentleman. He was always imagining himself; it is difficult to decide how much of genuine feeling he put into these imaginations. He had affairs with half-a-dozen ladies before he married; he went through ecstasy and anguish; they failed him or they did not deserve him; but he was never driven from his elegant and half quizzical attitude, like a man who is conscious that he has the eye of the audience upon him. "Come why do I allow myself to be uneasy for a Scots lass? Rouse me, my friend! I must have an Englishwoman. . . . You cannot say how fine a woman I may marry; perhaps a Howard or some other of the noblest in the kingdom."

Was it his vanity that made him such good company? For the vanity of Boswell was a rare quality. It kept him alive and it gave a point to him. He was not anxious merely to display all his emotions, but he was anxious to make them tell. He left out much that other people put in, and directly that he had a pen in his hand he became a natural artist. One may go further, indeed, and credit him with a sense that was oddly at variance with his egoism and his garrulity; a sense, as it seems, that something of value lay hidden in other people also beneath the babble of talk. "I got from my lord a good deal of his life. He says he will put down some particulars of himself if I will put them together and publish them." In order to get from a man a good deal of his life you must be able to convince him that you see something that he wishes to have seen, so that your curiosity is not impertinent. Boswell was not content, after all, with a view of a "visible progress through the world"; it was "a view of the mind in letters and conversation" that he sought, and sought with all the rashness of a hero. He had the gift, which is rare as it is beautiful, of being able "to contemplate with supreme delight those distinguished spirits by which God is sometimes pleased to honour humanity." Perhaps that was the reason why most people found something to like in him; it was a part of his wonderful sense of the romance and excitement of life.

His intense consciousness of himself made his progress like a pageant, and every day was a fresh adventure. If he dined out he noticed that there were "three sorts of ice creams"; he noticed the handsome maid; he noticed whether people liked him, and he remembered what clothes he wore. "It is hardly credible what ground I go over, and what a variety of men and manners I contemplate every day, and all the time I am myself *pars magna*, for my exuberant spirits will not let me listen enough." But as time went on this same exuberance was his undoing; he could never cease imagining, and settle to what lay before him. He made vows in St Paul's Church and under solemn yews; he vowed to reform and read the classics; he broke them the day after and was carried home drunk; and then "all the doubts which have ever disturbed thinking men" came over him, and he lay awake at night "dreading annihilation." It is characteristic that he helped himself out of his depression by remembering that worthy men like Temple cared for him. He used his friends to reflect his virtues. It is possible, too, that as the years failed to fulfil his hopes he was teased by a suspicion that other people had found something that he had missed. He had conceived too many possibilities to be content to realize one only, and now again he was able to see, as he saw everything, that he had somehow failed in life. "O Temple, Temple, is this realizing any of our towering hopes which have so often been the subject of our conversations and letters?" he exclaimed. Was there, perhaps, as he was wont to hint, some strain of madness in him that made his will shake always before an effort? "Why should I struggle?" he breaks out. "I certainly am constitutionally unfit for any employment." Was it madness or some power allied to genius that let him see in sudden incongruous flashes, as the scene shifted round him, how strange it all was? To get the full impression it would be necessary to quote letters at length; but when we read (for example) the letter upon the death of his wife with its grief for "my dear, dear Peggy," and its glory in the nineteen carriages that followed the hearse, and its repentance and its genuine cry of dismay and bewilderment, we feel that Boswell, as he sat and wrote it, had something of the clown in Shakespeare in him. It was granted to this scatter-brained and noisy man with a head full of vanity and grossness to exclaim with the poets and the sages, "What a motley scene is life!"

It would be more rash in his case than in another's to say what he felt or how strongly he felt it; and yet, whether it was due to his wife's death or whether his system really proved impossible, his fortunes from that time dwindled away. His hopes of preferment were disappointed; he failed at the English bar; and to hearten himself he drank more than ever. But we should underrate the amazing vitality that clung to the shreds of him if we believed that he shuffled out of life, a dejected and disreputable figure, by some back door. There was still a twinkle of curiosity in his eye; the great lips were moist and garrulous as ever. But there is a harsh strain henceforward in his chatter, as though some note had cracked with too much strumming. Someone stole his wig, "a jest that was very ill-timed to one in my situation," but was probably irresistible. Then he began to finger "several matrimonial schemes," to plume himself that his classical quotations had not deserted him, and to run after a certain Miss Bagnal. Mr Temple, near the end of their strange correspondence, had to admonish him, for Boswell answers, "Your suggestion as to my being carried off in a state of intoxication is awful." How was he "carried off" in the end? Were his wits fuddled with wine and was his imagination dazed with terror, and did some snatch of an old song come to his lips? It is strange how one wonders, with an inquisitive kind of affection, what Boswell felt; it always seems possible with him as with living people that if one watches closely enough one will know. But when we try to say what the secret is, then we understand why Boswell was a genius.

Shelley and Elizabeth Hitchener[1]

LOVERS of literature have once more to thank Mr Dobell for discharging one of those patient and humble services which only true devotion will take the pains to perform. Shelley's letters to Miss Hitchener have already been printed, indeed, but privately; and now we have them issued in a delightful shape, enriched with an introduction and with notes by Mr Dobell himself, so that one more chapter in the life of Shelley becomes plainer and more substantial. Nor can it be objected that the piety in this instance is excessive, for although the letters are chiefly remarkable because they illustrate the nature of a boy who was, five or six years later, to write consummate poetry, still Shelley's character is always amazing. And in spite of the verbosity and the pale platitudes of his style in 1811, it is impossible to read the letters without an exquisite sense of faded scenes come to life again, and dull people set talking, and all the country houses and respectable Sussex vicarages once more alive with ladies and gentlemen who exclaim, "What! a Shelley an Atheist!" and add their weight to the intense comedy and tragedy of his life.

Elizabeth Hitchener was a schoolmistress at Hurstpierpoint, and Shelley first knew her in 1811 when he was nineteen and she was twenty-eight. She was the daughter of a man who kept a publichouse and was, or had been, a smuggler; and all her education was due to a Mrs Adams, who is called, in the language of the letters, "the mother of my soul." Miss Hitchener was thin, tall, and dark, an austere intellectual woman with a desire for better things than the society of a country village could afford her, although she was not, as Shelley was eager to assure her, a Deist and a Republican. But she was probably the first clever woman he had met; she was oppressed, lonely, misunderstood, and in need of some one with whom she could discuss the pleasant agitations of her soul. Shelley rushed into the correspondence with enthusiasm; and she, no doubt, though a little mystified and awkward in her flight, was touched and anxious to prove herself as passionate,

[1] *Letters from P. B. Shelley to Elizabeth Hitchener*, edited by Bertram Dobell. *The Times Literary Supplement*, March 5, 1908.

as philanthropic, and almost as revolutionary as he was. Shelley's first letter indicates the nature of the friendship; he speaks of certain books which, in the manner of ardent young men, he had thrust upon her—Locke, "The Curse of Kehama," and Ensor's "National Education." He goes on to attack her Christianity, exclaims that "Truth is *my* God," and ends up, "But see Ensor on the subject of poetry." It would be delightful if we could have Miss Hitchener's letters also, for some allusions in Shelley's answers show the way in which, on occasion, she would try to cap his speculations. "All nature," she wrote, "but that of *horses* is harmonical; and *he* is born to misery because he is a horse." An Ode on the Rights of Women began,

All, all are men—women and all!

But it is clear enough, without her replies, that Shelley was not anxiously concerned with the state of her mind. He assumed easily that she was of a more exalted temper than he was; so that it was not necessary to investigate details, but he might pour forth to her, as to some impersonal deity, the surprising discoveries and ardent convictions which come, with such bewildering rapidity, when for the first time the world asks a definite question and literature supplies a variety of answers. The poor schoolmistress, we can gather, took vague alarm when she found to what a mate she had attached herself, to what speculations she was driven, what opinions she must embrace; and yet there was a strange and not laughable exhilaration in it, which urged her on. The relationship, moreover, was soon justified by Shelley's marriage with Harriet Westbrook, and her approval of the correspondence. It was to be a spiritual companionship, in no way inspired by carnal love of that "lump of organized matter which enshrines thy soul"; and, further, there was the insidious bait which Shelley offered, with his curious lack of humanity, in the letter which explains why he married Harriet. He begged the "sister of his soul" to help him in educating his wife. "Blame me [for the marriage] if thou wilt, dearest friend, for *still* thou art dearest to me; yet pity even this error, if thou blamest me." Miss Hitchener, it is clear, was keenly susceptible to praise of her mind which so subtly implied a closer tie; her letters became voluminous, and

showed, so Shelley declared, "the embryon of a mighty intellect."
But the prophetess kept one shrewd and sensible and, it must be
added, honourable eye upon the earth; she was well aware that
Harriet might become jealous, nor could she disregard the mis-
chievous chatter of Cuckfield gossips and attend only, as Shelley
bade her, to the majestic approval of her conscience. Tragedy, of
a sordid and substantial kind, was bound sooner or later to dissolve this incongruous alliance between the rushing poet, whose
wings grew stronger every day, and the painstaking but closely
tethered woman. The illusion was only sustained because for so
long Shelley was in Wales or Cumberland or Ireland, and the
lady remained at Hurstpierpoint, earning her living, which was
noble in itself, and teaching small children, which was yet nobler;
for to teach is "to propagate intellect . . . every error conquered,
every mind enlightened, is so much added to the progression of
human perfectibility." Then the first of the poet's illusions was
terribly destroyed; Hogg's treachery was discovered; and poor
Shelley, more in need than ever of understanding, turned wholly
to his "almost only friend," as he calls her in the letter which tells
her of the blow.

His desire, reiterated with the utmost emphasis, was that
Elizabeth should join his wandering household directly; and
Harriet, in some of the most interesting letters in the volume,
was made to add her entreaty to his, in a tone that tried, with
some pathos, to imitate his enthusiasm and generosity, but would
lapse easily, it is clear, into plaintive common-sense when he was
out of hearing. Miss Hitchener for a long while declined, for a
variety of reasons; she would have to give up her school, her only
support, depend entirely on Shelley, defy her father, and,
besides, people would talk. But these arguments, coming on the
top of so much impassioned rhetoric, were inadmissible; "the
hatred of the world," Shelley declared, "is despicable to you.
Come, come, and share with us the noblest success, or the most
glorious martyrdom. Assert your freedom. . . . Your pen . . . ought
to trace characters for a nation's perusal." Whatever the reason,
she yielded at length, and set off in July, 1812, on her disastrous
expedition to Devonshire. For a time all acted up to their high
missions; Portia (for "Elizabeth" was already sacred to Harriet's
sister), discussed "innate passions, God, Christianity, &c.,"

with Shelley, walked with him, and condescended so far as to exchange the name Portia, which Harriet did not like—"I had thought it would have been one more common and pleasing to the ear"—for Bessy. Professor Dowden gives us a singular picture of the time; Shelley and the tall dark woman, who is taken by some for a maidservant, wander on the shore together, and set bottles and chests stuffed with revolutionary pamphlets floating out to sea, uttering words of ecstatic prophecy over them. Within doors she wrote from his dictation and read as he directed. But the decline of this artificial virtue was inevitable; the women were the first to discover that the others were impostors; and soon Shelley himself veered round with childlike passion. The spiritual sister and prophetess became simply "The Brown Demon," "a woman of desperate views and dreadful passions," who must be got rid of even at the cost of a yearly allowance of a hundred pounds. It is not known whether she ever received it; but there is a very credible tradition that she recovered her senses, after her startling downfall, and lived a respectable and laborious life at Edmonton, sweetened by the reading of the poets, and the memory of her romantic indiscretions with the truest of them all.

Literary Geography[1]

THESE two books belong to what is called the "Pilgrimage" series, and before undertaking the journey it is worth considering in what spirit we do so. We are either pilgrims from sentiment, who find something stimulating to the imagination in the fact that Thackeray rang this very door bell or that Dickens shaved behind that identical window, or we are scientific in our pilgrimage and visit the country where a great novelist lived in order to see to what extent he was influenced by his surroundings. Both motives are often combined and can be legitimately satisfied; as, for instance, in the case of Scott or the Brontës, George Meredith or Thomas Hardy. Each of these novelists may be said to possess a spiritual sovereignty which no one else can dispute. They have made the country theirs because they have so interpreted it as to have given it an ineffaceable shape in our minds, so that we know certain parts of Scotland, of Yorkshire, of Surrey, and of Dorset as intimately as we know the men and women who have their dwelling there. Novelists who are thus sensitive to the inspiration of the land are alone able to describe the natives who are in some sense the creatures of the land. Scott's men and women are Scotch; Miss Brontë loves her moors so well that she can draw as no one else can the curious type of human being that they produce; and so we may say not only that novelists own a country, but that all who dwell in it are their subjects. It seems a little incongruous to talk of the Thackeray "country" or the Dickens "country" in this sense; for the word calls up a vision of woods and fields, and you may read through a great number of these masters' works without finding any reason to believe that the whole world is not paved with cobble stones. Both Thackeray and Dickens were Londoners; the country itself comes very seldom into their books, and the country man or woman—the characteristic product of the country—hardly at all. But to say that a man is a Londoner implies only that he is not

[1] *The Thackeray Country*, by Lewis Melville. *The Dickens Country*, by F. G. Kitton. *The Times Literary Supplement*, March 10, 1905.

one of the far more definite class of countrymen; it does not stamp him as belonging to any recognized type.

In the case of Thackeray any such definition is more than usually absurd; he was, as Mr Melville remarks, a cosmopolitan; with London for a basis he travelled everywhere; and it follows that the characters in his books are equally citizens of the world. "Man and not scenery," says Mr Melville, "was what he strove to portray"; and it is because he took so vast and various a subject that the only possible scene for a pilgrim in Thackeray's footsteps is the great world of London. And even in London, the scene of "Vanity Fair," of "Pendennis," of "The Newcomes," it is not easy to decide upon the exact shrine at which we are to offer incense. Thackeray did not consider the feelings of these devout worshippers, and left many of his localities vague. Whole districts rather than individual streets and houses seem to be his; and though we are told that he knew exactly where Becky and Colonel Newcome and Pendennis lived, the photographs of the authentic houses somehow leave one's imagination cold. To imprison these immortals between brick walls strikes one as an unnecessary act of violence; they have always tenanted their own houses in our brains, and we refuse to let them go elsewhere. But there can be no such risk in following Thackeray himself from one house to another; and we may perhaps find that it adds to our knowledge of him and of his books to see where he lived when he was writing them and what surroundings met his eye. But here again we must select. Charterhouse and the Temple, Jermyn-street, and Young-street, Kensington, are the genuine Thackeray country, which seems to echo not only his presence but his spirit; these are the places that he has interpreted as well as pictured. But it needs either a boundless imagination or a mind that holds sacred the boots and umbrellas of the great to follow Thackeray with un-flagging interest in his journeyings to Ireland, to America, and to all parts of the Continent; and at No. 36, Onslow-square, Brompton, the most devoted pilgrim might find it difficult to bend the knee.

We do less violence to the truth if, in our love of classification, we describe Dickens as a cockney. We might draw a very distinct line round London—even round certain districts of London—if we wished to circumscribe his kingdom. It is true that the late

Mr Kitton, who brought what we must consider a superfluous
zeal and a too minute knowledge to the task, begins his book with
two or three pictures of Portsmouth and Chatham. We are asked
to imagine the child Dickens as he looked at the stars from the
upper window of No. 18, St Mary's-place, and we are assured
that he enjoyed many a ramble with his sister and nurse in the
fields near Chatham. The imagination oppressed with these
details has to bear an altogether insupportable load before it has
followed Dickens to his last resting place. Mr Melville was wise
enough to ignore the "hundred and one places of minor importance" in writing of Thackeray and select only those that seemed
to him of primary interest—from which the reader will probably
make a further selection. But Mr Kitton, whose mind was a
unique storehouse of facts about Dickens, lets us have the full
benefit of his curiously minute scholarship. He knows not only
every house where Dickens lived, but every lodging that he took
for a month or two in the summer; he tells us how Dickens
seemed to prefer "houses having semi-circular frontages" and
describes the inns where Dickens lodged and the mugs from which
he is said to have drunk and the "stiff wooden chair" in which he
sat. A pilgrimage, if one followed this guide, would be a very
serious undertaking; and we doubt whether the pilgrim at the end
would know very much more about Dickens and his writings
than he did at the beginning. The most vivid and valuable part
of the book is that which describes the various dwelling places of
Dickens as a young man before he was famous and could afford
a "frightfully first-class family mansion," as he calls it. It was
while he lived in these dreary and dingy back streets in Camden-
town and the neighbourhood of the Debtors' Prison that Dickens
absorbed the view of life which he was afterwards to reproduce so
brilliantly. These early experiences, indeed, read like the first
sketch for David Copperfield. No one probably has ever known
his London so intimately as Dickens did, or has painted the life
of the streets with such first-hand knowledge. He was not really
happy when he was alone. He made one or two conscientious
expeditions into the country in search of local colour, but when it
had yielded the words he wanted he had no further use for it.
He spent his summer holidays at various seaside resorts, and in
London he lived in a variety of houses which leave no single

impression upon the mind. Indeed, the book is such an accumulation of detail that it is, after all, from his own writings that one must draw one's impression of the Dickens country.

And perhaps, when everything is said, this is always bound to be the case. A writer's country is a territory within his own brain; and we run the risk of disillusionment if we try to turn such phantom cities into tangible brick and mortar. We know our way there without signposts or policemen, and we can greet the passers by without need of introduction. No city indeed is so real as this that we make for ourselves and people to our liking; and to insist that it has any counterpart in the cities of the earth is to rob it of half its charm. In the same way too the great dead come to each of us in their own guise, and their image is more palpable and enduring than any shapes of flesh and blood. Of all books therefore the books that try to impress upon the mind the fact that great men were once alive because they lived in this house or in that are those that seem to have least reason for their being, for Thackeray and Dickens, having done with earthly houses, live most certainly in our brains.

Flumina Amem Silvasque[1]

IT is a proof of the snobbishness which, no doubt, veins us through that the mere thought of a literary pilgrim makes us imagine a man in an ulster looking up earnestly at a house front decorated with a tablet, and bidding his anaemic and docile brain conjure up the figure of Dr Johnson. But we must confess that we have done the same thing dozens of times, rather stealthily perhaps, and choosing a darkish day lest the ghosts of the dead should discover us, yet getting some true pleasure and profit nevertheless. We cannot get past a great writer's house without pausing to give an extra look into it and furnishing it as far as we are able with his cat and his dog, his books and his writing table. We may justify the instinct by the fact that the dominion which writers have over us is immensely personal; it is their actual voice that we hear in the rise and fall of the sentence; their shape and colour that we see in the page, so that even their old shoes have a way of being worn on this side rather than on that, which seems not gossip but revelation. We speak of writers; the military or medical or legal pilgrim may exist, but we fancy that the present of his heroes' old boots would show him nothing but leather.

Edward Thomas was as far removed from our imaginary pilgrim as well may be He had a passion for English country and a passion for English literature; and he had stored enough know-ledge of the lives of his heroes to make it natural for him to think of them when walking through their country and to speculate whether the influence of it could be traced in their writing. The objection that most writers have no particular country he met in a variety of ways, which are all excellent, and many of them illuminating, because they sprang from the prejudices and prefer-ences of a well-stocked mind. There is no need to take alarm, as we confess to have done, at finding that the counties are distributed among the poets; there is no trace whatever of the "one can imagine" and "no doubt" style of writing.

On the contrary the poets and the counties are connected on

[1] *A Literary Pilgrim in England*, by Edward Thomas. *The Times Literary Supplement*, October 11, 1917.

the most elastic and human principle; and if in the end it turns out that the poet was not born there, did not live there, or quite probably had no place at all in his mind when he wrote, his neglect is shown to be quite as characteristic as his sensibility. Blake, for instance, comes under London and the Home Counties; and it is true that, as it is necessary to live somewhere, he lived both in London and at Felpham, near Bognor. But there is no reason to think that the tree that was filled with angels was peculiar to Peckham Rye, or that the bulls that "each morning drag the sulphur Sun out of the Deep" were to be seen in the fields of Sussex. "Natural objects *always did and do* weaken, deaden, and obliterate imagination in me!" he wrote; and the statement, which might have annoyed a specialist determined to pin a poet down, starts Mr Thomas off upon a most interesting discussion of the state of mind thus revealed. After all, considering that we must live either in the country or in the town, the person who does not notice one or the other is more eccentric than the person who does. It is a fine opening into the mind of Blake.

But the poets, as Mr Thomas shows, are an extremely capricious race, and do for the most part show a bird's or butterfly's attachment to some particular locality. You will always find Shelley near the water; Wordsworth among the hills; and Meredith within sixty miles of London. Matthew Arnold, although associated with the Thames, is, as Mr Thomas points out in one of those critical passages which make his book like the talk of a very good talker, most particularly the poet of the garden and of the highly cultivated land.

I know these slopes; who knows them, if not I?

"has the effect of reducing the landscape to garden scale." There is, he points out, "a kind of allegorical thinness" about Arnold's country, "as if it were chiefly a symbol of escape from the world of 'men and towns.' " Indeed, if one takes a bird's-eye view of Arnold's poetry the background seems to consist of a moonlit lawn, with a sad but not passionate nightingale singing in a cedar tree of the sorrows of mankind. It is much less easy to reduce our vision of the landscape of Keats to something marked upon a map. We should be inclined to call him more the poet of a season than the poet of a place. Mr Thomas puts him down under London and the Home Counties because he lived there. But although he began as most writers do by describing what he saw, that was exercise work, and very soon he came to "hate descriptions." And thus he wrote some of the most beautiful descriptions in the language, for in spite of many famous and exact passages the best descriptions are the least accurate, and represent what the poet saw with his eyes shut when the landscape had melted indistinguishably into the mood. This brings us, of course, into conflict with Tennyson. The Tennysonian method of sifting words until the exact shade and shape of the flower or the cloud had its equivalent phrase has produced many wonderful examples of minute skill, much like the birds' nests and blades of grass of the pre-Raphaelite painters. Watching the dead leaves fall in autumn, we may remember that Tennyson has given precisely the phrase we want, "flying gold of the ruin'd woodlands"; but for the whole spirit of autumn we go to Keats. He has the mood and not the detail.

The most exact of poets, however, is quite capable of giving us the slip if the occasion seems to him to demand it; and as his theme is most often a moment of life or of vision, so his frozen stream, or west wind, or ruined castle is chosen for the sake of that mood and not for themselves. When that "sense of England," as Mr Thomas calls it, comes over us driving us to seek a book that expresses it, we turn to the prose writers most probably—to Borrow, Hardy, the Brontës, Gilbert White. The sense of country which both Mr Hardy and Emily Brontë possess is so remarkable that a volume might be spent in discussion of it. We should scarcely exaggerate our own belief if we said that both seem to forecast a time when character will take on a different aspect under the novelist's hand, when he will be less fearful of the charge of unreality, less careful of the twitterings and chatterings which now make our puppets so animated and for the most part so ephemeral. Through the half-shut eyes with which we visualize books as a whole, we can see great tracts of Wessex and of the Yorkshire Moors inhabited by a race of people who seem to have the rough large outline of the land itself. It is not with either of these writers a case of the word-painter's gift; for though they may have their detachable descriptions, the element we mean is rubbed deep into the texture and moulds every part. Ruskin, we observe, who did the description pure and simple to perfection, is not quoted by Mr Thomas; and the omission, which seems to us right, is a pleasant sign of the individual quality of the pilgrimage. We have seldom read a book indeed which gives a better feeling of England than this one. Never perfunctory or conventional, but always saying what strikes him as the true or interesting or characteristic thing, Mr Thomas brings the very look of the fields and roads before us; he brings the poets, too; and no one will finish the book without a sense that he knows and respects the author.

Haworth, November 1904[1]

I DO not know whether pilgrimages to the shrines of famous
men ought not to be condemned as sentimental journeys. It is
better to read Carlyle in your own study chair than to visit the
sound-proof room and pore over the manuscripts at Chelsea. I
should be inclined to set an examination on Frederick the Great
in place of entrance fee; only, in that case, the house would soon
have to be shut up. The curiosity is only legitimate when the
house of a great writer or the country in which it is set adds
something to our understanding of his books. This justification
you have for a pilgrimage to the home and country of Charlotte
Brontë and her sisters.

The *Life*, by Mrs Gaskell, gives you the impression that
Haworth and the Brontës are somehow inextricably mixed.
Haworth expresses the Brontës; the Brontës express Haworth;
they fit like a snail to its shell. How far surroundings radically
affect people's minds, it is not for me to ask: superficially, the
influence is great, but it is worth asking if the famous parsonage
had been placed in a London slum, the dens of Whitechapel
would not have had the same result as the lonely Yorkshire moors.
However, I am taking away my only excuse for visiting Haworth.
Unreasonable or not, one of the chief points of a recent visit to
Yorkshire was that an expedition to Haworth could be accomplished. The necessary arrangements were made, and we
determined to take advantage of the first day for our expedition.
A real northern snowstorm had been doing the honours of the
moors. It was rash to wait fine weather, and it was also cowardly.
I understand that the sun very seldom shone on the Brontë
family, and if we chose a really fine day we should have to make
allowance for the fact that fifty years ago there were few fine days
at Haworth, and that we were, therefore, for sake of comfort,
rubbing out half the shadows in the picture. However, it would be
interesting to see what impression Haworth could make upon the
brilliant weather of Settle. We certainly passed through a very

---

[1] *The Guardian*, December 21, 1904. The first of Virginia Woolf's essays to be
accepted for publication.

cheerful land, which might be likened to a vast wedding cake, of which the icing was slightly undulating; the earth was bridal in its virgin snow, which helped to suggest the comparison.

Keighley—pronounced Keethly—is often mentioned in the *Life*; it was the big town four miles from Haworth in which Charlotte walked to make her more important purchases—her wedding gown, perhaps, and the thin little cloth boots which we examined under glass in the Brontë Museum. It is a big manufacturing town, hard and stony, and clattering with business, in the way of these Northern towns. They make small provision for the sentimental traveller, and our only occupation was to picture the slight figure of Charlotte trotting along the streets in her thin mantle, hustled into the gutter by more burly passers-by. It was the Keighley of her day, and that was some comfort. Our excitement as we neared Haworth had in it an element of suspense that was really painful, as though we were to meet some long-separated friend, who might have changed in the interval—so clear an image of Haworth had we from print and picture. At a certain point we entered the valley, up both sides of which the village climbs, and right on the hill-top, looking down over its parish, we saw the famous oblong tower of the church. This marked the shrine at which we were to do homage.

It may have been the effect of a sympathetic imagination, but I think that there were good reasons why Haworth did certainly strike one not exactly as gloomy, but, what is worse for artistic purposes, as dingy and commonplace. The houses, built of yellow-brown stone, date from the early nineteenth century. They climb the moor step by step in little detached strips, some distance apart, so that the town instead of making one compact blot on the landscape has contrived to get a whole stretch into its clutches. There is a long line of houses up the moor-side, which clusters round the church and parsonage with a little clump of trees. At the top the interest for a Brontë lover becomes suddenly intense. The church, the parsonage, the Brontë Museum, the school where Charlotte taught, and the Bull Inn where Branwell drank are all within a stone's throw of each other. The museum is certainly rather a pallid and inanimate collection of objects. An effort ought to be made to keep things out of these mausoleums, but the choice often lies between them and destruction, so that we must be grateful for the care which has preserved much that is, under any circumstances, of deep interest. Here are many autograph letters, pencil drawings, and other documents. But the most touching case—so touching that one hardly feels reverent in one's gaze— is that which contains the little personal relics, the dresses and shoes of the dead woman. The natural fate of such things is to die before the body that wore them, and because these, trifling and transient though they are, have survived, Charlotte Brontë the woman comes to life, and one forgets the chiefly memorable fact that she was a great writer. Her shoes and her thin muslin dress have outlived her. One other object gives a thrill; the little oak stool which Emily carried with her on her solitary moorland tramps, and on which she sat, if not to write, as they say, to think what was probably better than her writing.

The church, of course, save part of the tower, is renewed since Brontë days; but that remarkable churchyard remains. The old edition of the *Life* had on its title-page a little print which struck the keynote of the book; it seemed to be all graves—gravestones stood ranked all round; you walked on a pavement lettered with dead names; the graves had solemnly invaded the garden of the parsonage itself, which was as a little oasis of life in the midst of the dead. This is no exaggeration of the artist's, as we found: the stones seem to start out of the ground at you in tall, upright lines, like an army of silent soldiers. There is no hand's breadth un- tenanted; indeed, the economy of space is somewhat irreverent. In old days a flagged path, which suggested the slabs of graves, led from the front door of the parsonage to the churchyard without interruption of wall or hedge; the garden was practically the graveyard too; the successors of the Brontës, however, wishing a little space between life and death, planted a hedge and several tall trees, which now cut off the parsonage garden completely. The house itself is precisely the same as it was in Charlotte's day, save that one new wing has been added. It is easy to shut the eye to this, and then you have the square, boxlike parsonage, built of the ugly, yellow-brown stone which they quarry from the moors behind, precisely as it was when Charlotte lived and died there. Inside, of course, the changes are many, though not such as to obscure the original shape of the rooms. There is nothing remark- able in a mid-Victorian parsonage, though tenanted by genius, and the only room which awakens curiosity is the kitchen, now used as an ante-room, in which the girls tramped as they conceived their work. One other spot has a certain grim interest—the oblong recess beside the staircase into which Emily drove her bulldog during the famous fight, and pinned him while she pommelled him. It is otherwise a little sparse parsonage, much like others of its kind. It was due to the courtesy of the present incumbent that we were allowed to inspect it; in his place I should often feel inclined to exorcise the three famous ghosts.

One thing only remained: the church in which Charlotte worshipped, was married, and lies buried. The circumference of her life was very narrow. Here, though much is altered, a few things remain to tell of her. The slab which bears the names of the succession of children and of their parents—their births and deaths—strikes the eye first. Name follows name; at very short intervals they died—Maria the mother, Maria the daughter, Elizabeth, Branwell, Emily, Anne, Charlotte, and lastly the old father, who outlived them all. Emily was only thirty years old, and Charlotte but nine years older. "The sting of death is sin, and the strength of sin is the law, but thanks be to God which giveth us the victory through our Lord Jesus Christ." That is the inscription which has been placed beneath their names, and with reason; for however harsh the struggle, Emily, and Charlotte above all, fought to victory.

PART TWO

MAINLY PORTRAITS

The Girlhood of Queen Elizabeth[1]

THERE is a memorable passage at the end of Froude's History, in which, before summing up the qualities of the great Queen and delivering judgment, he bids us consider what it is to be a Sovereign. Their mean thoughts "rise like accusing spirits . . . out of the private drawers of statesmen's cabinets.' They may not stand aside, but must always act. Their duties cling to them as their shadows. Their words and deeds live after them, and must bear a scrutiny to which few could look forward without dismay. Having pronounced this warning, he goes on to strip Elizabeth of every virtue that was claimed for her, save the virtue of her supreme bravery. In some degree such seems to be the fate of the majority of rulers of whom we can form a judgment. Human nature when set upon a throne seems unable to sustain the enormous enlargement. The very early kings alone, in whom courage was the essential virtue, are dubbed "the Good." The later ones, grown subtle, are deformed by vice, stupidity, or bigotry. And yet, partly because it is extraordinary, the spectacle of Royalty never fails to surprise us. To see the pageant is strange enough, but it is far stranger to look into the mind of one of the great actors themselves and to watch the normal human being struggling, an ant laden with a pebble, beneath the superhuman burden laid upon it by its fellows. The difficulty of framing an opinion arises from the necessity that such a person is under of conforming to an unnatural standard, so that it is only at rare moments that one can see how he behaves as an individual. For the rest, one must use one's imagination. Mr Rait, in introducing the present volume of Queen Elizabeth's private letters, enumerates other difficulties that must beset the student of early documents. With their formalities and encumbrances, the very language they write is different from ours; they have a thousand inducements to tell lies, nor can they always tell the truth if they wish it. But, allowing for all obstacles, "it remains true," he proceeds, "that in such letters as are contained in this book we have the very marrow of history." By the very marrow in this

[1] By Frank A. Mumby. *The Times Literary Supplement*, December 30, 1909.

case we mean the temperament of the woman who ruled England from the time she was twenty-five, and whose whims and qualities lay at the centre of the vast expansion of the Elizabethan age. If we can arrive at some knowledge of her nature and of the circumstances that formed it, we shall read our history with a greater understanding; and Mr Mumby's collection gives us a splendid chance at least, by laying the original matter out of which history is fashioned before us. He has restricted himself to supplying the necessary links as briefly and as lucidly as possible.

The story from the first is strange and violent. Her birth made enemies of her own kinsmen, for on that account her half-sister was degraded of her title and shorn of her household. Then three years later Elizabeth was deposed in her turn, without a mother, and left in the hands of a governess who confessed that she did not know what to do with her. The Princess, she wrote, had scarcely any clothes, and it was not good for a child of three who had "great pain with her great teeth and they come very slowly forth" to sup every day at the board of Estate. "For there she shall see divers meats, and fruits, and wine, which it would be hard for me to restrain her Grace from." It was the third stepmother, Catherine Parr, who first noticed her, and encouraged her to learn. Elizabeth, aged 11, recognizing her "fervent zeal . . . towards all goodly learning," dedicated to her a translation which she had made of "The Mirror, or Glass, of the sinful soul." Making allowance for the constraint put upon her, one may infer that Elizabeth was a very precocious and somewhat priggish child, whose precocity was sometimes disagreeable. At the age of fourteen she was ripe for a serious flirtation with her step-mother's husband, Thomas Seymour, and was so outspoken in this precocious love-making as to bring all those concerned into trouble and herself, finally, to disgrace. Yet, though Elizabeth was forward enough according to her governess, it seems pitiable that a girl of that age should have her feelings made the subject of inquisition by a council of noblemen. She subdued her passions, and in the retreat at Hatfield vanity drove her to excel in the only direction now open to her. Grave scholars like William Grindal and Roger Ascham had been her tutors from the first, and had predicted great things of "that noble imp." At the end of her sixteenth year Ascham reckoned up her accomplishments, and stated that she could speak French and Italian like English; Latin and Greek she could speak with fluency; she had read some of Cicero, Livy and Sophocles; she liked a style that was "chaste in its propriety and beautiful in perspicuity," but "greatly admired metaphors"; at that age (her tutor says) she preferred simple dress to "show and splendour." This was one stage in her development. Such an educational one was enough to isolate her from her sex, save for the half-dozen noble ladies, the Greys and the Cecils, who were also prodigies.

Then, when Mary came to the throne she had to summon all her ability and the composure which learning gives in order to devise a policy and steer "like a ship in tempestuous weather" between the two parties. The Protestant party endangered her by their favouritism and made her the Queen's most serious rival. Every movement was watched; after Wyatt's conspiracy the Queen's nerve was so much shaken that she dared the people's rage and sent Elizabeth to the Tower. The three years that followed were sufficient to give her the habit of telling lies all her life. But the memory of her unhappiness was bitter enough also to rouse in her the one "sustained and generous feeling" of her life; she showed, Mr Froude thinks, true pity for the Queen of Scots when, years afterwards, she too lay in prison. To be "cold and unemotional," the faults with which Elizabeth is oftenest charged, was the natural refuge for a woman of powerful intellect in the midst of spies. To think perpetually and never to act without a motive was the one safe policy. But it makes it unusually difficult to arrive at her genuine feeling. Thus, some one wishing to endow the magnificent young woman with human tenderness suggests that she was really fond of children, because when she walked in the Tower Garden she liked to play with a child of four who gave her flowers. Yet it was at once suspected that her motive was not tender after all, but that letters from Courtenay lay hid among the leaves. Perhaps it is a trifle, yet it is our certain knowledge of the incidents of life that inspires our conception of character, for there is much less individuality in the way great acts are done. It would be interesting to know how far we still make use of tradition in giving colour to the great figures of the past when we are without details. But there are more definite statements about her appearance: she was tall, with a swarthy skin, and fine eyes—

"above all a beautiful hand, of which she makes display." She liked to have it said that she resembled her father, for "she prides herself on her father and glories in him." In manner it is probable that she was overbearing and argumentative, insisting, "from vanity," in talking Italian to Italians, and because she spoke it better than Mary.

Thus, at the age of twenty-three she was a remarkable personage, impressing the Venetian Ambassador by her intellect and by her "astute and judicious" behaviour, and a perpetual menace to her sister. Some of the most interesting letters in the collection are the Bedingfeld papers concerning her imprisonment at Woodstock, which Froude, it seems, had never read. They show that Sir Henry Bedingfeld, far from ill-treating her as is commonly said, very much disliked his task and did what he could to help her. But Elizabeth was a formidable prisoner, very observant, silent if crossed, capable of a "most unpleasant" manner, and so Royal in her demeanour that it seemed impertinent to restrain her. There was nothing for her to do save to embroider the covers of a Bible and scratch plaintive verses on the window panes; she asked for books, a Cicero and an English Bible; she wanted to walk freely and demanded to write her complaints to the Council. Sir Henry had to check her in every way; he was made uneasy if a servant bringing presents of "freshwater fish . . . and two dead pheasant cocks" stayed too long gossiping with the servants. But such was the tone in which she issued "an importunate command" that in spite of all injunctions Sir Henry not only gave her pen and paper, but wrote at her dictation, although he spelt very badly, the Princess "saying that she never wrote to your Lordships but by a secretary." He pointed out the inconveniences of Woodstock as a residence in winter—how the wind and rain would come through the chinks, and how the villagers grumbled already at the soldiers who were quartered upon them. It is clear that he only wished to be rid of her.

When Mary died three years later no more seasoned woman of her age could be found in Europe than Elizabeth. She had known love, and seen death very close; she had learnt to suspect almost every one, and to let men struggle and plot before her without taking part. Her intellect was trained to wrestle with intricate arguments and to delight in flourishes of ornament. Her poverty had taught her to hoard money and to hint for gifts. In short, her education and her adventures had equipped her with a complete armour of cold and harsh feelings, under the control of a perfectly dauntless bravery. Thus, splendid and inscrutable, she rode through London on the day of her Coronation; arches, pyramids, and fountains stood in her way, from which boys sang greeting; a fine snow kept falling over her, but the gems and the golden collars shone clearly through the whiteness.

The Diary of a Lady in Waiting[1]

LADY CHARLOTTE BURY was the daughter of the fifth Duke of Argyll, and her beauty and her wit made her at once the talk of London when she came up to town in the last years of the eighteenth century. But her head was full of romance, and she preferred a marriage with her kinsman, Jack Campbell, who was handsome, "a great fellow," but badly off, to an alliance with some rich nobleman in England. They lived in Edinburgh for the most part, and Lady Charlotte was queen of the literary society there, scribbling her own verses, and receiving the compliments of Walter Scott, C. K. Sharpe, and Monk Lewis. Their circumstances, however, were never easy; nine children were born to them, and, when she was thirty-four, her husband died, and left her to bring them up as she might. The natural profession, for a woman with her connexions, was about the Court; and it is characteristic of her that she sought service with the Princess of Wales, with whom she had long sympathized, although the Princess was then in an uncomfortable situation, separated from her husband and estranged from the Royal family. At the same time Lady Charlotte began to keep a diary, and it is this work which is now reprinted, with the omission of certain unnecessary parts, and the addition of a great number of names which the discretion of previous editors thought fit to conceal beneath a dash. As it is, the size of the volumes is sufficiently formidable, and were it not for the watery Georgian atmosphere which they preserve we might wish that Lady Charlotte's sentiments had been curtailed. "Those evanescent emanations of spirit which are only cognisable to the very few, and which thrive not unless under the influence of congenial feelings" have fallen, to continue her metaphor, upon a barren soil, and are withered by the cold blight of criticism.

The Princess of Wales's court, if it has a right to the name, was a comfortless and incongruous place. She kept up all the forms of royalty at Kensington and Blackheath, but she was constantly

1 By Lady Charlotte Bury, edited by A. Francis Steuart. *The Times Literary Supplement*, July 23, 1908.

meeting with some insolence from the great nobles, and flouting them with an irresponsible outburst of wild spirits. She would walk solemnly with her ladies in Kensington-gardens and suddenly "bolt out at one of the smaller gates and walk all over Bayswater and along the Paddington Canal," asking at every door whether there were any houses to be let, and chuckling at her own ingenuity. Some respectable people stood by her, and gave her parties the semblance of dignity, but as soon as these gentlemen left she "felt a weight" off her. "She calls it *dull*" observes Lady Charlotte, or, in her own phrase, "Mine Gott! Dat is de dullest person Gott Almighty ever did born!" "and true enough," the moralist proceeds, "*good* society is often dull." Brougham and Whitbread were always coming with documents for her to sign, and good advice for her to follow. There was perpetual talk of policy, whether she should go to the opera, whether she should accept the Regent's terms, or hold out for her own rights; she was always acting on the spur of the moment, and upsetting calculations that were not, as Lady Charlotte guessed, entirely disinterested. They go over the whole story of her wrongs again and again, at those dreary dinner parties; and when that subject becomes intolerable, she chatters about books, or talks scandal, wishes people dead, or sings—"squall—squall—squall"—with the Sapios, for she loved to imagine herself the centre of a brilliant society. Lady Charlotte had much to deplore from the first, although her kind and sentimental heart was constantly touched by the poor lady's miseries, the cause, she guessed, of much of her levity; and she had sense enough to see that a little good management at this crisis might have invaluable results. The Princess occasionally would act with the utmost dignity, or endure some insult without a word, so that Lady Charlotte herself felt humiliated. A friend reported on one occasion that the Tsar of Russia meant to call upon her, an honour for which she said she would give both her ears, though they are "very ugly." She dressed in delight, and waited all the afternoon, with Lady Charlotte beside her, till it was seven o'clock. For four hours they sat opposite each other keeping up a miserable small talk; and, though the Tsar never came, the Princess would not own that she was disappointed. It was not wonderful, perhaps, that she should relapse after these fruitless efforts into wilder dissipation than ever. When there was no company she would sit over the fire after dinner modelling a little figure of her husband in wax, transfixing it with a pin, and holding it over the flames so that it melted away. Was one to laugh, or was it not unspeakably tragic? Sometimes, says Lady Charlotte, she had the feeling of one who humours a mad woman.

But advice and sentiment had no power to stay the course of the uneasy woman; she was too sensitive to ignore the slights which people who, as she observed, would eat her food thought fit to put upon her, and she was foolish enough to seek redress by making friends of her inferiors. The description which Lady Charlotte gives of "that incongruous piece of patchwork," the villa at Blackheath—"It is all glitter and glare and trick; everything is tinsel and trumpery about it; it is altogether like a bad dream"—represents very well the impression which her life makes upon us; it is like Cremorne or Vauxhall by daylight, when the lamps are out, and the pale minarets and pagodas are exposed to the sun, with all their stains and frivolities and their midnight grimace. Lady Charlotte's proprieties were constantly shocked; and, as she could in no way prevent the disaster, she left her mistress in 1814, without offending her, in order, she pretended, to take her children to Geneva. She was little more, however, than a correct and kindly woman, with a diffuse taste for sentiment of all kinds, whether in people, or art, or letters, and, when she had no point to concentrate her mind upon, her observations become insipid. The Princess of Wales, vulgar and flighty as she was, had the quality of making people interested in her, not for her fate alone, but because she had lively feelings and expressed them nakedly. Lady Charlotte when set adrift upon the Continent and exposed now to a picture, now to a church, now to the historical associations of Versailles, floats, with all her sails spread, upon a leaden sea. "I gazed once more at the undying beauties of the immortal Venus. I felt a spark of inspiration emanate from the divine Apollo. . . . Time and circumstance tore me away." She came at length to Geneva, and settled herself in the midst of the "literary and scientific republic," smiling and sighing when she remembered the "great stage of life" upon which she had acted so lately. But she was not to philosophize for long. The rumour spread that the Princess, with a motley court, was upon them, and some of the English ladies hastily made up a ball in her honour. With what an expression Lady Charlotte gazed upon the figure of her late mistress, dressed *"en Venus,"* waltzing all night long, we can imagine; it is a delightful picture. "I was unfeignedly grieved . . . and thought it would be my own fault if she caught me again in a hurry." But Lady Charlotte was too good-natured to desert any one in difficulties; she had a family to support; and after a few months she joined the Princess at Genoa as her lady in waiting. She found that Mr Craven and Mr Gell, her respectable English friends, had left her, and her own position was more odious than ever. Bergami, the tall Italian courier, was now the favourite, and the Princess drove about in a carriage shaped like a sea-shell, lined with blue velvet and drawn by piebald ponies. She protested that she meant to travel on and on, to visit Greece, and never to return to England. Lady Charlotte had to shut both eyes and ears; but her charity was at length exhausted, and she finally left the Princess in 1815, the last of the English courtiers to stay with her. Lady Charlotte went to Rome, and the Princess wandered about Italy, adding doubtful countesses "of decayed nobility" to her train, and abbés who could speak forty-four different languages, both living and dead, in perfection—so "they assure me." The last sight of her was reported by an English lady living at Florence, who came upon a procession of carriages at some little country village, drawn by the piebald horses, and occupied by a "rabble rout" of low-looking men and women, dressed like "itinerant show players," of all nationalities; among them was "one fat woman," who was said to be the Princess of Wales. Most readers will be tempted to skip the reflections which Lady Charlotte has to record about Rome, for she echoed the taste of her time, and it is not ours; but she corresponded still with the Princess and received from her a number of those odd ungrammatical letters, where all the t's are d's, which still sound so lively, so absurd, and so unhappy.

All de fine English folk leave me [she writes]. I not send them away, though, bye the bye, some of dem not behave as civil as I could like.

. . . I detest Rome. It is the burial-place of departed grandeur. It is very well to see it once, like a raree show . . . I shall die of

de blue devils, as you English call it. . . . Very often we cook
our own dinner! What voud de English people say if dey heard
dat? Oh, fie! Princess of Wales."

Lady Charlotte returned to London in 1819, in order to introduce
an orphan niece to the world. She was forty-four, and the diary,
though it is still as profuse as ever, describes merely the respectable
life of a lady living in good society, with the remains of beauty,
and many memories of happier days. Major Denham described
the interior of Africa; Tom Moore sang "The Parting of the
Ships," "each to sail over the lonely ocean! How very true it is to
nature! How thrilling to those who have witnessed the scene!"
Once she met Mrs Mee, the miniature painter, and "another
eccentric little artist, by name Blake," who talked to her about
his painting, and seemed to her full of imagination and genius.
She saw Sir Thomas Lawrence sneer as he watched them. But
the diary ends, fitly enough, with the death of Queen Caroline a
few days after she had knocked at the door of Westminster Abbey
in vain. Many people felt that there was an end to an awkward
situation; Lady Charlotte, as one might expect, had a final word
of regret for the poor woman, and in this case, at least, we may
believe that she meant it, for she had been a good friend.

Queen Adelaide[1]

"I REQUEST not to be dissected nor embalmed, and desire to give as little trouble as possible" wrote Queen Adelaide characteristically when she was considering the disposition of her dead body; and all the industry of Miss Sandars has not been able to violate the privacy of her spirit. For if Queen Anne is dead, we must invent some more absolute form of annihilation for Queen Adelaide. We cannot boldly affirm, after reading 289 pages about her, that she never existed; but we feel much as though we had been to visit some one in a large handsome house, and after wandering through all the state rooms and up the grand staircase and through the attics had heard only the swishing of a skirt and once—that was the most vivid moment of all—caught a glimpse of a "wonderful red and grey parrot," but never met the owner of the house, or heard more than the murmur of her voice in the next room. It is not Miss Sandars's fault. She has done her best to produce the Queen for us, and, as the Queen is dumb, has imagined what her feelings must have been on several very important occasions, as for example when she landed in England to marry a husband she had never seen.

> The sea was rough . . . and the Princess Adelaide's spirits were doubtless at a low ebb. . . . Nothing is reported of the interview between him and his future bride, and we can only guess the feelings of the Princess when, at the end of what must have been for one of her delicate physique a most exhausting fortnight, she was introduced to her middle-aged, garrulous, unpolished bridegroom. We may guess, however, that even were her agitation great, nothing of it appeared on the surface. Her manners were good, she was possessed of much reticence and self-control, and she doubtless behaved suitably and with the sense of propriety natural to her.

That is the style of the volume. We are made to feel that it is not permitted in the case of a great lady so recently dead to impute to her any feelings save those that she might show to the public

[1] *The Life and Times of Queen Adelaide*, by Mary F. Sandars. *The Times Literary Supplement*, January 13, 1916.

through the windows of her crystal coach on her way down the Mall when, although in constant fear of assassination, she made a point of sitting rather forward and very upright. She was always on her guard with the English, who disliked her, and she never lost the traces of her long girlhood in the pious, secluded Court of Meiningen, where a paternal Government issued decrees about coffins, and begging, and dancing on Sundays and wrestled, unsuccessfully it appears, with the problem of geese who stray from the flock. The Princess was well suited to pet and bully a state of devoted retainers, but only the arbitrary exigencies of politics could have forced a woman so trained to become the bride of William the Fourth, with his large family of illegitimate children, and given her the most corrupt Court and the least reputable Royal Family in Europe for her circle and surroundings.

As fate would have it, she became Queen Consort when England was struggling for reform. The mere thought of reform, were it merely the introduction of gas in a palace, affected Queen Adelaide like an explosion of gunpowder, and suggested immediate death on a scaffold. She would accept William and George the Fourth, and a large impertinent family of Fitz-Clarences with angelical sweetness and submission, as part of the lot of womanhood, but the idea of giving power to the people stiffened her into something like self-assertion. All the influence she had she brought to bear on the King against the Reform Bill, and drew on herself such hatred from the people that William paced the room anxiously if she were late home from the opera, and the newspapers bespattered her with names which nowadays would not be applied to any woman in the land.

But the Reform Bill passed and there was no martyrdom for Adelaide. Her head, that is, remained on her shoulders; but the discomforts of her lot surely amount in sum of agony to a beheading if it were possible to extract them and compute them. Doubtless, to borrow a very useful phrase from Miss Sandars, the manners of the Royal Family afflicted her considerably. They remind us of those astounding scenes in Dickens and George Eliot when uncles and aunts behave in such a manner at the dinner table that we are inclined to think it is put on for the reader's benefit; but William the Fourth had exactly the same method. At a birthday dinner he took the occasion to jump up and abuse the Duchess of Kent, who was sitting next to him:—"I have no hesitation in saying that I have been insulted—grossly and continually insulted—by that person now near me" upon which the Princess Victoria burst into tears, and the Duchess ordered her carriage. At another dinner party, to annoy the same lady's brother, he pretended to be deaf; and we have an appalling picture of the scene after dinner, when the chairs were placed in such a way that conversation was impossible, and the only diversion apparently for that silent company was to listen to the snores of the Duke of Somerset happily sleeping behind a pillar. But the domestic evenings of calm were no less trying, according to poor Lady Grey, who hoped that she might never see a mahogany table again after sitting for two evenings round the one at Windsor, while the Queen netted a purse, and the King slept, "occasionally waking for the purpose of saying, 'Exactly so, Ma'am' and then sleeping again." When he kept awake for any length of time, the King would pull out a "curiosity" for the company to look at, and then wander about signing papers, which a Princess blotted for him, while the Queen beckoned a small society of intimate friends into a corner and handed round her sketches. The nearest approach to the hypnotised boredom of that assembly is to imagine thirty people gathered nightly in a dentist's waiting room, with its round tables, and albums, its horsehair chairs, and diamond spotted carpet, and without even the excitement of the anticipated summons. This dreary scene dragged on until 1837, when the Queen found herself a widow, with an income of £100,000 a year. But her perpetual colds in the head and other indispositions had now developed into chronic ill health, which made her "rather fidgety about due attention being shown her," and her chief interest seems to have lain in seeking health, in suppressing dissent and providing Colonial Bishops, in smiling graciously upon assembled multitudes and, let us hope, in admiring the gifts and cherishing the plumage of that remarkable bird, the red and grey parrot.

Elizabeth Lady Holland[1]

TWO handsome volumes, with large print and wide margins, portraits, annotations, and introduction, give us after a lapse of almost a century the diary which Lady Holland kept from the year 1791 to the year 1811. At the same time Mr Lloyd Sanders publishes "The Holland House Circle," a thick volume with many chapters. Each chapter represents a different group of men and women, of all ranks and callings, and is distinguished generally by one important name. But the chief interest of these groups lies in the fact that they were once dispersed about the great drawing-rooms at Holland House, and that the people composing them had been picked out from the tumult of London, and drawn to this one spot by the power of Lady Holland and her husband. Indeed, so much time has passed that it begins to seem strange to us that the imperious-looking lady who sits with her foot displayed in Leslie's picture, as though subjects bowed to her throne, should once have gone upstairs to her room, taken out a sheet of paper, and written down what she thought of the scene. We are told continually how she snubbed people, how she dropped her fan, how she sat at the head of her table and listened to the cleverest talk in England until she was bored, and cried out: "Enough of this, Macaulay!" But it is hard to remember that she passed through many more experiences than usually fall to the share of women, so that when she sat at her table she may have been thinking of different scenes and marvelling at the accidents that had brought her to this position. Until Lord Ilchester published her diaries there was only material for such a book as that by Mr Lloyd Sanders; we only knew what impression she had made on other people, and had to guess what she had been feeling herself. She was the daughter of a wealthy gentleman of Jamaica, Richard Vassall, and he married her to Sir Godfrey Webster, of Battle Abbey, when she was but fifteen. By her own account she had run wild, picked up her learning where she might, and come by her views without help from anyone else. It was not from lack

[1] *The Journal of Elizabeth Lady Holland*, edited by the Earl of Ilchester, two vols. and *The Holland House Circle* by Lloyd Sanders. *The Cornhill Magazine*, December, 1908.

of care on her parents' part; they were too fond of her to tame her; and it was quite consistent with their affection that when they saw her grown a fine girl with a proud spirit they should think that she deserved to marry. A baronet who was almost twenty-three years her elder, who owned a country seat, was Member of Parliament, and was "immensely popular in the county, perhaps partly on account of his liberality and extravagance," must have appeared to them mainly in the light of a fine career for their daughter; there could be no question of love. At the time of their marriage Sir Godfrey lived in a small house close to the Abbey; the building itself was tenanted by his aunt. One may gather something of young Lady Webster's temper from the question which she used to send across to the Abbey in the mornings: "If the old hag was dead yet." The days in the little Sussex village were dreary enough, for Elizabeth amused herself by rambling over the great house, which had fallen into ruins, and rattling chains, like a naughty child, to frighten her aunt. Her husband was busy with local affairs, and, though he had some of the simple tastes of a country gentleman, was not a husband whom a clever young woman could ignore; he was not merely rough, but his temper was violent; he gambled, and he sank into fits of depression. From all these circumstances Lady Webster conceived such a picture of life in the country that she always shuddered at the thought of it afterwards, and wrote, on leaving a country house, that she felt as though she had "escaped from some misfortune." But even as a girl it was not her way to suffer when anything could be done by protesting. She worried her husband with her restlessness until he consented to travel. One must not deny that he made some effort to see her point of view, and had enough affection to try to satisfy her, for to travel in those days of coaches and to leave his own corner of Sussex must have been a genuine hardship for an important man. Lady Webster, at all events, had her way, and it is likely that she gave her husband fewer thanks for the sacrifice than he deserved. They set off for Italy in 1791, and it was then, being twenty years of age, that Lady Webster began to keep a diary. An English traveller in the eighteenth century could not profit completely by the experience unless he wrote down what he had seen and reflected; something was always left over at the end of the day which had to be disposed of thus, and Lady Webster began her diary from such an impulse. It is written to propitiate her own eye when she reads it later in Sussex; to assure her that she was doing her duty with all her faculties, and that she was going about the world as a sensible young Englishwoman, much like other people. But one imagines that she would never feel on easy terms with this version of herself, and would turn to the pages more and more for a date or a fact, and would soon dissociate herself entirely from her reflections. Her case differs a little, however, from the usual one. From her earliest youth Lady Webster seems to have had a quality which saved her diary from the violent fate of diaries, and spared the writer her blushes; she could be as impersonal as a boy of ten and as intelligent as a politician. How far she really cared to know that flax is grown by the inhabitants of Kempten, and that they must consume their produce themselves, "for there are no navigable rivers," one cannot tell; but she thought it worth while to observe the fact, and proceeded quite naturally to moralise "perhaps they are happier without facility of intercourse," for commerce breeds luxury, and luxury leads to a love of gain, and thus "simplicity of manners" is destroyed, which the moralist felt to be a pity. What strange conversations and what gloomy silences there must have been in the post-chaise! The young lady was indefatigable, and honestly scorned her husband because he had no enthusiasms and no theories.

When they got to Rome the situation was even worse. Lady Webster was beginning to be aware of the fact that she was a remarkable young woman, and all the masterpieces of the world were here to prove it. She set out directly upon her "course of *virtu*," tramped through galleries, craned her neck back, looked intently where "old Morrison" bade her look, and wrote stiff sentences of admiration in her diary. When her husband came with her he either hurried her along, so that she could not see the pictures, or flew into such a passion that she could not distinguish them. The pictures, it is clear, threw a disastrous light upon Sir Godfrey. At Rome, too, there were sympathetic married ladies who assured Elizabeth that her husband was a monster, and encouraged her to see herself in a tragic light. She sobbed herself sick, reflected that human miseries must have an end, and pitied herself for thinking so. But there is no doubt that she was unhappy, however one may apportion the blame; for one must pity any young woman of twenty-two who leans out of her window at night, snuffs the air, sees water gleaming, and feels a strange stir in her spirit, and yet must write a few days later that she is now able to laugh at her husband's menaces, although they used to terrify her. It is natural to dread one's own faults, and to feel a peculiar dislike for the circumstances that develop them, for they make you ignoble in your own eyes; and the strain of bitterness which we trace in Lady Webster's diaries points to the presence of this discomfort. She knew that she was disposed to be hard, and she resented treatment which drove her to it, for she was a proud woman, and would have liked to admire herself unreservedly. In Italy, too, she felt often what she had seldom felt in England: hours of confused happiness in which the land was fair and she was young, and wonderful capacities stirred within her. She could not soothe such ecstasies with any of her "cold maxims of solitary comfort," but admitted the thought of "another" for her "heart to open itself into." Directly that other had shown what he could do in relieving her she dismissed him in agitation, comforting herself with the reflection that there was a "want of passion" in her nature which would save her from many disasters. "But what will be my resource if both head and heart accord in their choice?" Her honesty drove her to ask herself that question, but it is evident that it alarmed her still as much as it excited her.

It was in Florence, not a year after the words were written, that she met Lord Holland for the first time. He was a young man of twenty-one, just returning from his travels in Spain. Her first impression is as direct as usual: "Lord H. is not in the least handsome." She notes his "pleasingness of manner and liveliness of conversation"; but it was the "complex disorder" in his left leg "called an ossification of the muscles," that interested her most, for, like other practical women, she had a great curiosity about physical disease and loved the society of doctors. She repeats their phrases as though she flattered herself that they meant more to her than to most people. One cannot trace the friendship accurately, for it was not the purpose of her diary to follow her feelings closely, or indeed to record them at all, except to sum them up now and then in a businesslike way, as though she made a note in shorthand for future use. But Lord Holland became one of

that singular company of English people, travelling in Italy in the
last years of the eighteenth century, whom we come upon later in
the first years of the nineteenth when we read the story of Shelley,
Byron, and Trelawny. They went about together, like adventurers
in a strange land, sharing carriages and admiring statues, had their
own little society in Florence and Rome, and were allied generally
by birth and wealth and the peculiarity of their taste for the fine
arts. Sir Godfrey (it is no wonder) grew restive, and was impatient
to put an end to this aimless wandering with a family of small
children in a land of foreigners, among pictures and ruins which
bored him acutely. One entry, made at Rome, shows us what was
going on in the spring of 1794: "Almost the whole of our
Neapolitan set was there . . . we all made an excursion to Tivoli.
I conveyed Lord Holland, Mr Marsh and Beauclerk. . . . We got
back late at night. . . . In the course of our evenings Lord H.
resolved to make me admire a poet . . . Cowper. My evenings were
agreeable. . . . A sharp fit of gout, brought on by drinking Orvieto
wine did not increase the good temper of (my husband)." One of
the attractive features of those early Italian travels is the leisure
that people had, and the instinct, natural in a beautiful land far
from all duties, which made them fill it with long hours of aimless
reading. Lady Webster says of herself that she "devoured books,"
histories, philosophies, serious books for the most part, to increase
her knowledge. But Lord Holland made her read poetry; he read
Pope's "Iliad" aloud, besides a translation of Herodotus, "a good
deal of Bayle and a great variety of English poetry." Her head was
conquered, and that, in Lady Webster's case, was the only way
to her heart. Sir Godfrey left her alone in Italy for months together; finally, in May 1795, he returned to England without her.
The diary is still as sensible as ever; one might imagine her a cultivated British matron with all the natural supports. But, remembering that she had now determined to defy the law and to honour
her own passion, there is something more highly strung than usual
in the record of her days. She never repents, or analyses her conduct; her diary is still occupied with Correggio and the Medici
family and the ruts in the roads. She drove about Italy with her
own retinue, spending a few days in one place, a week in another,
and settling in Florence for the winter. Lord Holland's name occurs
again and again, and always as naturally as another's. But there

is a freedom in her manner, a kind of pride in her happiness, which seems to show that she was perfectly confident of her own morality. In April, Lord Holland and Lady Webster travelled back to England together; Sir Godfrey divorced his wife in July 1797, and in the same month she became Lady Holland. Something remarkable might have been expected from such a marriage, for the feeling between a husband and wife who have won each other by such means will not be conventional or easy to explain. One does not know, for instance, how far Lady Holland was led to live the life she did from a sense of gratitude to her husband, and one suspects that Lord Holland was tender and considerate beyond what was natural to him because his wife had made an immense sacrifice on his behalf. He saw, what other people did not see, that she was sometimes made to suffer. One can be sure at least that the oddities were only superficial, and that Lord and Lady Holland, grown old and sedate, never forgot that they had once been in league together against the world, or saw each other without a certain thrill. "Oh, my beloved friend," exclaimed Lady Holland, "how hast thou, by becoming mine, endeared the everyday occurrences of life!"

> *I loved you much at twenty-four;*
> *I love you better at three-score*

was, so Lord Holland wrote when they had been married for thirty-four years, the

> *One truth which, be it verse or prose,*
> *From my heart's heart sincerely flows.*

If that is so, we must admire them both the more for it, remembering what a reputation Lady Holland won for herself in those years, and how difficult she must have been to live with.

She may well have taken possession of Holland House with a vow to repay herself for wasted time and a determination to make the best of herself and of other people at last. She was determined also to serve Lord Holland in his career; and those unhappy years when she had roamed about the Continent, making her sensible observations, had taught her, at least, habits that were useful to her now, "to talk the talk of men" and to feel keenly the life in people round her. The house at once, with such a mistress, came to have a character of its own. But who shall say why it is that people agree to meet in one spot, or what qualities go to make a *salon*? In this case the reason why they came seems to have been largely because Lady Holland wished them to come. The presence of someone with a purpose gives shape to shapeless gatherings of people; they take on a character when they meet which serves ever after to stamp the hours so spent. Lady Holland was young and handsome; her past life had given her a decision and a fearlessness which made her go further in one interview than other women in a hundred. She had read a great deal of robust English fiction, histories and travels, Juvenal in a translation, Montaigne and Voltaire and La Rochefoucauld in the French. "I have no prejudices to combat with," she wrote; so that the freest thinker could speak his mind in her presence. The reputation of this brilliant and outspoken young woman spread quickly among the politicians, and they came in numbers to dine or sleep or even to watch her dress in the morning. Perhaps they laughed when they discussed her afterwards, but she carried her main point triumphantly—that they should come to see her. Two years after her marriage she notes: "Today I had fifty visitors." Her diary becomes a memorandum book of anecdotes and political news; and it is very seldom that she raises her eyes for a moment to consider what it is all about. But at one point she gives us a clue, and observes that although she cares for her old friends best she seeks new acquaintances "with avidity," because "mixing with a variety of people is an advantage to Lord H." One must live with one's kind and know them, or "the mind becomes narrowed to the standard of your own set," as the life of Canning had shown her. There was so much good sense always in what Lady Holland said that it was difficult to protest if her actions, in their excessive vigour, became dangerous. She took up politics for Lord Holland's sake, with the same determination, and became before long a far greater enthusiast than he was; but, again, she was able and broadminded. Such was her success, indeed, that it can be said by a student of the time[1]—nearly a hundred years after it has all faded away—"Holland House was a political council chamber . . . and the value of such a centre to a party under exclusively aristocratic

[1] Mr Lloyd Sanders.

leadership was almost incalculable." But, however keen she became as a politician, we must not pretend that she inspired Ministers, or was the secret author of policies that have changed the world. Her success was of a different nature; for it is possible even now, with her diaries before us, to reconstruct something of her character and to see how, in the course of years, it told upon that portion of the world which came in contact with it.

When we think of her we do not remember witty things that she said; we remember a long series of scenes in which she shows herself insolent, or masterful, or whimsical with the whimsicality of a spoilt great lady who confounds all the conventions as it pleases her. But there is some quality in a scene like the following, trivial as it is, which makes you realise at once the effect of her presence in the room, her way of looking at you, her attitude even, and her tap with her fan. Macaulay describes a breakfast party. "Lady Holland told us her dreams; how she had dreamed that a mad dog bit her foot, and how she set off to Brodie, and lost her way in St. Martin's Lane, and could not find him. She hoped, she said, the dream would not come true." Lady Holland had her superstitions. We trace it again in her words to Moore, "This will be a dull book of yours, this 'Sheridan,' I fear"; or at dinner to her dependant, Mr Allen, "Mr Allen, there is not enough turtle soup for you. You must take gravy soup or none." We seem to feel, however dimly, the presence of someone who is large and emphatic, who shows us fearlessly her peculiarities because she does not mind what we think of them, and who has, however peremptory and unsympathetic she may be, an extraordinary force of character. She makes certain things in the world stand up boldly all round her; she calls out certain qualities in other people. While she is there, it is her world; and all the things in the room, the ornaments, the scents, the books that lie on the table, are hers and express her. It is less obvious, but we expect that the whole of the strange society which met round her board owed its flavour to Lady Holland's freaks and passions. It is less obvious, because Lady Holland is far from eccentric in her journal, and adopts more and more as time goes by the attitude of a shrewd man of business who is well used to the world and well content with it. She handles numbers of men and women, rough-hews a portrait of them, and sums up their value. "His taste is bad; he loves society, but has no selection, and swallows wine for quantity not quality; he is gross in everything. . . . He is honourable, just, and true." These characters are done in a rough style, as though she slashed her clay, now this side, now that. But what numbers of likenesses she struck off, and with what assurance! Indeed, she had seen so much of the world and had such knowledge of families, tempers, and money matters, that with greater concentration she might have shaped a cynical reflection in which a lifetime of observation was compressed. "Depraved men," she writes, "are in a corrupt state of things, but yet they like the names of virtues as much as they abhor the practice." La Rochefoucauld is often on her lips. But merely to have dealt with so many people and to have kept the mastery over them is in itself the proof of a remarkable mind. Hers was the force that held them together, and showed them in a certain light, and kept them in the places she assigned to them. She took in the whole sweep of the world, and imprinted it with her own broad mark. For not only could she subdue all that happened ordinarily in daily life, but she did not falter when the loftiest heights, which might well have seemed beyond her range, lay across her path. She sent for Wordsworth. "He came. He is much superior to his writings, and his conversation is even beyond his abilities. I should almost fear he is disposed to apply his talents more towards making himself a vigorous conversationalist . . . than to improve his style of composition. He holds some opinions upon picturesque subjects with which I completely differ. . . . He seems well read in his provincial history."

Monstrous and absurd as it is, may we not find there some clue to her success? When anyone is able to master all the facts she meets with, so that they fall into some order in her mind, she will present a formidable figure to other people, who will complain that she owes her strength to her lack of perception; but at the same time so smooth a shape of the world appears in her presence that they find peace in contemplating it, and almost love the creator. Her rule was much abused in her lifetime, and even now we are disposed to make little of it. We need not claim that it was ever of very great importance; but if we recall her at all we cannot, after all these years, pretend that it has no existence. She still sits on her chair as Leslie painted her—a hard woman perhaps, but undoubtedly a strong and courageous one.

Lady Hester Stanhope[1]

THE writers in the Dictionary of National Biography have a
pleasant habit of summing up a life, before they write it, in
one word, thus—"Stanhope, Lady Hester Lucy (1776-1839),
eccentric." The reason why her life is written at all is that she
differed from other people, but never converted them to her own
way of thinking. Mrs Roundell, who has written the latest account
of her, is sympathetic and respectful, but she is clearly no convert.
One feels that she is smoothing over eccentricities, as though we
were all at a tea party together. It would be polite there to remark,
"Lady Hester is very fond of cats," but in private, and writing is
private, one should allow oneself to luxuriate in the fact that she
kept forty-eight of them, choosing them for the harmony of their
stars with her own, joining in a deep bass voice with their music at
night, and accusing her doctor of a lumpish, cold, effeminate
disposition if he found the noise intolerable. But the merit of Mrs
Roundell's work, together with its simplicity and its quotations
from later writers, is that it brings or recalls to our notice a most
entertaining book, "The Memoirs and Travels of Lady Hester
Stanhope," by Dr Meryon, in six volumes. The charm of Dr
Meryon's work lies in its comprehensiveness. He lived with her
off and on for twenty-eight years, and the people we live with are
the last we seek to define in one word. Dr Meryon never attempted
it. To him she was not an eccentric by profession, but a lady of
exalted birth, who condescended when she shook hands with him,
a woman of political greatness, inspired at times, with a spell like
Circe. As a middle-class Englishman, as a doctor, as a man
respecting woman's courage but a little touched by the need for
it, he felt her charm. She treated him like a servant, but the
"magical illusion which she ever contrived to throw around
herself in the commonest circumstances of life" kept its glamour.
Happily the conditions of life on Mount Lebanon in the 'thirties
of the last century allowed him to write profusely, and gave him
only the one subject to treat. When he got back at dawn from those

[1] By Mrs Charles Roundell. *The Times Literary Supplement*, January 20, 1910.

long audiences, by the end of which the lady was hidden in smoke, he tried to put down the stories and to express the kind of stupefaction with which she overwhelmed him.

Very little, unfortunately, is known of Lady Hester's early life. When she kept house for William Pitt she made herself disliked, presumably, from the account that she gives of her triumphs. With a scanty education but great natural force, she despised people without troubling to give them a reason for it. Intuition took the place of argument, and her penetration was great. "Fort grande, fort maigre, fort décidée, fort independante" a French lady describes her as a girl in the ball-room; she herself recalled her complexion of alabaster and her lips of carnation. Further, she had a conviction of the rights of the aristocracy, and ordered her life from an eminence which made her conduct almost sublime. "Principle!" she exclaimed; "what do you mean by principle?—I am a Pitt." Unluckily her sex closed the proper channels. "If you were a man, Hester," Mr Pitt would say, "I would send you on the Continent with 60,000 men, and give you carte blanche; and I am sure that not one of my plans would fail, and not one soldier would go with his shoes unblacked." But, as it was, her powers fermented within her; she detested her sex, as though in revenge for the limitations with which ordinary women cramp remarkable ones; and drove herself as near madness as one can go by feeding a measureless ambition upon phantoms.

When her uncle died she had a pension of fifteen hundred a year and a house in Montague-square; but she pointed out in a remarkable conversation how these conditions are precisely the most intolerable if you are a person of rank. They condemn you to nothing less than imprisonment in your own drawing-room, for you cannot do yourself justice in the streets upon such a pittance. She preferred to sacrifice her health rather than lower her standards, until it occurred to her that simplicity, so extreme that no one can connect it with necessity, is the other way of being distinguished. Accordingly she retired to a cottage at Builth, in Wales, where she lived in a room "not more than a dozen feet square," "curing the poor" and keeping a dairy. She was then thirty-two. With a mixture of true greatness and grandiloquence, she determined that English ways of life are made to suit timid herds, and that a remarkable person must seek a land less corrupted by hypocrisy, where nature prevails. With what expectations she set sail for the East we know not, but she emerged in Syria, astride her horse, in the trousers of a Turkish gentleman. For the rest of her life she did nothing but shake her fist at England, where the people had forgotten their great men.

As usual, her sublimity was accompanied by a touch of the ridiculous. It is impossible not to feel that the presence of Mrs Fry, the respectable English maid, impaired the romance of the cavalcade. Dressed in men's clothes, she was expected to ride like a man, but with the heroism of her class she persisted in sitting "in the decorous posture customary with women in England," and was thus "often exposed to the danger of falling from her ass." Then, how pathetic were her attempts to redeem the wild Eastern names to the semblance at least of Christianity—Phillippaki became Philip Parker and Mustapha Mr Farr. Lady Hester and Dr Meryon saw nothing in this but the feebleness of a womanish disposition. A convent on the slopes of Mount Lebanon was bought, and there Lady Hester settled down to exert her mysterious spells. All round the house, which was perched on the top of a hill, she dug an elaborate garden, from whose terraces one could see the Mediterranean between the hills. Her influence at one time was vast, though vague; the children for twenty miles round Constantinople had heard her name. The apparition of this Englishwoman, with her large frame and her cadaverous face and her connexion with august personages in England, was in itself a miracle; the natives thought her neither man nor woman, but a being apart. The chiefs came to her for counsel, because she was absolutely without fear and loved to intrigue. The English Consuls all along the coast held her in horror. Sitting on her hilltop, she thought that she arranged the affairs of the countryside and overheard the faintest whispers. A sponge diver called Logmagi was sent to pick up news in the seaports and the bazaars of Constantinople, and in particular to report the first tidings of unrest among the people. At once new rooms and secret tunnels were added to the house, till it was shaped like a labyrinth, for she believed that "events and catastrophes" would come to pass, when people of all nations would fly to her, and she would lead them forth to Jerusalem itself, mounted upon one of the two sacred mares which now fattened in her stalls. Upon the other "a boy without a father" would ride, who was none other than the Messiah Himself. For some time the Duke of Reichstadt was the boy of the prophecy, but when he died she "fixed on another."

Talk, since nothing ever happened, became the solace of her life. The memoirs are made out of talk. Wrapped in a white cloak, with a great turban on her head, she sat in the dusk, so that you might not notice how her skin was wrinkled "like the network which we see on the rind of some species of melons," picking spoonfuls of meat and sweetstuff from saucers, and pouring forth her soliloquy. Nothing that had happened in the years she lived with Mr Pitt was forgotten: she remembered how she had snubbed Admiral ——, what the Duchess of D. had worn, what a leg had Sir W—— R——; in particular, how Mr Pitt had praised her, and he liked his food. She gossiped as though she were talking over the events of the night before, although she sat among broken crockery, in the Syrian mountains, smoking pipes with her doctor, twenty years or more after it had all faded away. Thus she rambled on:

> What can be the reason? I am now always thinking of Sir G. H——. I have been thinking how well he would do for Master of the Horse to the Queen, and I have a good way of giving a hint of it through the Buckleys; for I always said that, next to Lord Chatham, nobody ever had such handsome equipages as Sir G.; nobody's coaches and horses were so neatly picked out as theirs. Sir G. is a man, Doctor, from what you tell me, that would have just suited Mr Pitt. That polished and quiet manner which Sir G. has was what Mr Pitt found so agreeable in Mr Long. It is very odd—Mr Pitt always would dress for dinner, even if we were alone. One day I said to him, "You are tired, and there is no one but ourselves; why need you dress?" He replied, "Why, I don't know, Hester; but if one omits to do it to-day, we neglect it to-morrow, and so on, until one grows a pig."

Her spirits fell, and she went on:

> To look at me now, what a lesson against vanity! Look at this arm, all skin and bone, so thin, so thin that you may see through it; and once, without exaggeration, so rounded that you could not pinch the skin up. My neck was once so fair that a pearl necklace scarcely showed on it; and men—no fools, but sensible

198

men—would say to me, "God has given you a neck you really may be proud of; you are one of Nature's favourites, and one may be excused for admiring that beautiful skin." If they could behold me now, with my teeth all gone and with long lines in my face—not wrinkles, for I have no wrinkles when I am left quiet and not made angry; but my face is drawn out of composure by these wretches. I thank God that old age has come upon me unperceived. When I used to see the painted Lady H., dressed in pink and silver, with her head shaking, and jumped by her footman into her sociable, attempting to appear young, I felt a kind of horror and disgust I can't describe. I wonder how Lady Stafford dresses now she is no longer young; but I can't fancy her grown old.

Fierce storms of rage possessed her, and then she would weep with a wild howl painful to hear, as though Bellona should weep. More and more, as time passed without any revolution and her influence waned, and debts crushed her, did she seek the support of magic. Although she had failed to subdue the forces of this world, and the Queen and Lord Palmerston were against her, she was mistress of arts that the vulgar knew nothing of. She saw the sylphs perched on her chest of drawers and clumsy fellows tripped up for ignoring them; seated in the convent at Dar Djoun, she could look into the heart of Paris or of London; she knew the cavern where the King of the Serpents lived, with the head of a man; she knew where to find the lost book of Adam and Eve's language written in letters a span high; "I believe in vampires, but the people in England know not how to distinguish them."

After a time she never left her hilltop; then she scarcely went beyond her room, but sat in bed, arguing, scolding, and ringing bells perpetually, the floor littered with pipes and bits of string; she was never to ride into Jerusalem upon her mare, and the aristocratic ideal remained high. She would let no European come near her, and at last she turned even Dr Meryon away. In June, 1839, the news came to Beirut that she had died with only native servants round her. Rooms were found full of mouldy stores hoarded for the great emergency, but her valuables had been stolen while she lay helpless. The dead lady looked "composed and placid," but she was so much in the habit of hiding her feelings that her expression told nothing. She was buried in a corner of her rose garden in the grave of a certain prophet, where she had not wished to be buried. Ten years later the place was a thicket of brambles and roses; now there are lines of mulberry trees. But Lady Hester, the last of the great English aristocrats, lives on in despite of the plough.

The Memoirs of Sarah Bernhardt[1]

THERE are good reasons why, when an actress promises to give us her memoirs, we should feel an unusual interest and excitement even. She lives before us in many shapes and in many circumstances, the instrument of this passion and of that. Meanwhile, if we choose to remember it, she also sits in passive contemplation some little way withdrawn, in an attitude which we must believe to be one of final significance. It might be urged that it is the presence of this contrast that gives meaning to the most trivial of her actions, and some additional poignancy to the most majestic. We know, too, that each part she plays deposits its own small contribution upon her unseen shape, until it is complete and distinct from its creations at the same time that it inspires them with life. And when she undertakes to show us what manner of woman this has become, should we not feel an exceptional gratitude and an interest that is more than usually complex?

Perhaps no woman now alive could tell us more strange things, of herself and of life, than Sarah Bernhardt. It is true that when she comes to this final act of revelation she makes use of certain conventions, poses herself with greater care than we could wish, before she allows the curtain to rise; but that, too, is characteristic, and, to drop all metaphor, her book surely should do what none of her parts has done, and show us what cannot be shown upon the stage.

She was brought up in the Convent of Grands Champs at Versailles, and her life at once forms itself into separate and brightly coloured beads; they succeed each other, but they scarcely connect. She was so intensely organized even then that there were explosions when she came into contact for the first time with hard things in the world outside her. When she was confronted by the sad walls of the convent, she exclaimed: "Papa, papa! I won't go to prison. This is a prison, I am sure." But at that moment a "little round short woman" came out veiled to the mouth. After she had talked for a time she saw that Sarah was trembling, and with some strange instinct she raised her veil wholly for a second. "I then saw

[1] *Cornhill Magazine*, February, 1908.

the sweetest and merriest face imaginable. . . . I flung myself at once into her arms." Her actions within the walls were as sudden and as passionate. Her hair, for example, grew thick and curled, and the sister who had to comb it in the early morning tugged callously. "I flung myself upon her, and with feet, teeth, hands, elbows, head, and indeed all my poor little body, I hit and thumped, yelling at the same time." The pupils and the sisters came running, they muttered their prayers and waved their holy signs, at a distance, until the Mother Prefect had recourse to a further charm and dashed a spray of holy water over the active devil of Sarah Bernhardt. But after all this spiritual display it was the good Mother Superior, with her sure instinct for effect, who conquered by no more potent charm than "an expression of pity." But such tempers were partly the result of the extreme fragility of her health. It is more significant to read how she built up for herself the reputation of a "personality" among her fellows. She carried about with her little boxes full of adders and crickets and lizards. The lizards generally had their tails broken, for, in order to see whether they were eating, she would lift the lid and let it fall sharply "red with surprise" at their assurance in rushing forwards. "And *crac*—there was nearly always a tail caught." So, while the sister taught she was fingering the severed tails and wondering how she could fasten them on again. Then she kept spiders, and when a child cut her finger, " 'Come at once,' I would say, 'I have some fresh spider web, and I will wrap your finger in it.' " With such strange crafts and passions, for she was never good at her books, she touched the imagination. And of course all this intensity of feeling went, in the convent, to paint some beautiful dramatic picture in which she acted the chief part as the nun who had renounced the world, or the nun who lay dead beneath a heavy black cloth, while the candles flared, and the sisters and pupils cried out in delightful agony. "You saw, O Lord God," she prayed, "that mamma cried, and that it did not affect me!" for "I adored my mother, but with a touching and fervent desire to leave her . . . to sacrifice her to God." But a violent escapade which ended in a bad illness finished the religious career that promised so well. She left the convent, and though she still cherished only one ambition, to take the veil, it was decided in the most casual fashion in a remarkable family council to send her to the Conservatoire.

Her mother, an indolent charming woman, with mysterious eyes and heart disease and a passion for music, who was at any rate no ascetic, was in the habit of assembling relations and advisers when any family business had to be transacted. On this occasion there were present a notary, a godfather, an uncle, an aunt, a governess, a friend from the flat above, and a distinguished gentleman, the Duc de Morny. Most of these people Sarah had some reason to hate or to love—"he had red hair planted in his head like couch grass," "he called me 'ma fil' "—"he was gentle and kind . . . and occupied a high place at Court." They discussed whether, with the 100,000 francs which her father had left her, it would not be best to find her a husband. But upon this she flew into a passion and cried "I'll marry the Bon Dieu . . . I will be a nun, I will," and grew red and confronted her enemies. They murmured and expostulated, and her mother began to talk in a "clear drawling voice like the sound of a little waterfall." . . . Finally the Duc de Morny was bored, and rose to go. "Do you know what you ought to do with this child?" he said. "You ought to send her to the Conservatoire."

The words, as we know, were to have tremendous consequences, but it is worth while to consider the whole scene apart from them as an example of that curious gift which gives to so many passages in this autobiography the precision and vitality of coloured and animated photographs. No emotion that could express itself in gesture or action was lost upon her eye, and even though such incidents had nothing to do with the matter in hand, her brain treasured them and could, if necessary, use them to explain something. It is often something quite trivial, but for that reason, perhaps, almost startling in its effect. Thus the little sister was sitting on the floor "plaiting the fringe of the sofa"; Madame Guérard came in "without a hat; she was wearing an indoor gown of indienne with a design of little brown leaves." Later, a little drama is given thus. "My godfather shrugged his shoulders, and getting up, left the box, banging the door after him. Mamma, losing all patience with me, proceeded to review the house through her opera-glasses. Mdlle de Brabender passed me her hand-kerchief, for I had dropped mine and dared not pick it up." That perhaps may be taken as a simple example of the way in which it is natural for an actress, be she only twelve years old, to see things.

It is her business to be able to concentrate all that she feels into some gesture perceptible to the eye, and to receive her impressions of what is going on in the minds of others from the same tokens also. The nature of her gift becomes increasingly obvious as the memoirs proceed, and the actress matures and takes her station at this point of view. And when, as is here the case, the alien art of letters is used to express a highly developed dramatic genius, some of the effects that it produces are strange and brilliant, and others pass beyond this limit and become grotesque and even painful. On the way back from her examination at the Conservatoire, in which she had been successful, she prepared a scene for her mother. She was to enter with a sad face, and then, when her mother exclaimed "I told you so," she was to cry "I have passed!" But the faithful Madame Guérard spoilt the effect by shouting the true story in the courtyard. "I must say that the kind woman continued so long as she lived ... to spoil my effects ... so that before beginning a story or a game I used to ask her to go out of the room." Not seldom we find ourselves in the same position as Madame Guérard, although perhaps we might be able to offer an excuse. There are two stories, out of a bewildering variety, which will serve to show how it is that Sarah Bernhardt sometimes crosses the boundary, and becomes either ludicrous or painful—or is it that we, like Madame Guérard, should leave the room?

After her astonishing exertions in the Franco-Prussian war she felt the need of a change, and went accordingly to Brittany. "I adore the sea and the plain ... but I neither care for mountains nor for forests ... they crush me ... and stifle me." In Brittany she found horrid precipices, set in the "infernal noise of the sea," and rocks to crawl beneath, which had fallen there " in unknown ages, and were only held in equilibrium by some inexplicable cause." There was a crevasse also, the Enfer du Plogoff, which she was determined to descend in spite of the mysterious warnings of her guide. Accordingly she was lowered by a rope attached to a belt, in which additional holes had to be pierced, for her waist "was then but forty-three centimetres." It was dark, and the sea roared, and there was a din as of cannons and whips and the howling of the damned. At last her feet touched ground, the point of a little rock in a swirl of waters, and she looked fearfully about her. Suddenly she saw that she was observed by two enormous eyes; a little further, and she saw another pair of eyes. "I saw no body to these beings . . . I thought for a minute that I was losing my senses." She tugged violently, and was slowly raised; "the eyes were lifted up also . . . and while I mounted through the air I saw nothing but eyes everywhere—eyes throwing out long feelers to reach me." "Those are the eyes of the shipwrecked ones," said her guide, crossing himself. "I knew very well that they were not the eyes of shipwrecked ones . . . but it was only at the hotel that I heard about the octopus." It might puzzle a scrupulous chronicler to assign their original parts in this drama to the octopus, the fisherman, and to Sarah Bernhardt; for the others it does not matter.

Then, again, "my dear governess, Mdlle de Brabender," was dying, and she went to visit her.

"She had suffered so much that she looked like a different person. She was lying in her little white bed, a little white cap covering her hair; her big nose was drawn with pain, her washed-out eyes seemed to have no colour in them. Her formidable moustache alone bristled up with constant spasms of pain. Besides all this she was so strangely altered that I wondered what had caused the change. I went nearer, and bending down, kissed her gently. I then gazed at her so inquisitively that she understood instinctively. With her eyes she signed to me to look on the table near her, and there in a glass I saw all my dear old friend's teeth."

There is one quality that most of the stories she tells have in common: they are clearly the productions of a very literal mind. She will accumulate fact upon fact, multiply her octopuses indefinitely, in order to achieve her effect, but she will never invoke any mystical agency. How could one manage "the souls of the drowned"? All the vast unconscious forces of the world, the width of the sky and the immensity of the sea, she crinkles together into some effective scenery for her solitary figure. It is for this reason that her gaze is so narrow and so penetrating. And although her convictions as an artist hardly enter these pages, it may be guessed that something of her unmatched intensity on the stage comes from the capacity which she shows for keen and sceptical vision where character is concerned; she is under no illusions. "I had played badly, looked ugly, and been in a bad temper." One figures her the most practical of women when she chooses, a cheapener of fowls with the best of them, who will only suffer herself to be cheated from the same cynicism with which, no doubt, she would cheat herself if she wished it. For so clear an insight does not seem in her case at least consistent with a very exalted view of her kind; if she had it by nature she may have found that it would not lend itself easily to the resources of her art, that the effects to be got by it were uncertain, and it is her glory to make any sacrifice that her art demands. Certainly, when you have read some way in the book you become aware of a hardness and limitation in her view, which perhaps may be accounted for by the fact that all these violent scenes are the result of certain well-contrived explosions which serve but to illumine the curious face, so unlike any other face, of the actress. And in a world thus lit for us in lurid bursts of violet and crimson light the one figure in all its poses is always vivid enough, but the others which fall just outside the circle are strangely discoloured. Thus, she saved a lady from falling downstairs on board ship, who murmured "in a voice that was scarcely audible 'I am the widow of President Lincoln' . . . A thrill of anguish ran through me . . . her husband had been assassinated by an actor, and it was an actress who prevented her from joining her beloved husband. I went to my cabin and stayed there two days." And what was Mrs Lincoln feeling meanwhile?

Such a multiplication of crude visible objects upon our senses wearies them considerably by the time the book is finished, but what we suffer—it is the final triumph of "the personality"—is exhaustion and not boredom. Even the stars, when she draws her curtain at night, shine not upon the earth and the sea, but upon "the new era" which her second volume will reveal to us also.

With our eyes dazzled by this unflinching stare we are urged to say something of the revelation—and vainly, no doubt. For the more you are under the obsession of a book the less of articulate language you have to use concerning it. You creep along after such shocks, like some bewildered animal, whose head, struck by a flying stone, flashes with all manner of sharp lightnings. It is possible, as you read the volume, to feel your chair sink beneath you into undulating crimson vapours, of a strange perfume, which presently rise and enclose you entirely. And then they draw asunder and leave clear spaces, still shot with crimson, in which some vivid conflict goes forward between bright pigmies; the clouds ring with high French voices perfect of accent, though so strangely mannered and so monotonous of tone that you hardly recognise them for the voices of human beings. There is a constant reverberation of applause, chafing all the nerves to action. But where after all does dream end, and where does life begin? For when the buoyant armchair grounds itself at the end of the chapter with a gentle shock that wakes you and the clouds spin round you and disappear, does not the solid room which is suddenly presented with all its furniture expectant appear too large and gaunt to be submerged again by the thin stream of interest which is all that is left you after your prodigal expense? Yes—one must dine and sleep and register one's life by the dial of the clock, in a pale light, attended only by the irrelevant uproar of cart and carriage, and observed by the universal eye of sun and moon which looks upon us all, we are told, impartially. But is not this a gigantic falsehood? Are we not each in truth the centre of innumerable rays which so strike upon one figure only, and is it not our business to flash them straight and completely back again, and never suffer a single shaft to blunt itself on the far side of us? Sarah Bernhardt at least, by reason of some such concentration, will sparkle for many generations a sinister and enigmatic message; but still she will sparkle, while the rest of us—is the prophecy too arrogant?—lie dissipated among the floods.

Lady Strachey[1]

THERE are some people who without being themselves famous seem to sum up the qualities of an age and to represent it at its best. Lady Strachey, who died last week at the age of eighty-eight, was among them. She seemed the type of the Victorian woman at her finest—many-sided, vigorous, adventurous, advanced. With her large and powerful frame, her strongly marked features, her manner that was so cordial, so humorous, and yet perhaps a little formidable, she seemed cast on a larger scale, made of more massive material then the women of to-day. One could not but be aware even to look at her that she was in the line of a great tradition. She came of a family famous for its administrators and public servants; she married into one of the great Anglo-Indian families of the nineteenth century. One could easily imagine how, had she been a man, she would have ruled a province or administered a Government department. She had all that instinct for affairs, that broad-minded grasp of politics that made the great public servant of the nineteenth century. But, in addition, like all Victorian women of her stamp, she was emphatically a mother and a wife. Even while she wrote dispatches at her husband's dictation and debated—for she was in the counsels of the men who governed India—this problem, that policy, she was bringing up, now in India, now in England, a family of ten children. She was presiding over one of those vast Victorian households which, chaotic as they seem now, had a character and a vitality about them which it is hard to suppose will ever be matched again. Memory provides a picture of the many-roomed house; of people coming and going; of argument; of laughter; of different voices speaking at once; of Lady Strachey herself a little absent-minded, a little erratic, but nevertheless the controller and inspirer of it all, now wandering through the rooms with a book, now teaching a group of young people the steps of the Highland reel, now plunging into ardent debate about politics or literature, now working out, with equal intentness, some puzzle

[1] *The Nation & Athenæum*, December 22, 1928.

in a penny paper which if solved would provide her with thirty shillings a week and a workman's cottage for life.

In her old age she wrote down a few memories of the past which show, very briefly, how naturally, how as a matter of course, she was in touch with the great figures of the Victorian world. She joked with Huxley; she exchanged spectacles with Tennyson; she was a special favourite with George Eliot, and, "though much ashamed of my vanity in recording it," could not help remembering how "Lewes told a friend of mine that I was his idea of Dorothea in Middlemarch." She sat up to all hours of the night, "eagerly discussing every aspect of humanity," with the most distinguished men of her time, openly but impersonally, rather as if they were in full evening dress, so it seems to a less formal age. For together with her keen interest in public questions, particularly in the education and emancipation of women, went an interest as vigorous in music and the drama, and especially in literature. She had a vast capacity for enthusiasm which fed happily and confidently as was common with the Victorians upon her own contemporaries and their works. She had no doubts whatever about the greatness of the men she knew and the lasting importance of their books. When she met Browning for the first time at a concert she wrote on her programme:

> *"And did you once see Browning plain?*
> *And did he stop and speak to you?"*

and kept it, a sacred relic. She counted it one of her great pieces of good luck that she was born contemporary with Salvini. She went to the theatre every night on which he acted. But she was not only attracted by the great figures of her own age. She was an omnivorous reader. She had her hands upon the whole body of English literature, from Shakespeare to Tennyson, with the large loose grasp that was so characteristic of the cultivated Victorian. She had a special love for the Elizabethan drama, and for English poetry—Beddoes was one of the obscure writers whom she championed and discovered—a little incongruously perhaps, for her own affinities seemed rather with the age of reason and the robust sense of the great English prose writers. She was, above all things, rational, positive, agnostic, like the distinguished men who were her friends. Later in life, after her husband's death, when her

activities were somewhat lessened, though they were still varied
enough to have filled the life of a younger woman, she would
spend an entire winter's afternoon in reading an Elizabethan play
from end to end. For reading aloud was one of her great natural
gifts. She read with fire and ardour, and with a great clarity and
distinction of utterance. Often she would pause to point out the
beauty of some passage, or propound with extreme ingenuity
some emendation, or impart a curious illustration that had stuck
in her mind from her wide and miscellaneous foraging among
books. Then, when the reading was over, she would launch out
into stories of the past; of Lord Lytton and his sky-blue dressing
gown; of Lord Roberts helping to mend her sewing machine;
of Lawrence and Outram (she never passed the statue of Outram
without making a salute, she said); of Pattles and Prinseps; of
bygone beauties and scandals—for though she observed the
conventions she was not in the least a prude; of Indian society
fifty years, eighty years, a hundred years ago. For she had the
Scottish love of following family histories and tracing the friend-
ships and alliances of the present back to their roots in the past.
Thus a haphazard party would come in her presence to have a
patriarchal air, as she recalled the memories and the marriages
that had bound parents and grandparents together years ago, in
the distant past.

Gradually, though the vigour of her mind was as great as ever,
it seemed to withdraw from modern life and to focus itself more
and more upon the past. She did not remember clearly what had
happened the week before, but Calcutta in 1870, Robert
Browning's laugh, some saying of George Eliot's, were as clear, as
dear, and as vivid as ever. It was her hard fate to lose her sight
almost entirely some years before she died. She could no longer
go foraging and triumphing through English literature—for it
seemed as if she carried on even the passive act of reading with
something of the vigour with which she strode the streets, peering
forward with her short-sighted eyes, or tossed her head high in a
shout of laughter. But she could talk, she could argue, she could
join in the disputes of the younger generation and follow with pride
the successes of her children. Her mind was still busy with literature, still active with suggestions for reviving forgotten plays, for
editing old texts, for bringing to light some hidden splendour in

those old books which she could no longer read herself, but almost commanded the younger generation to love as she had loved them. Her memory, grown to be the strongest part of her, still kept unimpaired in its depths some of the loveliest things in English poetry. When she was past eighty, she stopped one summer evening under a tree in a London square and recited the whole of "Lycidas" without a fault. Last summer, though too weak to walk any more, she sat on her balcony and showered down upon the faces that she could not see a vast maternal benediction. It was as if the Victorian age in its ripeness, its width, with all its memories and achievements behind it were bestowing its blessing. And we should be blind indeed if we did not wave back to her a salute full of homage and affection.

John Delane[1]

I F, in the middle days of the last century, you had seen the figure
of a certain tall young man, ruddy of complexion and powerful
of build, you might have foretold a dozen successful careers for him,
as squire, lawyer, or man of business, but perhaps you would not
have fitted him at once with his indubitable calling. That spark
of genius, for surely it was not less, flashed in the brain of John
Walter, proprietor of the "Times," when he saw the second son of
a neighbour of his in the country riding to hounds or conducting
a successful election on his behalf. John Thadeus Delane went to
Oxford and distinguished himself there rather as a bold rider—
"Mr Delane is part and parcel of his horse," wrote his tutor—a
tennis-player, or a boxer (for the hot Irish blood in him would rise)
than as a nice scholar or a mathematician. His letters to his friend
George Dasent show him something of a Philistine, with a command of vigorous and wholesome English, lending itself happily to
such casual remarks as those he had to make about his studies and
his sports. He did not know, for instance, "how I am to cram a
sufficient store of divinity into my head. As the premises will
only be occupied a short time with the last-named commodity,
the trouble of storing it should be slight. [I must] try to secure a
patent safety vehicle. . . . This is a most glorious country—capital
people, excellent horses, prime feeding, and very fair shooting."
Such is the slang of the 'forties, which, with its comfortable lapse
from the dignity of contemporary prose, reveals a young man
lazily conscious of his power, with a capacity for shooting words
straight if need be, and for distorting them at will, which is the
despair of lady novelists who seek to reproduce it.

Directly he had taken his degree, in 1840, he went to Printing-
house Square, and was occupied with various duties about the
paper. Little is said of their nature, or of the way in which he
discharged them, for he had now entered that unnamed world
which is crowded but unchecked; there are duties which belong
to no profession, nor are the limits of work bounded so long as the

---

[1] *The Life and Letters of John Thadeus Delane*, by Arthur Irwin Dasent.
Cornhill Magazine, June, 1908.

brain urges on. He made himself familiar with the House of
Commons, we are told, "summarising the remarks of the principal
speakers." We must imagine how swiftly he took the measure of
the world around him, gauging silently the capacity of his machine
for reporting and perhaps for directing the turmoil. A year later,
at any rate, when Mr Barnes, the editor, died, Mr Walter had no
hesitation in choosing "the youngest member of all the staff,"
whose age was then twenty-three, to succeed him. Sense and industry and ability were his, but the easy margin of strength, as of
a loosely fitting coat, which may be detected in his Oxford letters,
marked him, to a discriminating eye, as the man who would put
forth greater power than he had yet shown, with a competent tool
in his hand, or would so weld himself to his instrument that their
joint stroke would be irresistible. But it is one of the mysteries that
tempt us and baffle us in this biography that the transition is almost unmarked. We hear Mr Delane exclaim once, in "tremendous spirits," "By Jove, John, . . . I am editor of the 'Times,'" but
in future the editor and the "Times" are one, as in the old days
the undergraduate was part of his horse. What the condition of
the paper was when he came to it, or what private estimate he had
formed of its scope, we are not told. But as all agree that the
age of Delane was the great age, and that the paper grew with its
editor, we may believe that he undertook the task without articulate reflection, conscious of a power within him that would soon
fill all the space permitted it. "What I dislike about you young
men of the present day is that you all shrink from responsibility,"
he was wont to laugh, when people wondered.

Much of the paper's industry as chronicler and reporter and
simple publisher was merely that of a gigantic natural force,
sucking in and casting forth again its daily cloud of print impartially; and the editor was lost in its shade. But almost at once
the brain of the monster, which expressed itself daily in the four
leading articles, was given cause to show its quality. There was a
"Ministerial crisis" and Delane had not only to anticipate the rest
of the world in publishing the news, but to express an opinion.
No study, were there material for it, could be more fascinating
than the analysis of such an opinion. Hawthorne himself might
have found scope for all his imagination, all his love of darkness
and mystery, in tracing it from its first secret whisper to its final

reverberation over the entire land. A great Minister sends for the editor to his private room, and speaks to him; a note from someone who has picked up a word at Court is left on him; instantly, with an audacity that may land him in disaster, he fits the parts together, and instructs his leader-writer to embody them in a column of English prose; to-morrow a voice speaks with authority in Court and market and Council Chamber. But whose voice is it? It is not the voice of Mr Delane, the urbane gentleman who rides along Fleet Street on his cob, nor is it the voice of Dr Woodham, the learned Fellow of Jesus. It has the authority of Government and the sting of independence: Downing Street trembles at it and the people of England give ear to it, for such is the voice of the "Times."

It is easy to submit to the fascination of the idea, and to conceive a monster in Printing-house Square without personality but with an infallible knowledge of persons, ruthless as a machine and subtle as a single brain. And there are facts in this book which seem to justify the most extravagant statement that we can make. There is, of course, the romantic story of the "Times" and the repeal of the Corn Laws; we read also how Louis Philippe and Guizot thought it worth their while to impede the paper's correspondence; how the Czar heard of the Ultimatum of 1854 through the "Times" and not through the Foreign Office; how it was objected in the House of Lords that Cabinet secrets were made public, and the "Times" answered, "We are satisfied that it was useful to the public and to Europe"; how the "Times" foretold the Indian Mutiny, and was the first to reveal the state of the army in the Crimea; how the "Times" was foremost with the Queen's Speech and with texts and resignations innumerable; making Ministries, deciding policies, exalting statesmen, and casting them down. The list might be lengthened, but surely without avail; for already there is some risk lest we grow beyond our strength and forget, what these volumes should recall, the character, the individual will, directing this giant force and placing its blows in such tender quarters. His contemporaries certainly did not forget, for it was the independence of the paper that was chiefly valuable, or dangerous, as fortune chanced, and the spirit that preserved it from the blunt blow and shapeless mass of a machine was of course the spirit of Mr Delane. Together with these triumphs of organization we read of other triumphs that are no less remarkable. Prime Ministers and Secretaries of State lay aside (with relief one guesses) their impassive public countenance, and entrust Mr Delane not only with State secrets, but with private prejudices of their own. Here was one with greater knowledge than the best instructed of Ministers, with whom no secrecy availed, who was moreover so sequestered from the public eye that you might approach him without reserve, as patients their physician, or penitents their confessor. A letter from Lord Palmerston begins, "I am told you disapprove . . ." and goes on to justify his action with allusions to foreign politics and the gout which, though each had a share in his behaviour, would not have been used to explain it either to the public or to his friends.

The anonymity which Delane took such care to preserve was no doubt of the utmost value in the conduct of the paper, investing it with an impersonal majesty; but there is reason to think that it came from no mere professional policy but was a deeply seated instinct in the character of the man. He was infinitely receptive, and so far "anonymous" by nature that the broad columns of the "Times," filled with the writing of other men but sharpened and guided by himself, expressed all of him that he chose to express. When he left his rooms in the morning he rode about London, followed by a groom, calling at the House of Commons or at Downing Street, and took his lunch with one great lady and his tea with another. He dined out almost nightly, and met frequently all the great nobles and celebrities of the time. But his demeanour, we are told, was inscrutable; he was of opinion that society should be exclusive; and his attitude generally was one of "observant silence." He never mentioned the "Times" after he had left the office, though the paper was always in his thoughts. At length, when he had stored his mind with observations, he returned to Printing-house Square, and, with his energies at full play and his staff circling round him, shaped the course of the paper in accordance with his own view until it was three or four in the morning and he must rest before the labours of the day. And yet, in spite of his silence—his broad way of looking at tendencies and institutions rather than at individuals—men and women, we read, gave him their confidences. They were sure of able consideration from a man who had infinite experience of men, but, as it appears from his letters, they were sure also of a massive integrity which inspired absolute trust, both that he would respect your secret, and that he would respect more than you or your secret, what was right. His letters, however, can seldom be said to add anything that the columns of the "Times" have not already supplied; but they are token again of the literal truth of his phrase, when there was talk of his retirement, "All that was worth having of [my life] has been devoted to the paper."

There was not sufficient space between his professional life and his private life for any change of view or difference of code. We may find in that fact some clue to the amazing authority which he wielded, for it is easy to see that if you disproved some opinion of his or disparaged some method, you aimed a blow at the nature of the man himself, the two being of one birth. When he travelled abroad and visited towns famous for their beauty or their art he was unconscious of their appeal, but was inclined to adopt on such occasions the attitude of a portly gentleman with pretty children. Perhaps he had noticed some new factory or some stout bridge from the train window, and had found in it the text of a leading article. He travelled much, and visited any place that might become the centre of action; and in time of peace he went on pilgrimage through the great houses of England, where the nerves of the country come nearest to the surface. It was his purpose to know all that could be known of the condition and future of Europe, so far as certain great signs reveal it, and if he ignored much there was no wiser or more discriminating judge of the symptoms he chose to observe.

One quality seems to mark his judgments and to add to their value—they are so dispassionate. The indifference he always showed to what was thought of him came, naturally, from his well-founded trust in himself; but there was another reason for it, once or twice hinted in the course of this book, and once at least outspoken. The paper was more to him than his own fortunes, and, thus divested of personality, he came to take a gigantic and even humorous view of the whole, which sometimes seems to us sublime, sometimes callous, and sometimes, when we read certain phrases near the end, very melancholy. He was the most attentive observer of the political life of his age, but he took no part in it. When he was attacked he gave, with one exception, no answer. His anonymity, his reticence—no man was to take his portrait or to make him look ridiculous—are allied surely with the casual bluntness of speech and indifference to praise or blame which gave his opinion its peculiar weight. "Something like consternation prevailed at the War Office and at the Horse Guards when it became known that Delane intended to be present upon Salisbury Plain." But could he have cared so much for the world, for politics, for the welfare of numbers had he not been indifferent to his personal share in it? or again, would he so soon have tired of the scene had some part of it touched him more nearly? Again and again the phrase recurs, "The New Year found me, as the last had done, alone at Printing-house Square," and the loneliness deepened as life drew on until we find such a sentence as this: "Nobody now [his mother being dead] cares about me or my success, or my motives, and that weariness of life I had long felt has been gaining on me ever since. . . . I have much to be thankful for, [but] I have become so indifferent to life . . . weary both of work and idleness, careless about society and with failing interests." But it would be unwise to allow such a sentence to set its seal upon the rest, or to colour too sadly that colossal erection of courage and devotion which he called "the Paper"; his success only was tinged with "a browner shade" than it might otherwise have worn.

When he was middle-aged he bought himself a tract of common near Ascot, and busied himself in reclaiming the land and in playing the farmer. It is easy to see him there, looking much like a country squire with the interests of his crops at heart, as he rode about and drew in great draughts of the open air. From the clods of earth and the watery English sky he received a passive satisfaction, and came perhaps to enjoy an easier intercourse with these dumb things than with human beings.

Body and Brain[1]

ONE might read the lives of all the Cabinet Ministers since the accession of Queen Victoria without realizing that they had a body between them. To imagine any of the statues in Parliament Square running, climbing, or even in a state of nudity is not only impossible but also unseemly. The life, dignity, character of statesmen is centred in the head; the body is merely a stalk, smooth, black and inexpressive, whether attenuated or obese, at the end of which flowers a Gladstone, a Campbell-Bannerman, or a Chamberlain. But you have only to look at a photograph of Theodore Roosevelt to see that he and his body are identical. The little round pugnacious head with the eyes screwed up as if charging an enemy is as much part of his body as a bull's head is part of his body. Decency requires that the man's body shall be cut off from his head by collar, frock coat and trousers, but even under that disguise we still see, without any sense of unseemliness, bones, muscles, and flesh.

As Mr Thayer remarks in the course of his witty and sensible biography, very little is yet known of the interaction between mind and body. The mind in biography as in sculpture is treated as a separate and superior organ attached to an instrument which is, happily, becoming obsolete. If Cabinet Ministers exercise their bodies for a few hours it is only in order to clarify their brains. But Roosevelt, though given by nature a sickly and asthmatic body which might have claimed the pampered life of a slave, always treated his body as a companion and equal. Indeed, his education until he left college was more the education of the body than of the mind. It was not until he had wrought a light weak frame into a tough thick body capable of immense endurance that his brain came into partnership. If he used his brain at all it was not to think about books but about animals. He was taken on a tour through Europe as a small boy, but what did he see? Only that there are flocks of aquatic birds on the banks of the Nile, and that in Cairo there is a book by an English clergyman that tells you a

[1] *Theodore Roosevelt*, by William Roscoe Thayer, *The New Statesman*, June 5, 1920.

great deal about them. In Venice he wrote in his diary, "We saw a palace of the doges. It looks like a palace you could be comfortable and snug in (which is not usual)." "The poor boys have been dragged off to the orful picture galery" wrote his little sister. Roosevelt had no artistic sense either as boy or man, so that we are not able to consider the effect upon an artist of owning a body. But directly the body and mind came into partnership it was plain that for political purposes no combination is more powerful.

American politics in the 'eighties appear to an English reader as a rough-and-tumble shindy of public house loafers in which the only serviceable weapon is a strong right arm. When Roosevelt said on leaving college "I am going to try to help the cause of better government in New York; I don't exactly know how," his ambition seemed to his friends "almost comic." Politics were not for "gentlemen." Jake Hess, the Republican Boss, and his heelers were equally amused. What business had a youth of the "kid glove and silk stocking set" among such as them? After a little experience of him they owned that he was "a good fellow"—"a good mixer." Both friends and enemies were wont to expatiate upon his luck. Directly Roosevelt was safely shelved for life as Vice-President, President McKinley was shot dead. The greatest prize in the United States fell into his hands without an effort. That was the sort of thing that always happened to Roosevelt. But it is impossible to feel that his progress had anything accidental about it. Fortune, indeed, showed herself quite ready to suppress him had he been made of suppressible material. The year 1883 found him out of politics, alienated from many of his best friends, and bereaved of his wife. Intellectually and emotionally he was disillusioned and disheartened. Then flooded in to his rescue that strange passion for using muscles and breathing fresh air and throwing oneself naked upon nature and seeing what happens next which cannot be called intellectual but which is certainly not merely animal. He became a ranchman. His companions were uncivilized; his duties were those of a primitive man. He lived with horses and cattle and at any moment might have to shoot or be shot. The same thing happened with the desperadoes of Little Missouri as had happened with Boss Hess and his heelers. They began by despising his spectacles and ended by thinking him the same kind of man as themselves. When he was President of the

United States a cowboy came up to him and said, " 'Mr President, I have been in jail a year for killing a gentleman.' 'How did you do it?' asked the President, meaning to inquire as to the circumstances. 'Thirty-eight on a forty-five frame,' replied the man, thinking that the only interest the President had was that of a comrade who wanted to know with what kind of tool the trick was done." No other President, it is said, from Washington to Wilson would have drawn that answer.

Undoubtedly, it was not his fight against Trusts, or his action in ending the Russo-Japanese war, or any other political faith of his that gave him his popularity so much as the fact that his development was not limited to the organs of the brain. He was a good mixer. We have seen the effect upon bosses and cowboys. Now let us go to the other extreme and see how the President affected a highly cultivated Frenchman, the ambassador, M. Jusserand. Desired by his government to sketch some account of the President's temperament, M. Jusserand sent a dispatch describing "a promenade" in Washington. "I arrived at the White House punctually in afternoon dress and silk hat. . . . The President wore knickerbockers, thick boots and soft felt hat, much worn. . . . On reaching the country, the President went pell-mell over the fields, following neither road nor path, always on, on, straight ahead! I was much winded, but I would not give in, nor ask him to slow up, because I had the honour of La Belle France at heart. At last we came to the bank of a stream, rather wide and too deep to be forded. I sighed relief. . . . But judge of my horror when I saw the President unbutton his clothes and heard him say, 'We had better strip, so as not to wet our things in the creek.' Then I, too, for the honour of France, removed my apparel, everything except my lavender kid gloves. The President cast an inquiring look at these but I quickly forestalled any remark by saying, 'With your permission, Mr President, I will keep these on, otherwise it would be embarrassing if we should meet ladies.' And so we jumped into the water and swam across." They came out on the other side firm friends. That is the result of taking off everything except one's lavender kid gloves.

It was the combination of brain and body that was remarkable—for neither, separately, excelled immensely those of other men. Was it not the essence of his teaching that almost any man can achieve great things by getting the utmost use out of "the ordinary qualities that he shares with his fellows?" Put an ordinary man under a microscope and you see President Roosevelt. Unfortunately, many shadows are needed even in the crudest snapshot. Directly you are conscious of being ordinary you cease to be ordinary. And, after all, can we call the President a perfect example of a successful man? Are we not conscious towards the end of his life of a lack of balance which destroys his value as a magnified specimen of the human race? The slaughter of animals played too large a part in his life. And why start exploring the Brazilian River of Doubt at the age of fifty-five? Nature, outraged, sent him back with a fever in his bones from which he died years before his time. So difficult is it at this late stage of civilization for one and the same person to have both body and brain.

*Books by Virginia Woolf
available in paperback editions
from Harcourt Brace Jovanovich, Inc.*

The Voyage Out
Night and Day
Jacob's Room *and* The Waves
The Common Reader: First Series
Mrs. Dalloway
To the Lighthouse
Orlando
A Room of One's Own
The Second Common Reader
Flush
The Years
Three Guineas
Roger Fry: A Biography
Between the Acts
The Death of the Moth and Other Essays
A Haunted House and Other Short Stories
The Moment and Other Essays
The Captain's Death Bed and Other Essays
A Writer's Diary
Granite and Rainbow
Contemporary Writers
Mrs. Dalloway's Party
The Letters of Virginia Woolf, Vol. I: 1888–1912
The Pargiters: The Novel-Essay Portion of *The Years*